T0063201

THE GREAT
BAHAMAS HURRICANE
of
1929

*The story of the Greatest
Bahamian Hurrricane of the 20th Century*

WAYNE NEELY

iUniverse LLC
Bloomington

THE GREAT BAHAMAS HURRICANE OF 1929
THE STORY OF THE GREATEST BAHAMIAN
HURRRICANE OF THE 20TH CENTURY

iUniverse books may be ordered through booksellers or by contacting:

iUniverse
1663 Liberty Drive
Bloomington, IN 47403
www.iuniverse.com
1-800-Authors (1-800-288-4677)

ISBN: 978-1-4917-1613-7 (sc)
ISBN: 978-1-4917-1615-1 (hc)
ISBN: 978-1-4917-1614-4 (e)

Library of Congress Control Number: 2013921660

Printed in the United States of America.

iUniverse rev. date: 12/10/2013

DEDICATION

This book is dedicated first and foremost to all of the victims of the *Great Bahamas Hurricane of 1929.* It is my hope that their stories will live on for future generations of Bahamians to read about and to appreciate why this storm was regarded as "The Greatest Bahamian Hurricane of the 20th Century!"

To Mr. Les Brown, who at a conference held here in the Bahamas through his own unique way and method reminded me: 1) "Pass it on"; 2) "It is important how you use your down time"; 3) "Someone's opinion of you doesn't have to become a reality"; and 4) "In the time of adversity, expand!" To Dr. Myles Munroe, who always reminds me: 1) "Die empty!" 2) "Pursue your purpose!" 3) "Sight is the function of the eyes and vision is the function of the heart,"; and 4) "Maximize your potential." I listened to them, and this book is the end result . . .

Thank you, Mr. Les Brown and Dr. Myles Munroe, for your invaluable contribution to my life.

Dr. Martin Luther King, Jr., once said: 1)"Faith is taking the first step even when you don't see the whole staircase."; and 2)"If you can't fly, then run. If you can't run, then walk. If you can't walk, then crawl- but whatever you do, you have to keep MOVING FORWARD."

Mahatma Gandhi once said, "You must be the change you want to see in the world!" and "There are 2 types of people in this world, those that take the credit and those that actually do the work. Take my advice and follow the latter, as there is a lot less competition there."

Michelle Obama once said, "Success isn't about how much money you make, it's about the difference you make in people's lives!"

CONTENTS

FOREWORD

"Hurricanes cause the most severe natural disasters in the Western Hemisphere. Impacts range from wind-borne damages, freshwater flooding from rainfall, storm surge, salt-water flooding from the ocean, destructive ocean waves, and tornadoes in the hurricane's outer rainbands. Today, hurricanes commonly cause massive disruptions to society and can often take the lives of hundreds of people or more. Because of the wide geographic range of the Bahamas spread across Hurricane Alley, this island country is affected almost annually by these cyclonic disturbances.

Mr. Wayne Neely, the foremost Hurricane Historian of the Bahamas, has recounted the stories of many hurricanes, as well as the people who were impacted by them. In this newest book, Mr. Neely recounts the life cycle, destruction, and long-lasting impacts from one of the most devastating of Bahamian hurricanes: the Great Bahamas Hurricane of 1929. The effects from this Saffir-Simpson Hurricane Wind Scale Category 4 hurricane were extreme for the island nation. The impacts were even more severe because of the extremely slow movement of the hurricane, which caused winds, rain, surge and waves for several days.

It is crucial that such events be recalled in detail so that our society can best prepare for the inevitable return of such devastating events. Mr. Neely successfully provides the reader with this information and does his part in helping us all be ready for the great hurricanes of the future."

Christopher Landsea
Science and Operations Officer
NOAA/NWS/NCEP/National Hurricane Center

Christopher W. Landsea (born 1965) is an American meteorologist, formerly a research meteorologist with the Hurricane Research Division of Atlantic Oceanographic & Meteorological Laboratory at NOAA, and now the Science and Operations Officer at the National Hurricane Center. He is a member of the American Geophysical Union and the American Meteorological Society. Landsea earned his doctoral degree in Atmospheric Science at Colorado State University. He served as chair of the American Meteorological Society's Committee on Tropical Meteorology and Tropical Cyclone. Landsea was recognized with the American Meteorological Society's Banner I. Miller Award for "best contribution to the science of hurricane and tropical weather forecasting."

In January 2005, Landsea withdrew from his participation in the IPCC (Intergovernmental Panel on Climate Change) Fourth Assessment Report, criticizing it for using "a process that I view as both being motivated by pre-conceived agendas and being scientifically unsound." Landsea claimed the IPCC had become politicized and that the leadership ignored his concerns. Landsea does not believe that global warming has a strong influence on hurricanes: "Global warming might be enhancing hurricane winds, but only by 1 percent or 2 percent." He strongly questions the accuracy of the historical global hurricane database for comparisons with current observations, citing an uncounted, catastrophic 1970 storm as an example.

Over the years, Landsea's work has involved the general hurricane FAQ currently on the Atlantic Oceanographic and Meteorological Laboratory website and the Atlantic hurricane reanalysis. Landsea has contributed to Science, Bulletin of the American Meteorological Society, Journal of Climate, *and* Nature. *He has been vocal on the lack of a link between global warming and current hurricane intensity change. Landsea has published a number of research papers on cyclones and hurricanes. He is the author of* Hurricanes, Typhoons, and Tropical Cyclones: FAQ. *He also has been the lead scientist in the Atlantic hurricane reanalysis since 1997.*

PREFACE

Over the last 23 years of my life as a professional Bahamian meteorologist, hurricanes and their impact on my country of the Bahamas and the region as a whole has led me to write eight books on hurricanes. These books have allowed me to procure some of the best meteorologists in the business to write the foreword for me, from Bryan Norcross, Herbert Saffir, Phil Klotzbach, Professor William Gray, Steve Lyons and in this book Chris Landsea. This was done not only to add credibility to these books but also to show the importance of hurricanes and their great impact on the lives of people of all walks of life here in the Bahamas and around the region. The weather affects everyone, whether we like it or not. It is our constant companion - as tranquil, as turbulent, as phenomenal, and sometimes as unpredictable as life itself.

Many years ago, when I had the idea to write the first volume of *The Great Bahamas Hurricane of 1929,* I did something unique and different from many local authors. I travelled to many of the islands in the Bahamas to interview numerous persons who had experienced this storm. One thing that surprised me back then was how great an impact this storm had on their lives. Many of them cried as they related their stories of this storm, and others recalled with great details the impact of this storm. The majority of the persons I've interviewed have since passed on, but thankfully I was able to extract from them a vital part of Bahamian history. This information will be passed on for future generations of Bahamians to realize and appreciate how great an impact this storm had on the Bahamas at the time.

Devastating and deadly hurricanes, like this one in 1929 are nothing new to the Bahamas. For example, in September of 1866, a destructive hurricane struck the Bahamas killing 387 persons. In 1899, another deadly hurricane wreaked havoc here in the Bahamas, killing over 334 persons. Then in July 1926, a massive hurricane struck the Bahamas at peak intensity of 140 mph, killing 268 persons. As these events illustrate, Earth is a restless planet, a work in progress, where hurricanes can wreak havoc on both the most advanced and the most impoverished islands here in the Bahamas. This book will explore all aspects of this deadly hurricane, which occurred in 1929 and lay claim to 134 victims. Furthermore, I will also explore all aspects of hurricanes and illuminate the science behind them. Additionally, I will seek to astonish and educate many residents, as I investigate and explain the meteorological processes behind hurricanes.

The Great Bahamas Hurricane of 1929 never had a name because the naming system we presently use did not exist at the time. Today, most people know this hurricane as "the Great Bahamas Hurricane of 1929," "the Storm or Gale of 1929," "the Great Bahama Storm," "the Three-day Storm," or "the Great Andros Hurricane of 1929." Whichever name you mention, chances are those who were unlucky enough to be around at that time would know exactly what you were referring to. And in most cases, they would give a detailed account of what took place on those fateful three days of utter destruction and mayhem. To the average Bahamian at the time, this hurricane had a tremendous impact. As such, it deserves a much bigger place in Bahamian history than it currently holds. Chances are that most young people will not know of this storm, and while older people may have heard about it from their parents or grandparents, they probably won't know much about what happened. This book will educate readers about this hurricane and the impact that it had on the Bahamian Islands. I believe this storm deserves more than just a footnote, bookmark or sentence in Bahamian history.

English and Spanish colonizers of the New World expected to encounter a harsh and threatening physical environment. The deep, dark forests, the unexpectedly extreme climate, the unknown flora and fauna - all were perceived as menacing and potentially disruptive to the colonial explorers. But perhaps nothing was more threatening to colonists in the Caribbean than the powerful and deadly hurricanes and tropical storms. These storms regularly swept across the region, devastating cities and leveling plantations, disrupting trade and commerce, and plunging society into general disarray. Hurricanes were an entirely new phenomenon for the early Spanish and English colonial explorers, and these explorers and colonists learned the hard way in which these storms devastated their new-found homes here in the Caribbean. Fortunately, over the years we've come a long way in our understanding and appreciation of the nature and character of these deadly storms. It is a great storm like this one in 1929 that allowed us as meteorologists to use this deadly storm as a template to help forecast future storms and in the final analysis help to save lives.

Each day, it seems as if there is a new report or article published regarding changes in weather, climate, global warning, or even a new storm that ravaged some remote or populated corner of the Earth. Claims of a hotter planet, a stormier ocean, more violent winters, more frequent hurricanes, never before have we been more tuned in to the local and international weather reports. Is it that the weather is more severe, as some experts claim, or is it simply that we have more access to weather news? Today, we have more access to weather news, 24-hour cable TV channels dedicated solely to weather, stronger emphasis in newspapers, magazines, the Internet, and news stations, and they all reminds us of how vulnerable we are to the weather. It has a lot to do with the fact that advanced technology has allowed weather forecasters and scientists to broadcast the latest weather information within seconds, but the technology of forecasting and the unilateral communications between countries - even the most remote - has never been better. So it can be said that readers, viewers, and everyday people have never been more aware of their surroundings, thanks to improvements in technology. Nowadays, Bahamians can watch hurricanes like Wilma of 2005, Frances of 2004 or Irene of 2011 raging through the Bahamas from their living rooms. They can watch film footage of storm surge or flood damage along the coast of Grand Bahama or some other populated island of the Bahamas. So, now is a great time to be engaged in why the weather is important, not only here in the Bahamas where I live, but all over the planet.

Hurricanes are born over the warm waters of the North Atlantic. As the summer sun heats down on the oceans, the warm water vapour rises into the atmosphere, forming cumulonimbus clouds. Rich with moisture and energy from the ocean, these clouds may combine to form vast, low pressure whirlpools. Strong winds start the clouds spinning; in the Northern Hemisphere, the spin is counterclockwise because of the Coriolis Effect. This is an apparent curving motion of anything, such as wind, caused by the Earth's rotation. It was first described in 1835 by French scientist Gustave-Gaspard Coriolis. Such tropical depressions generally move west, then northwest, gathering energy and moisture as they travel throughout the region. When a tropical depression develops to the point at which the maximum sustained winds reach a speed of 75 miles an hour, it is classified as a hurricane. In this stage, the storm begins a west or northwest track, gathering additional energy from the warm tropical waters of the North Atlantic. Evaporation of surface waters feeds water vapour into the ascending currents of the storm. In the meantime, the atmospheric pressure continues to drop and the eye forms, eventually becoming a full-fledged hurricane destroying any and everything in its path.

By definition, hurricanes are out of the ordinary, the antitheses of our everyday lives during the summer months. Meteorologists, scholars and even students concerned with the slower, steadier rhythms of hurricanes of the past and present realize that when it comes to hurricanes, we should try to avoid them, and then if that is not possible we should make all of the necessary preparations for the impending storm and then bunker down in a home or some hurricane shelter and witness one of nature's most awesome atmospheric shows. But if studying hurricanes allows us to observe these familiar patterns at moments of heightened danger, it also invites us to see that the 'normal' workings of culture, society, and politics are far from smooth. Hurricanes evoke the defense of established ways precisely because they so dramatically reveal the challenges to established ways.

As the September hurricane drew near, old-timers lifted their heads, studying the birds' movement and other animals' behavior, sky and the small, fast-moving low clouds called scuds, sniffing the air, peering at the sea. There were signs of approaching trouble; something was brewing, but what? Most of them never expected a storm of this magnitude and duration, considering they had just been struck by several deadly storms within the space of three years. Many persons after experiencing this storm wondered if this was an omen from the gods or the Almighty God, because these storms were striking the Bahamas too frequently. Today's thorough hurricane warnings were unheard of in 1929 and for some years thereafter. To make matters worse, many persons on the Out Islands had very limited advanced warnings, and in some instance none at all. In fact, in 1928, another deadly hurricane struck the Bahamas, killing over 18 persons. It was not a killer storm like this one, but it brought to Nassau British Royalty, Prince George, the youngest son of King George V and Queen Mary, who was serving with the Royal Navy. His ship, attached to Bermuda and West Indies Station, was sent to lend assistance to this hurricane-prone colony. The excitement was great, as His Royal Highness Prince George was the first member of a British Royal Family to pay us a visit in almost seventy years, when Queen Victoria's youngest son, Prince Albert, spent a short time in Nassau. He, too, came in a ship of the Royal Navy.

Prior to 1929, before the development of modern methods for tracking weather, people had little warning that a dangerous and powerful storm was bearing down upon them. Today, storms are watched carefully from the moment they first begin to form near the African Coast to the time they hit some country in the Caribbean, Central or North America. Weather satellites in geostationary orbit above the equator can keep a constant watch on the areas where these storms are born. When a storm is spotted, 'Hurricane Reconnaissance Aircrafts' are dispatched to investigate the area. The aircraft fly directly into the growing storm, at a significant risk to the pilot and scientists onboard, to collect data on pressure, temperature, humidity, wind speed and direction, and rainfall. As the storm approaches land, radars also track it continuously. Each change in the storm's track is noted in order to predict the storm's exact landfall and give area residents the earliest possible warning of the approaching storm.

The autumn of 1929 arrived, and with it came a raging devil of a storm. A hurricane was known to be east of the islands of the Bahamas Islands and appeared to be passing to the north. It turned in a southwesterly direction and bore down on Nassau and other islands in the Northwest Bahamas. It shook the long-suffering capital and the settlements of Fox Hill, Adelaide, Gambier and others like a crazed thing. For three consecutive days, the winds blew from the northeast. The rain lashed at houses and trees, at gardens and crops, at docks and boats. Nothing was sacred to this storm. Churches lost their roofs or were blown to bits-along with dance pavilions. The scene in the city was chaotic. Royal palms stood bravely, their tops frizzled like the hair of rock 'n' roll singers. Sponge beds and flamingo breeding grounds at Andros, directly in the hurricane's path, were almost washed away.

This gigantic storm departed Nassau and then went on to devastate the island of Andros, leaving a massive death toll in its wake. The history of Andros can be traced back to pre-Columbus times, when the island was inhabited by the Lucayan Indians. The early inhabitants of the island were known as the invisible people because no one could see them due to the fact that they coated themselves with a special mud comprising the blue-green algae found on the island. That made them invisible in sunlight and only visible under ultraviolet light. When the Europeans came to the island, they saw evidence of human inhabitants but could not see them. The first recorded "discovery" of Andros—or "La Isla del Espiritu Santo" (The Island of the Holy Spirit) as the Spanish named it—was in 1550 while they were searching for slave labour. They referred to the island by that name because of its vast forest and the interplay of land and water, which made Andros one of the truly unique and mystical land forms in the Caribbean at the time. However, by 1782, the island was called San Andreas, possibly named after the 1,400 inhabitants of St. Andreas Island off the Mosquito Coast who came to inhabit the island in 1787. Although no one really knows for sure, the modern name Andros is believed to be in honor of Sir Edmond Andros, Commander of His Majesty's Forces in Barbados in 1672.

Several factors are involved in why storms become extreme or great, including their strength, frequency, duration, and most importantly-who's in the storm's path. Sure, we all see the damage of extreme storms (such as what this one in 1929 caused), but how they form can be somewhat of a guessing game. Meteorologists have a good lead on why most weather goes bad, but not always. And it's not just Mother Nature who controls the spin of a storm. Man also has a hand in some of the heavy weather and climate changes planet Earth has been witness to. Weather might be all around us, but where 'great' hurricanes strikes is the last place you want to be around. Each year, hurricanes kill and injure thousands of people and cause billions of dollars in damage worldwide. Tragedy could be averted with a good dose of common sense and an eye toward the forecast, but severe hurricanes are complicated systems of nature because hurricanes are notoriously unpredictable, especially when it comes to the track and intensity of these systems because they can bring a major city or even a country to its knees. Add to the fray that more people than ever are over-crowding the coastal areas of countries within this region, and you have the perfect recipe for great devastation of cataclysmic proportions. Storm damages in the Bahamas in the busy 2004 and 2005 seasons stretched into over 300 million dollars, and flooding in low-lying areas further exacerbated the devastation.

People have tried to forecast the weather for at least as long as there has been recorded history. All modern forecasting methods involve observations of current conditions, along with a combination of historical data, scientific method, and computer modeling. Before people had instruments to measure parameters such as temperature, humidity, and barometric pressure, there were ways in which the weather could be forecast, or at least ways in which attempts at forecasting could be made. People noticed that certain observations or events were usually followed by fair weather, while other observations or events were usually followed by foul weather. Here in the Bahamas, many of the older folks looked at the large flock of birds flying in from many of the cays back to the mainland as a sign of an approaching storm. While others simply looked at the behavior of other animals such as, pigs, goats, dogs and cats to determine whether there was an approaching hurricane over that island. Tropical storms and hurricanes have been influencing people for centuries, but only in the past one hundred years have we been able to track their progress with increasing proficiency. Each tropical cyclone we monitor contributes to our very short hurricane climatology. Memorable hurricanes such as the Great Bahamas Hurricane of 1929 have left their mark on coastal areas, towns, and people around the world. Some devastating hurricanes have been 'retired.' Their names will no longer be used for future storms. Other names are repeated every six years in the North Atlantic.

The term 'hurricane' refers generally to a revolving storm that forms over tropical waters of the North Atlantic, where the sustained winds exceed 74mph. Such hurricanes are about 300 to 500 miles across and can cause widespread damage on landfall. Hurricanes are the most widely publicized of all storms. They occur every year in this hemisphere and form over these warm waters of the tropics and subtropics, but they often end up in the temperate regions, where they die out or merge with some mid-latitude system. In this book, we will discuss hurricanes and then go into great details about one of the greatest storms to impact the Bahamas in 1929

INTRODUCTION

Hurricanes are quite possibly the most dramatic, feared, and intense of all the Earth's natural phenomena. The very name "hurricane" conjures up the screaming roar of winds gone mad, torrential rains that beat down on the Earth like a musician's drum, and the erratic movements of a spinning top. Hurricanes are marvels of nature that are today, thankfully, spotted and charted well in advance of landfall. But a new dimension of suspense has been added to them because for hours, days and perhaps weeks, we here in the Bahamas lie in the path of these dangerous storms already battened down, tense, fearful and feeling vulnerable waiting for the storm to strike. The year 1929 was a time of recession in the Bahamas and worldwide. Worldwide prices of Bahamian sponge and sisal plummeted when wartime demand ended abruptly and remittances dried up as servicemen and migrant workers returned to swell the labour market. Tourism was in its infancy, and the little tourism trade we had did not recover quickly because passenger shipping was in short supply, and an unfavorable currency ratio between sterling and dollar penalized a colony that was more than ever dependent on imports. These setbacks were exacerbated by natural disasters, especially this one in 1929 and two in 1926. Prolonged droughts hampered any efforts to increase food production. Even though this storm only struck Nassau and Andros directly, it still scourged many of the Out Islands indirectly and had a direct impact on the sponge industry.

It didn't help that there was a severe drought in the central and southeast Bahamas, and it was further exacerbated by the worldwide Great Depression of 1929. As a result, the Bahamas had to rely almost exclusively on itself to bring the country back to some degree of normalcy after this hurricane. The Great Depression was an economic slump in North America, Europe, and other industrialized areas of the world that began in 1929 and lasted until about 1939. It was the longest and most severe depression ever experienced by the industrialized Western world. Though the U.S. economy had gone into depression six months earlier, the Great Depression may be said to have begun with a catastrophic collapse of stock-market prices on the New York Stock Exchange in October 1929.

During the next three years, stock prices in the United States continued to fall, until by late 1932 they had dropped to only about 20 percent of their value in 1929. Besides ruining many thousands of individual investors, this precipitous decline in the value of assets greatly strained banks and other financial institutions, particularly those holding stocks in their portfolios. Many banks were consequently forced into insolvency; by 1933, 11,000 of the United States' 25,000 banks had failed. The failure of so many banks, combined with a general and nationwide loss of confidence in the economy, led to much-reduced levels of spending and demand and hence of production, thus aggravating the downward spiral. The result was drastically falling output and drastically rising unemployment; by 1932, U.S. manufacturing output had fallen to 54 percent of its 1929 level, and unemployment had risen to between 12 and 15 million workers, or 25-30 percent of the work force. The Great Depression began in the United States but quickly turned into a worldwide economic slump owing to the special and intimate relationships that had been forged between the United States and European economies after World War I. So once the American economy slumped and the flow of American investment credits to Europe dried up, prosperity tended to collapse there as well. The Bahamas was not a major tourist destination during this storm, but the select few winter residents who visited our shores were drastically curtailed due to this storm and the Great Depression of 1929.

It must be noted, however that the effects of the Volstead Act rapidly lifted the gloom hanging over the Bahamas, especially for Nassau and those Bahamians most able to benefit from Americans' desire to evade Prohibition. The Bahamian capital was ideally situated as an entrepôt, easily capable of expanding its normal inflow of West Indian rum, English gin and Scotch whiskey, which was then filtered through the northern islands to an American coast almost impossible to blockade effectively-especially by way of Bimini and West End, Grand Bahama, only fifty miles from Florida. The flow of illicit liquor became a flood, and the infusion of new wealth into the Bahamas was immediate.

The Great Bahamas Hurricane of 1929 shocked Nassau and Andros out of its apathy towards such great damage from these storms. Where builders had grown careless, sacrificing durability for a more modern and affluent look, there was major destruction throughout the city of Nassau and settlements in Andros. Weak old houses, particularly porches and verandahs, succumbed to the strong winds of this three-day storm, while fallen trees spanned across many roadways and many large trees were uprooted. Many small houses, some of them a little more than just small cabins comprised of just one room, collapsed completely, and many roofs were seen flying through the air during the storm. Heavy rains flooded all low-lying areas and prevented any kind of movement through the main thoroughfares of New Providence and Andros. Parts of the southern district of Nassau and the Pond area south of East Bay Street were over four feet deep in water for several days.

Families devastated by the storm took shelter with a select few kind neighbours, both here in Nassau and on the island of Andros, often for a few weeks to several months after the storm. In this book, I will take you back to a time when others were not as fortunate as we are today. The year was 1929, during the month of September, a time when Bahamians felt the full fury of a hurricane that left an extra large set of footprints in the sands of Bahamian history. The research for this book was worth the torture of trying to find any and everyone who experienced agony and grief from this monster of a storm. Sometimes it required me to walk communities like Bain Town, Johnson Road, The Bluff, High Rock and Yellow Elder, searching for anyone over the age of 88 (because anyone younger would not have clear memories of this storm).

I spoke to many persons, and all were accommodating and helpful. Most stopped what they were doing and often took hours of their time to recall their experiences, others found friends and relatives who had experienced the storm. Individuals like Illford Forbes, Macushla Hazelwood, Hilbert Pinder, Dorothy Davis, Jerry Gibson and Daniel Rahming Sr. gave first-hand accounts of living through three long, agonizing days of this monster storm. I found it intriguing to actually sit and talk with them about their recollections of some 84 years ago. It was noteworthy to see how in-depth most of them could recall the events of those days and the havoc caused to their lives. The more people I spoke to, the more important and significant this project became to me. I followed the research wherever it took me. Sometimes that meant jumping on a plane at short notice to interview a man in Abaco, or Andros, or parking my car and walking the streets of Nassau communities or visiting the old folk's homes or the local churches to talk with those who had lived through the storm.

Sadly, the majority of persons I spoke to have since passed away, including Illford Forbes, Macushla Hazelwood, Daniel Rahming Sr., Edward Bain, Melsheva Ferguson, Hilbert Pinder and many others. Had I not had the opportunity to speak with them, their information would have gone to the grave with them. I feel a debt to them and all others who contributed in one way or another. For this, I will be eternally grateful to all of those persons who contributed their recollections of this storm. My job from here on is to see that this storm is placed in its rightful shelf in the archives of Bahamian history and that the lessons learned from this storm are never forgotten. This book will provide a record of this historical storm drawn from all levels of society, leaving you better informed about the Hurricane of 1929 and about hurricanes in general.

Modern weather forecasting depends on gathering, assessing and disseminating millions of observations and measurements of atmospheric conditions from all over the world. No single system of measurements or instruments can give meteorologists a complete picture, so information is fed in from a wide range of sources. Most important are the many land-based weather stations, from city centers to remote islands. Ships and radio signals from drifting weather buoys and ships report details of conditions at sea. Balloons and specially equipped airplanes take measurements up through the atmosphere, while in space satellites beam back pictures of cloud and temperature patterns. It is difficult to imagine what it was like during the Hurricane of 1929. Meteorologists are now able to follow a hurricane from its origin as it comes off the African coast as a tropical wave, to a tropical disturbance, to a tropical depression, to a tropical storm, and finally to a full-fledged hurricane. In the Bahamas, we take this for granted and often never realize the importance of modern technology and man's advancement over the last 50 to 75 years.

Weather satellites did not exist until the 1960s, but they revolutionized the field of meteorology in a way that no other instrument ever did. This led to more refined forecasts and answered a lot of meteorological questions that ultimately save many lives. In 1929, there were no computers or televisions, and few people had radios, which were considered a luxury item. No radar was available for storm tracking. Today, with our sophisticated early detection and warning equipment, storms produce minimal death tolls, and property damage is reduced. Today, we can turn on our radios and get up-to-date weather reports every six hours from the Bahamas Meteorological Office, and if there is a hurricane within striking distance, updates are reported every three hours. We can log onto our computers and track storms 24 hours a day to get up-to-the-minute information. In 1929, none of these modern conveniences was available, and storms caused mass confusion, total devastation, and lots of casualties.

Andrew McKinney, who lived with his father on the Eastern Road, said his family was fortunate to have both a radio and a telephone at the time of the storm. But they were of little use because there was little being broadcast on the radio (this was before ZNS was started as a hurricane warning service in the 1930s). If there was an emergency telephone call to make, you had to go to Miami. At that time, you could count the number of people in Nassau with telephones on one hand.

There are now all types of instruments to measure the different elements of a hurricane, including marine barometers, tide gauges, wave poles, and radiosondes weather balloons, to name a few. The radar was introduced during the Second World War. It was used to track airplanes in-flight, but people began to realize that the radars also depicted areas of severe weather. After the war, military radars were used as forecasting tools. Nowadays, advanced systems like Doppler radars can detect areas of precipitation and measure rainfall intensity, as well as the speed of precipitation movement. A Doppler radar can give a three-dimensional, cross-sectional view of a thunderstorm cell, a hurricane or tornado funnel and gather vital information that can lead to saving lives. The satellite is another recent technological advancement that allows meteorologists to track storms more accurately. The satellite allows meteorologists to see the origins of a hurricane and study these storms in much more detail, resulting in a better forecast.

Reconnaissance aircraft are another major advancement in the study and forecasting of hurricanes. Flying into the eye of a hurricane is a great way to gather vital information about the storm. On July 27, 1943, Major Joseph P. Duckworth and navigator Ralph O' Hair took an aircraft from a base in Texas without permission to see what it was like to fly inside a hurricane. When they returned, their senior officer, Lieutenant William Jones Burdick, complained bitterly, not because they removed an aircraft without permission, but because he had not been taken along. So, a second trip was made the same day. Major Duckworth was later decorated for the flights.

We now take for granted the low death tolls in hurricane, but this was not always the case. For example, the Great Galveston Hurricane of 1900 killed over 6,000 people in Texas. The Great Lake Okeechobee Hurricane of 1928 killed over 2,500 persons, and Hurricane Camille in 1969 killed 256 persons in Mississippi, Louisiana, and Virginia. Today, death tolls have dropped while property damage has increased because more people live on or near the coast.

In 1929, local fishermen discerned the weather by watching the movements of low clouds (called 'scuds'), birds, trees and other animals. Some islanders used a 'Parameter Shell' to forecast the weather. The animal matter inside of the shell was removed, and the shell was painted in a blue dye called 'Iniqua Blue.' The shell would be found in most homes of the day, and it turned speckled white if it was going to rain. For heavy rain, the speckles would be larger and the ink would turn a deeper shade of blue. If it was calm or fair weather, the shell would turn ashy white. Although many people swore by this method, it was an unreliable way to forecast the weather compared to the modern instruments we have today. Meteorologists still use an instrument called a barometer to measure air pressure, but in 1929 there was no Bahamas Meteorological Office, so people had to rely on their own instruments or natural instincts. In those days, islanders referred to the barometer or the barograph as a 'parameter.' In some settlements, it was located at the district commissioner's residence and was a crude version of today's Aneroid Barometer. A steep drop in pressure would move the indicator to suggest some sort of disturbed weather in the vicinity.

The district commissioner would inform citizens that severe weather was approaching and they should take the necessary precautions. This would mean hauling boats out of the water or moving them to safe harbour, battening houses, stocking up on food and water, harvesting whatever crops they could and securing livestock. People would ride out the storm in their houses or at a designated shelter. Many farm animals were slaughtered and cooked, salted or smoked because they would likely be lost in the storm anyway. Refrigerators and freezers were out of the reach of the regular population.

Andrew McKinney provided me with the only known barograph chart of this storm-a rare find since no Bahamian meteorological records were kept in those days. This chart was from an instrument called a barograph, which is a continuous recording barometer. As the storm approached, the pressure reading dropped. The reading also gives some idea on the date, time, size and strength of the storm-information that a regular barometer would not be able to give. There is no mistaking the steep drop in pressure reading on the chart between Wednesday and Thursday, an indication that this was a very strong and intense hurricane. We do not know the accuracy or condition of the barometer that recorded this chart, but it is nonetheless a very valuable piece of evidence showing the passage of this hurricane.

Another method of forecasting was the observation of tidal changes. Water levels were often much higher at low and high tide just before the onset of a hurricane, and this gave people a small window of opportunity to prepare. This increase in the height of the water is because the low pressure at the centre of a hurricane pushes down on the water with great force, and because of the storm's rotation, the water piles up (or bulges) ahead of the storm. Today we refer to this as the storm surge. Some citizens would have their own barograph or barometer to give them warning. A hurricane is a low pressure system, so the closer it approaches, the lower the pressure reading. The eye of the storm has the lowest pressure. People also resorted to the Beaufort Wind Scale to estimate the proximity of storms and the speed of the wind.

A hurricane causes massive destruction to anything along its path. A hurricane can cause severe weather and high wind speeds, which leaves damage for miles and miles. Flooding, loss of homes, businesses, and even someone's life all accounts for the negative effects from these storms.

The effects of one hurricane, such as Hurricane Andrew, which left $250 million worth of damage here in the Bahamas alone. When Andrew came ashore on North Eleuthera, it left more than 20 to 25 feet of storm surge, which resulted in 4 causalities in Eleuthera. Hurricanes are the most devastating of all natural disasters, affecting thousands of people each year. During each hurricane season, innocent people are injured or killed, properties are demolished, and money is forever lost. Hurricanes cause damage in a variety of ways, including strong winds, storm surges, flooding, tornadoes, and rip tides. The strong winds of a hurricane are most often associated with the widespread damage from a hurricane. The rapidly moving winds can uproot trees, destroy cars, and level buildings. A storm is first classified as a hurricane when its winds exceed 74 miles per hour, though many may even reach as dangerously high as 200 miles per hour in gusts.

Hurricanes also cause storm surges, the rising of the sea level caused by low pressure, high winds, and high waves. These are characteristic of hurricanes as they reach land. Storm surges cause significant flooding, and being caught in one is almost certain death. The storm surge from the storm occurs as strong winds blow toward the shore push water in its direction, causing much of the coastal flooding. The central pressure of the hurricane is low enough in altitude that the lack of atmospheric weight above the eye and eye wall of the hurricane causes a bulge in the ocean surface. This low pressure lifts up the ocean surface in the center. Storm surges vary in height based on the hurricane's intensity, ranging from 5 to 25 feet. The distance that a storm surge travels inland is determined by the landscape. In flat areas, a surge can intrude as far as a mile, leading to flooding and the destruction of property

Flooding is caused by the storm surges and the heavy rainfall associated with the storm. Even when the hurricane moves inland and begins to deteriorate, there still may be a tremendous amount of rainfall. Many people are unaware of tornadoes that form during hurricanes. These tornadoes are found relatively close to the eye wall of a hurricane, where the conditions are ideal for their formation. The tornadoes occur in heavy areas of rain, making them extremely difficult to track. Storm surge is the final source of damage from hurricanes. Rip tides are very powerful sea currents moving outward from the shore when a strong storm is nearby. They are formed by the strong winds pushing water toward the shore, similar to storm surges. Winds from tropical cyclones push waves up against the shoreline even if the storm is hundreds of miles away, making rip tides the first indications of an approaching hurricane. The incoming waves create an underwater sandbar close to shore and the waves continuously push water in-between the sandbar and the shore until a section of this sandbar collapses. The excess water is forced through the gap, creating a very strong but narrow current away from the shore. Rip tides are so powerful that a person physically cannot overcome the pull of the tide. However, these tides are narrow enough that if a person swims parallel to the shore, it is possible to escape the current.

There is no other single regular producer of hurricanes in the North Atlantic like the so-called Atlantic conveyor belt. It is exactly what it sounds like: a surge of wind off the northwestern African coast that spirals over increasingly warm water as it heads toward the Caribbean and Central and North America, gaining strength from the warm temperatures. When the winds inside the storm reach 74 miles per hour, it's a Category 1 hurricane. At 111 miles per hour, it becomes a Category 3 hurricane, and it is then considered a major hurricane. Here in the North Atlantic, storms spin counter-clockwise. This is due to the Coriolis effect, which is a product of the planet's rotation. The Coriolis effect is the apparent curvature of global winds, ocean currents, and everything else that moves freely across the Earth's surface. The curvature is due to the rotation of the Earth on its axis. The effect was discovered by the nineteenth century French engineer Gaspard C. Coriolis. He used mathematical formulas to explain that the path of any object set in motion above a rotating surface will curve in relation to objects on that surface. Once air has been set in motion, it becomes deflected from its path as a result of that rotation. The force and frequency of storms in the North Atlantic may vary, but they are all measured on the Saffir-Simpson Hurricane Wind Scale.

The term 'climate' describes the average 'weather' conditions over a long period of time that can prevail at any given point around the world at a given time of the year. Daily weather may differ dramatically from that expected on the basis of climatic statistics. Energy from the sun drives the global climate system. Much of this incoming solar energy is absorbed in the tropics and provides the perfect conditions for hurricanes to form and strengthen over these vast warm tropical waters. Outgoing solar radiation, much of which exits at high latitudes, plays a vital role in balancing incoming solar radiation. To achieve a balance on a global scale, huge amounts of heat are moved from the tropics to polar regions by both the atmosphere and the oceans, thereby providing for life on Earth as we know it today.

Hurricanes are huge, spiraling tropical storms that can pack wind speeds of over 155 miles an hour and unleash more than 2.4 trillion gallons (9 trillion liters) of rain a day. These same tropical storms are known by different names around the world, such as cyclones in the northern Indian Ocean and Bay of Bengal, and typhoons in the western Pacific Ocean. The Atlantic Ocean's hurricane season peaks from mid-August to late October and averages twelve named storms, six hurricanes, and three major hurricanes per year. Hurricanes begin as tropical disturbances in warm ocean waters of the North Atlantic with surface temperatures of at least 80 degrees Fahrenheit (26.5 degrees Celsius). These low pressure systems are fed by energy from the warm seas. If a storm achieves wind speeds of up to 38 miles an hour, it becomes known as a tropical depression. A tropical depression becomes a tropical storm and is given an assigned name when its sustained wind speeds top 39 miles an hour. When a storm's sustained wind speeds reach 74 miles an hour, it becomes a hurricane and earns a category rating of 1 to 5 on the Saffir-Simpson Hurricane Wind Scale.

Hurricanes are enormous heat engines that generate energy on a staggering scale. They draw heat from warm, moist ocean air and release it through condensation of water vapour in thunderstorms. Hurricanes spin around a low-pressure center known as the "eye." Sinking air makes this 20 to 30 mile-wide area notoriously calm. But the eye is surrounded by a circular "eye wall" that hosts the storm's strongest winds and rain. These storms bring destruction ashore in many different ways. When a hurricane makes landfall, it often produces a devastating storm surge that can reach 20 feet high and extend nearly 100 miles. Seventy-five percent of all hurricane deaths result from storm surges. A hurricane's high winds are also destructive and may spawn tornadoes. Torrential rains cause further damage by spawning floods and landslides, which may occur many miles inland. The best defense against a hurricane is an accurate forecast that gives people time to get out of its way and provide adequate preparation and planning. The Bahamas Department of Meteorology (in collaboration with the National Hurricane Center in Florida) issues hurricane Alerts for storms that may endanger communities within 60 hours, watches for storms that may endanger communities within 48 hours, and hurricane warnings for storms that will make landfall within 36 hours.

Hurricane effects can create major problems. The maximum effects of a hurricane are usually felt within the right-front quadrant. Here, the winds are usually the strongest, storm surge is highest, and the possibility of tornadoes is greatest. It is important to know whether or not your area will be affected by the right-front quadrant. It could mean the difference between maximum hurricane conditions or a glancing blow. Storm surge is the fast uprising of sea level that happens when a hurricane approaches the coast. Two factors that cause storm surge are: first, strong winds that push the water toward the coast; and second, suction created by the storm's low pressure.

The Great Bahamas Hurricane of 1929 devastated some of the islands in the Northwest Bahamas, many of which sustained great damages due to the hurricane-caused storm surge. Long Wharf, which had been built to help reduce the damage caused by hurricane surge, was reduced to rubbles. Heavy rainfall is also produced by hurricanes. The average amount of rainfall usually varies between 6 and 12 inches. The most deadly rainfall occurs inland because a hurricane produces destructive floods. The flooding is the major cause of hurricane-related deaths. The danger from flooding depends on the storm's speed, other weather systems in the same area, the ground saturation, and the terrain.

Rains are heaviest in the six hours before and the six hours after the hurricane reaches landfall. Sometimes a hurricane can last for days and produce massive floods. The high winds from these storms are another cause of great devastation. The wind speed and potential damage of a hurricane is expressed as categories according to the Saffir-Simpson Hurricane Wind Scale. These high winds can easily destroy homes and buildings. Debris, such as signs or broken materials, can become airborne and penetrate just about anything with missile-like force.

Over the past 20 years, improvements in hurricane computer modeling, observational instrumentation and better training for forecasters have greatly increased forecast accuracy. Despite these advances, the many complex interactions that occur within the atmosphere are not fully understood or adequately modeled, producing errors in forecasts. The Bahamas Department of Meteorology here in the Bahamas, the National Hurricane Center in Miami along with other local and international agencies have several tools used to monitor hurricanes. While they are still far out in the ocean, indirect measurements of tropical storm and hurricane dimensions, as well as their wind speeds, use the 'Dvorak technique' and satellite imagery as their main tools, although ships and buoys also provide observations. The Dvorak technique (developed between 1969 and 1984 by Vernon Dvorak) is a widely used system to estimate tropical cyclone intensity (which includes tropical depression, tropical storm, and hurricane/typhoon/intense tropical cyclone intensities) based solely on visible and infrared satellite images. Once the storm comes closer to land, more direct measurements such as reconnaissance aircraft, radiosondes (upper air measurements), and automated surface observing stations (surface conditions) are also used. Once the system is within about 200 miles of the coast, radar provides important indirect measurements of the storm.

CHAPTER ONE

The impact and Dynamics
of Hurricanes

A tropical cyclone is a low-pressure system that forms in the tropics. 'Hurricane' is the name given to fully developed tropical cyclones that are found in the Atlantic Ocean, Caribbean Sea, Gulf of Mexico and the North Pacific Ocean east of the International Date Line. When local residents of an area refer to a hurricane, they are speaking of the violent, stormy weather system that brings torrential rains and destructive, high velocity winds of over 74 miles per hour. Hurricanes are also characterized by a heavy cloud cover, which reduces sunshine and makes visibility and temperatures very low. In other parts of the world, tropical cyclones are given other names. For example, in Australia they are known as Willy Willies, in India there are known as Tropical Cyclones and in the Pacific they are known as Typhoons. Hurricanes can only form in tropical regions due to their need for certain atmospheric and weather conditions only found there. Most hurricanes originate on the west coast of Africa, in the form of thunderstorms. As these thunderstorms move westwards over the ocean, they become low-pressure systems; first in the form of tropical depressions, then tropical storms and finally hurricanes.

Hurricanes usually take a matter of days to develop from a depression to a full-fledged hurricane, but this time period can vary depending on certain prevailing atmospheric conditions at the time. For a hurricane formation to take place, warm waters of temperatures higher than 26.5 degrees Celsius must be present. From these warm waters, evaporation takes place at a high rate. Warm, moist air above the ocean surfaces rises via convection currents. As this air rises, it condenses and storm clouds form. During condensation, energy is released in the form of heat, known as latent heat of condensation. Latent heat of condensation powers a hurricane. This latent heat warms air and causes it to rise. The risen air is replaced by more warm moist air from the ocean surfaces. This process is repeated continuously in a cycle. As heat is transferred from the surface to the atmosphere continually, a circular wind pattern (counter-clockwise in the Northern Hemisphere) is formed. Converging winds and a steep pressure gradient also help in hurricane formation, as they cause warm, moist air to rise, causing low pressure and circular wind patterns also.

Although hurricanes are low-pressure systems, they differ from the lows of the temperate latitudes. The hurricane is more symmetrical than the cyclone storms familiar to inhabitants of Europe, the interior United States, and other temperate regions. The hurricane, in its tropical stage, does not contain frontal systems. The isobars are almost a perfect circle, especially in a well-developed storm. The central pressure is usually lower (and sometimes much lower) than that of a cyclone in the temperate region. When a hurricane contains nearly circular isobars near its center, it is said to have 'tropical characteristics.' As a storm moves over land or over cold water, fronts develop and the isobars are no longer circular near the center. Such a hurricane is then said to have become 'extratropical.'

A hurricane is made up of three main parts: the eye, the eye wall and the rain bands. The eye is the calm region found in the centre of the hurricane. Here, pressure is at its lowest. Conditions within the eye are humid and not very windy. The eye wall surrounds the eye and is made of thick cumulonimbus clouds. Here, winds are most intense and rainfall heaviest. The rain bands are made of many thunderstorms circulating out from the eye. These play a key role in the evaporation/condensation cycle, which provides the system with energy it needs to sustain itself. Hurricanes are perhaps the most devastating of all natural disasters affecting the Earth today. They have a major impact of the physical and human environments. The physical environment can be defined as the structural features of the land, air and sea. The passing of a hurricane is always destructive to this environment. Most of the destruction is caused by the high-velocity winds and torrential rainfall that occur. These high-velocity winds along with a low pressure center leads to the formation of storm surges. Storm surges, sometimes many meters tall, crash against coastal areas; eroding beaches and damaging coastal homes and buildings. Storm surges also cause major damage to boats anchored in harbours.

Strong gusts of winds easily blow down power lines, uproot trees, bushes and other vegetation types. The pressure of the wind against the trees is so powerful that the trees have no choice but to fall down. Since many animals live in trees and bushes, many habitats are destroyed during this process. Powerful, destructive winds also push down communication poles, causing communication and utility lines to snap. The torrential rains (and sometimes the storm surge) are responsible for the flooding that occurs during hurricanes. Flooding is a natural disaster in itself. Houses and vehicles are swept away during a flood, possessions are destroyed and water supplies are polluted. Heavy torrential rainfall over a country during the passage of a hurricane can cause severe flooding in low-lying areas. If this occurs, buildings and crops could be destroyed. Together, torrential rains and powerful winds batter homes and other buildings, sometimes completely destroying them. They also bring on the death of crops and livestock, usually by uprooting and drowning respectively. The rains and wind can often damage road and bridges and other carriageways.

The human environment is the people that inhabit the Earth. Hurricanes impact on the human environment in a largely negative way. Due to the destruction of homes, many people are left exposed during hurricanes. Many of these people often die. The death-toll tends to be high and can range from under a hundred to even thousands of persons. Repair and restoration of damaged buildings and reconstruction of destroyed buildings can cost a country millions to billions of dollars. This greatly affects the economy and financial situation of a country. It also affects the lives of the citizens, as the rebuilding process can take many years. After the passage of a hurricane the ground water becomes polluted and contaminated, and this polluted and contaminated water supply cannot be used. If they do drink this water, diseases and infection can be contracted and spread. Damaged roads and workplaces make everyday functions hard to carry out. Trade and exchange are disrupted and life is made uncomfortable. The breakage of communications and utility lines leading to loss of power are a major inconvenience to many persons. They have to find means of living without electricity, telephone and sometimes television.

The destruction of crops and livestock have profound effects on the human environment. These provide food sources for people. When hurricanes occur, fields of crops can be lost, and many animals can die. When this occurs, there are food shortages, and hunger and starvation increase, causing an increase in crime. Hurricanes have a negative impact on both the human and physical environment. They are natural disasters, which cannot be prevented or stopped from occurring. Due to technological advancements made in the last few decades, though, hurricane formation can be spotted very early and their progress tracked and predicted. Hurricane warnings are then issued to places possibly and definitely in danger. Warnings give people time to reinforce their homes by boarding them up, etc., to stock up on food supplies and to move to "safer locations" if necessary and possible. Nonetheless, you can never guarantee your safety in the world's greatest natural disaster, the hurricane.

Each year, an average of twelve tropical storms develops over the Atlantic Ocean, Caribbean Sea, and the Gulf of Mexico. Many of these remain over the ocean, with approximately six of these storms becoming hurricanes each year. In an average 3-year period, roughly two hurricanes strike or brush the Bahamas coastline, anywhere from Inagua in the south to Grand Bahama in the north. Whether you live on the coast, have a condo in the Bahamas or are vacationing in the warm tropics of the Caribbean, hurricanes pose an enormous threat to humans and their habitat. The magnitude of these storms can devastate towns, tearing down power lines, ripping buildings apart and causing disastrous flooding hundreds of miles inland.

Tropical cyclones, which are simply low-pressure systems that have developed over tropical or sub-tropical waters, are the starting point for a hurricane. When winds of a tropical storm (39-73 mph) reach a constant speed of 74 mph or greater, the storm can then be classified as a hurricane. Typically, the season for the North Atlantic Basin (Atlantic Ocean, Caribbean Sea and the Gulf of Mexico) runs from June 1 to November 30, with hurricanes on average ranging from 200 to 600 miles in diameter. The term 'hurricane' is adapted to any such storm occurring in the North Atlantic, but be aware that in other parts of the world they are referred to as typhoons and severe tropical cyclones.

A cross-sectional view into a hurricane:

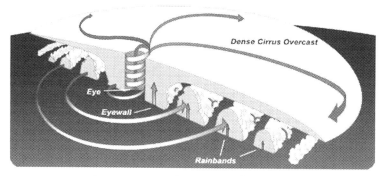

A cross-sectional view into a hurricane.

The eyewall surrounds the eye and is composed of intense thunderstorms, which have the strongest winds in the entire system. Changes in the structure of the eye and eyewall can cause changes in the wind speed, which is an indicator of the storm's intensity. The eye can grow or shrink in size, and double (concentric) eyewalls can form. The storm's outer rainbands are made up of dense bands of thunderstorms, which spiral slowly counterclockwise (in the northern hemisphere), ranging in width from a few miles to tens of miles. They can be 50-300 miles long and can extend hundreds of miles from the centre, usually having hurricane or tropical storm-force winds. Sometimes the bands and the eye are obscured by higher-level clouds, making it difficult for forecasters to use satellite imagery to monitor the storm. Hurricanes gain their strength from low surface pressure, evaporation of water from the warm seas; any condensation in the air and clouds that may already be present in the area. As a general rule of thumb, the hurricane's right side (relative to the direction it is travelling) is the most dangerous part of the storm because of the additive effect of the hurricane wind speed and the speed of the larger atmospheric flow (steering winds). The increased winds on the right side increase the storm surge; wreaking havoc on cities located to the top right of a hurricane when it makes landfall.

The extensive damage done to inland homes is due to these extremely strong winds that can tear the roofs off houses, uproot trees and throw debris around with ease. Rocks, tree limbs, and solid objects are picked up, become flying missiles and are hurled into buildings by the wind.

Being forceful enough to break windows and doors, these projectiles allow unforgiving winds inside a home. In extremely strong hurricanes, such as this hurricane in 1929, the winds can be strong enough to collapse any weak parts of a house. Even though hurricane winds are deadly enough on their own, hurricanes also bring with them storm surges, floods and tornadoes that have their own devastating effects. The danger with tornadoes spawned by hurricanes is the lack of warning signs that people associate with them. Usually, hail or a lot of lightning accompanies tornadoes, but in this case they come as a surprise. It is, therefore best if you remain indoors, in the centre of your house and away from doors and windows.

The risk of flooding depends on a number of factors: the speed of the storm, its interactions with other weather systems, the land or surface terrain it encounters, and ground saturation. Flooding is not only caused by storm surges, but also by torrential rains that hurricanes bring, which can reach hundreds of miles inland. A typical hurricane brings at least 6 to 12 inches of rainfall to the area it crosses. The resulting floods can cause considerable damage and loss of life, especially in mountainous areas where heavy rains produce flash floods and as a consequence result in devastating mudslides.

Although all these factors are dangerous, the most deadly force of all is the storm surge. A storm surge is a large dome of water, 50-100 miles wide, which sweeps across the coastline near where a hurricane makes landfall. Driven by high winds, any hurricane that makes a perpendicular landfall or hits at high tide creates tremendous damage. Approximately 75% of all hurricane related fatalities can be attributed to storm surge or flooding. The life of a hurricane can last more than two weeks over open waters and can run a path across the entire length of the eastern seaboard. Many Lay persons often ask how a hurricane forms, and why they are so destructive. Although tropical storms can rapidly intensify, very few of them ever become hurricanes at all. There are certain factors and stages that a storm must go through in order to develop into a threatening tropical cyclone.

The components needed for a hurricane include a pre-existing weather disturbance, warm tropical oceans (at least 80 degrees Fahrenheit to a depth of about 150 feet), moisture, and relatively light winds in the upper atmosphere. If the right conditions persist long enough, they can combine to produce the violent conditions of a hurricane. In these early stages, the system appears as a relatively unorganized cluster of thunderstorms, usually forming in the Caribbean or off the west coast of Africa. They slowly drift westward, fueled by the warm waters of the tropics, and if the conditions are just right, the system can develop into a tropical depression. Heat and energy for the storm are gathered through contact with warm ocean waters. The winds near the ocean surface spiral into the disturbance's low-pressure area, and the warm, moist air moves in toward the centre of the storm. At this point, the storm begins to take on the familiar spiral appearance due to the flow of the winds and the rotation of the Earth. The warm air then condenses into drops as it spirals upward, producing torrential rains and releasing more heat. This additional heat further powers the storm and brings the tropical depression to tropical storm status. As the updrafts suck up more water vapour, it triggers a cycle of strengthening that can be stopped only when it has made contact with the land or cooler waters. Bands of thunderstorms form, and the storm's cloud tops rise higher into the atmosphere. If the wind forces at these high elevations remain relatively small (no wind shear), the storm can remain intact and continue to strengthen. When the winds reach a minimum of 74mph (64 kt), it is classified as a hurricane and its characteristic eye forms.

CHAPTER TWO

Fundamentals of a Hurricane

Tropical cyclones are the broad class of all low-pressure systems that form in the tropics and have a closed wind circulation with sustained winds of at least 39 mph. When sustained winds reach 74 mph, the storm is classified according to its geographical location:

1) Hurricane (the North Atlantic Ocean, the Northeast Pacific Ocean east of the International Dateline or the South Pacific Ocean east of 160E);
2) Typhoon (the Northwest Pacific Ocean west of the International Dateline);
3) Severe Tropical Cyclone (the Southwest Pacific Ocean west of 160E or Southeast Indian Ocean east of 90E);
4) Severe Cyclonic Storm (the Southwest Indian Ocean).

For the ease of describing these intense tropical cyclones, I will simply refer to them as hurricanes, unless there's a specific geographical focus. Once winds in a closed tropical low-pressure system reach 39 mph, the system is named either a tropical storm or tropical cyclone, depending upon its location. Then, a name is assigned according to WMO's international naming conventions. These names are drawn from the Region IV naming list for the North Atlantic. Names are used to help focus attention to particular storms, especially when several storms are occurring at the same time. The names also provide easy recognition for the past historical and destructive hurricanes. Storms that are especially deadly or destructive have their names retired. Evolving from a tropical wave, through a tropical depression, to a tropical storm and finally a hurricane, tropical cyclones often capture our attention, not only because of their power, but also because of their wide-ranging societal, economic and physical impacts.

What distinguishes hurricanes from other types of low-pressure or another storm system is that hurricanes are 'warm-core' systems. This means that the entire storm system is composed of warm air. Middle-latitude low-pressure systems often have cold and warm sectors separated by weather fronts. Most hurricanes form over warm tropical oceans during the summer and early fall months. The peak of the hurricane season is usually about two months after the summer solstice. Hurricane season extends far beyond the warmest months of the year because ocean waters warm more slowly and retain their heat longer than either air or land. Scientists now realize that hurricanes are most likely to form and intensify when ocean water temperatures are at least 80°F.

Tropical cyclones are systems of large, rotating thunderstorms that form over warm tropical waters where the winds and the seas are conducive to the development and growth of these storms. There is nothing like hurricanes in the atmosphere. Even seen by remote sensors on satellites thousands of miles above Earth, the uniqueness of these powerful, tightly coiled storms is clear. Hurricanes are not the largest storm systems on Earth, nor the most violent-but they do combine those qualities as no other phenomenon does, as if they were designed to be powerful engines of death and destruction. Due to the effects of the Earth's rotation, these storms rotate in a counter clockwise direction in the northern hemisphere, and clockwise in the southern hemisphere. They are found in all areas of the tropical regions of the world with the exception of the southern Atlantic Ocean (although there was a case where a tropical cyclone called Cyclone Catarina formed there in 2005, but this was a rare exception to the rule).

In the northern hemisphere, these storms are called hurricanes, a term that echoes colonial Spanish and Caribbean Indian words for evil spirits and big winds created by their gods. The word 'hurricane' has its origins in the names given to the storm gods by various tribes of local Indians within this region. In the Bahamas, it is certain that the Lucayan Indians, who were the first people to inhabit the land we now call the Bahamas, experienced the high winds, rough seas and heavy rains of these storms. Unfortunately, they left no written accounts of their experiences with these storms. According to the edited abstracts taken from Spanish Priest

Bartholomew de Las Casas, he said that these Indians believed that the islands of the Bahamas were comprised of one giant complete landmass but had been separated by the howling winds and rough seas of the hurricane.

When the Europeans first attempted to establish permanent settlements in the Caribbean, they quickly learned about these storms when they destroyed their first built up settlements in the New World on the island of Hispaniola. In the Bahamas, Christopher Columbus was lucky enough not to have encountered any storms on his first voyage, but in 1499, Vicente Yañez Pinzón captain of Columbus' ship *'the Niña',* lost two ships in the fleet here in the Exuma Cays due to a hurricane. Furthermore, she was the only ship to survive the famous 1495 hurricane, battered but safely returning to Spain in 1496. In 1495, Christopher Columbus encountered a hurricane near Hispaniola, and it was the earliest hurricane reported by Christopher Columbus, who also encountered a tropical storm on one of his voyages to the New World.

Fortunately, here in the Caribbean, as time passed and these European settlers learned more about their new homeland, they experienced these storms on such a regular basis that they became accustomed to them. Eventually, they began calling them 'equinoctial storms,' as the storms normally hit in the weeks around the period of the fall equinox, which in the northern hemisphere occurs in late September. Now, thanks in part to over four hundred years of observations and advances in technology, we now know that hurricanes can strike at any time between June and November. The peak of the season in the North Atlantic is on September 11th, of each year, and August and September are the most active months for hurricanes to strike any part of this region. These storms are products of the tropical oceans and atmosphere and they are powered by heat from the warm seas, steered by the easterly trades and temperate westerlies, and driven by their own fierce energy. Around their tranquil core, called the eyewall, winds blow with lethal velocity and the ocean develops an inundating surge. In addition, as they move ashore, tornadoes may descend from the advancing bands of the surrounding thunderstorms. Hurricanes, as poorly understood as they are today, seem to have two main benefits—first, they are a major source of rain for many tropical and subtropical land areas; and second, they are responsible for redistribution of heat from the equator to the poles which allow us as humans to live and survive on an otherwise very volatile planet.

A hurricane represents the most advanced stage of a tropical cyclone. A cyclone refers to those types of storms having low atmospheric pressure at the center and cyclonic or rotating wind circulation. Thus, a tropical cyclone is a low pressure storm system that originates in tropical (or less often subtropical) areas. The tropics are defined as that area of the Earth that lies between the Tropic of Cancer, 23.5 degrees north of the equator, and the Tropic of Capricorn, 23.5 degrees south of the equator. Hurricanes vary greatly in size, intensity, behavior and path, but they have enough characteristics in common that some generalizations can be made. A hurricane can be visualized as an organized system of thunderstorm-type clouds generally assembled into spiral bands called rainbands. Much of the rain generated by a hurricane occurs within these spiraling bands of clouds, with rainfall between the bands generally being much less intense or even absent. Thunder and lightning are not always present, but when occurring will generally be found within those rainbands and the eyewall. There are generally from one to seven bands in a hurricane, with each band commonly 50 miles long. This accounts for the average diameter of the major area covered by a hurricane being roughly 100 miles, although diameters have ranged from less than 100 miles to over 500 miles. Tropical storm force winds (39 to 73 miles per hour) may occur at a distance from the center of the storm that is several times the diameter of the major cloudy portion of the hurricane.

One of the most distinctive features shared by nearly all hurricanes is the eye. This central portion of the storm varies greatly in size among hurricanes, with some only 3 miles in diameter and others extending to well over 38 miles across. The average eye is about 15 to 20 miles in diameter. The winds in the eye are greatly reduced, often blowing only 15 miles per hour, and the sky may be nearly rain-and-cloud-free. Many people who have been in the eye of a hurricane tell of finding clear blue skies above them as the eye passed over. The eye is also where the lowest atmospheric pressure and highest temperatures of the storm occur, and in many cases birds are frequently trapped in the eye, often found in large numbers clinging in desperation to the rigging of ships. They are blown into the eye and trapped there as the storm intensifies, then cannot escape

11

through the violent winds that surround the eye. As a matter of fact, several bird species have entered the United States, especially Florida, in this manner from the Bahamas and other Caribbean countries, including the Black Anis from Haiti, the Bahamas Honeycreeper, the Bahamas Shallow, the Cuban Cliff Swallow, several West Indian Doves and Pigeons, and most recently the Cattle Egret from the Antilles.

The eye is completely surrounded by the most intense portion of the hurricane, the eyewall. The clouds that compose this imposing feature of the storm reach heights of over 50,000 feet. The eyewall consists of very intense cumulonimbus clouds and within these clouds contains massive amounts of water vapour brought into this area by the rainbands, which are forced upwards, converting the water vapour into water and in the process releasing a tremendous amount of heat. This process helps to produce the high winds and the torrential rainfall found within the hurricane. The strongest winds and the heaviest rainfall are often found within or near the eyewall. Many persons have been fooled as the eye passes them into thinking that the storm is over, individuals venture out, only to be surprised as the other side of the eyewall approaches, bringing winds of equal destruction but now blowing from the opposite direction. Together, the eye and eyewall represent the heart of a hurricane.

For a tropical disturbance to develop into a hurricane, several environmental factors must be present, and they must interact in rather specific ways. This interaction is most likely to occur in late summer or early fall, which is the main reason for the higher incidence hurricanes forming during this time. The official hurricane season for the North Atlantic runs from June 1st to November 30th. September is especially significant, since more hurricanes have hit this region during this month than any other month, and as stated before, the peak of the hurricane season in the North Atlantic is September 11th of each year. As previously mentioned, a hurricane represents the ultimate stage of a tropical cyclone. The different stages of a tropical cyclone development can be described in a number of ways. The classification scheme most commonly used in this region recognizes four stages, based on formation and intensity. The stages of the tropical cyclone are:

1) Tropical disturbance: no strong winds (this stage is actually a precursor to a tropical cyclone).
2) Tropical depression: some rotary circulation at the surface and sustained winds speed of less than 39 miles per hour.
3) Tropical storm: distinct rotary circulation with highest sustained wind speed of 39 to 73 miles per hour.
4) Hurricane: very pronounced rotary circulation with sustained winds of 74 miles per hour or greater.

Several factors account for this particular seasonality. Hurricanes nearly always develop from low-pressure disturbances within the trade-wind belt, the area from approximately 30 degrees north latitude to within five degrees of the equator, which experiences consistent winds blowing from east to west. Several mechanisms are known to produce areas of low pressure in the trades, and these mechanisms are most prevalent during the summer and early fall. If the Bermuda or subtropical high pressure system is particularly weak and displaced south of this normal position, a condition quite common in early summer and fall, a region of low pressure may be introduced into the trade-winds belt. For example, higher-latitude low pressure systems can more easily penetrate into the tropics when the Bermuda high is displaced southward. The southern end of such systems may become trapped in the trades and provide the seeds of a hurricane.

Another mechanism generating low-pressure disturbances in the trades involves a low-pressure belt called the Intertropical Convergence Zone (ITCZ), which is located near the equator. In the summer, most frequently during the month of August, the ITCZ is at its northernmost location, about 12 degrees north latitude. A rotating low-pressure system forming where the ITCZ meets the trades can become a westward-migrating system in the trades. When this happens the conditions are favorable for the necessary rotation of the newly formed low-pressure system to be achieved.

One more extremely common type of low-pressure disturbance is an easterly wave. This is not an oceanic wave, but an atmospheric low-pressure feature embedded in the trade winds belt that moves east to west. The eastern portions of these waves are often very cloudy with heavy rain showers. These systems are nearly always present in abundant numbers during the hurricane season in the North Atlantic. The African continent, especially the very southern edge of the Sahara Desert, is the dominant source for easterly waves in the North Atlantic during the peak of the hurricane season. In fact, it is a bit ironic that one of the driest places on Earth is the birthplace for storms that have produced some of the greatest rainfall records on Earth. These easterly waves in any given year often number somewhere between 50 to 70 (but can be as high as 80) per year and are very common during May through November. Hurricanes that develop in this manner are called Cape Verde-type hurricanes.

After a hurricane develops, a tremendous amount of energy is released. A moderate hurricane is capable of taking up from the ocean approximately 15 million tons of water vapour per minute through the process of evaporation. The amount of energy released into the atmosphere by the transformation of this vapour back into liquid by the hurricane is the major driving force of the hurricane, and a true driving force it is. An average hurricane will release in 24 hours the energy equivalent to one-half million Nagasaki-type atomic bombs or 400 20-megaton hydrogen (fusion) bombs. This energy, if converted to electricity, would satisfy the electrical needs of the United States for more than six months. This transformation of tremendous amounts of energy is why tropical cyclones are called 'heat engines.' One of the most important requirements for the growth and development of a hurricane is the need for warm oceanic waters of 80°F or higher to supply the system with a continuing supply of warm and moisture rich air to allow the system to develop and strengthen.

In the North Atlantic, there are four different types of hurricanes that influence us in some way or the other. Each is uniquely different and has unique and different characteristics that are found in that type of hurricane alone in terms of formation and strength. The first is the Cape Verde type hurricane, which as its name suggests, originates off the African Coast in the vicinity of the Cape Verde Islands. Initially, it moves in a westerly direction and then in a west-northwest to a northwesterly direction as it makes its way through the Caribbean, Central America, the Bahamas and the United States. The Cape Verde Islands is an archipelago about 400 miles off the West African Coast and are volcanic in nature. It was colonized by Portugal in the fifteenth century and became an independent country in 1975. At one point in their history, these islands served as an outpost station for the movement of African slaves on the 'Middle Passage' to the Americas. This type of hurricane forms over the Atlantic mainly during the early to mid-part of the season, June through mid-September months, when the easterly waves are the most dominant weather features in the Caribbean region. This type of hurricane tends to produce the strongest hurricanes in this category because of the great distance they have in traversing the warm waters of the Atlantic before they get to any landmass, giving them the time and the opportunity to strengthen before hitting some landmass in the Caribbean, North or Central America.

At the beginning and the middle of the hurricane season, storms also tend to form near the Bahamas, mainly from upper-level systems or TUTT (tropical upper tropospheric trough) low pressure systems, and this type of hurricane has come to be known as '*Bahama Busters*', according to world renowned Professor William Gray from Colorado State University, who gave it that name. An example of this type of storm was Hurricane Katrina in 2005, which formed just east of the Bahamas from the remnants of Tropical Depression #10 and became Tropical Depression #12. This system initially moved westward and then northwestward into the Gulf of Mexico and then over Louisiana. This type of storm tends to produce hurricanes of moderate to intense hurricanes, and it all depends on the environmental factors at the time but also how long it remains in the Gulf of Mexico before hitting any landmass on the Gulf Coast States.

Another type of hurricane is the Gulf of Mexico type, which as its name suggests, originates in the Gulf of Mexico and travels northward or westward from its inception and mainly influences Latin America and the Gulf Coast of the United States. This type of hurricane tends to be the weakest of all four types of hurricanes because of the short distance from its formation to the time it hits any land area and begins the weakening or dissipating stage. Finally, there is the Western Caribbean type, which forms during the early and late parts of the hurricane season and forms in the most favoured location near the Gulf of Honduras or the southern Caribbean Sea, mainly in May through June and mid-September through late November. The formations of these cyclones are due in part to the seasonal movement of the Inter-Tropical Convergence Zone, also known as the Equatorial Trough. From its inception, this type of hurricane seems to take a westward or northward movement, which normally takes a track over Central America if it moves westward or over the island of Cuba, and into the Bahamas if it moves northward. The severity of which is influenced by how long the storm remains over the mountainous terrain of Cuba. One notable example of this type of storm affecting the region was Hurricane Michelle in 2001.

Hurricanes are born in low latitudes and are nurtured by warm tropical waters. They die by moving into higher latitudes with colder waters or by leaving the water and crossing over land or occasionally by coming under the influence of unfavorable upper-air wind flow. Hurricanes exists an average of about nine days, although life spans have varied from less than 12 hours to more than 28 days. During this time, they cover about 300 to 400 miles a day for a total of approximately 2,700 to 3,600 total miles during their lifetime. Nearly all hurricanes in the North Atlantic are eventually steered by large-scale, global wind patterns onto land or into higher latitudes, where the process of decay begins. Most of these storms recurve, that is, change direction from a predominantly west or northwest track to a more northerly and even a northeasterly direction. This recurvature, which occurs on average at about 25 degrees latitude, is produced largely by clockwise-moving winds around the Bermuda high pressure system in the Atlantic, and by the interaction of the hurricane with the prevailing westerlies of the mid-latitudes. A hurricane will often reach its maximum intensity just before or at the point of recurvature, at which time many hurricanes slow their forward progress. Once the path of the hurricane has changed, it will often increase its forward speed, attaining its greatest speed soon after recurvature.

As a hurricane moves into higher latitudes while still over water, the ocean temperatures become too cold to sustain the heat engine of the storm, and some would eventually become 'extra-tropical' in nature. The decaying process is especially evident once the storm moves up to oceanic regions of approximately 40 degrees latitude. Hurricane decay due to landfall is a much more complicated process. Once over land, several processes combine, which together lead to the demise of the storm. Friction is involved, but to a much lesser degree than originally thought. In fact, the friction that a hurricane encounters from the extremely agitated ocean surface and tremendous amounts of spray thrown into the air is greater than the friction a hurricane would encounter over relatively flat terrain, such as the Florida Everglades.

Much more significant than friction, and the prime reason for a hurricane's demise over land, is the rapid cooling experienced by the inner core of the hurricane soon after it makes landfall. This cooling results from the loss of a hurricane's major energy source, which are heat and moisture derived from the ocean, and the conversion of water vapour into liquid water. The cooling of the inner core is immediately followed by a process called filling. During this process, more air is coming in toward the central portion of the storm than is being exhausted upward through the system. The pressure in the central part of the hurricane increases, the area of maximum winds becomes more spread out and diffuse, and eventually the hurricane simply 'unravels' and dies. Some hurricanes are transformed into extratropical cyclones or combine with existing middle-latitude storms once they move into higher latitudes. Extratropical cyclones, sometimes called mid-latitude cyclones, baroclinic storms or wave cyclones, are a group of cyclones defined as synoptic scale low pressure weather systems that occur in the middle latitudes of the Earth (outside of the tropics), having neither tropical nor polar characteristics, and are connected with fronts and horizontal gradients in temperature and dew point otherwise known as "baroclinic zones." When a hurricane combines with such a storm, there may actually be a brief period of intensification of the hurricane, but this is often short-lived, as the cool air quickens the demise of the hurricane and it quickly dies or turns into a much weaker mid-latitude storm.

The movement of hurricanes from the lower to higher latitudes serves a very useful, in fact essential, purpose in the world's climate on a global scale. Between about 35 degrees north and south of the equator, heat (shortwave radiation) from the sun absorbed by the Earth and atmosphere is greater than the heat (longwave radiation) that is radiated from the Earth and atmosphere back into space. If the heating that results from this imbalance is not carried away, the tropical and subtropical regions of the Earth would be constantly growing warmer. Fortunately, nature has provided two mechanisms to transfer this excess energy to the higher latitudes, where there is an energy deficit, and therefore maintain a global balance. A portion of this excess heat is carried away by ocean currents. For example, the Gulf Stream carries warmth away from the equatorial areas into the coolers waters of the North Atlantic. However, most of the heat transfer is accomplished in the atmosphere. Tropical cyclones are a part of this atmospheric heat movement process. Hurricanes are, therefore, necessary for the Earth to maintain an energy balance to support life on this planet. In this respect, these generally hated and despised storms might be viewed as 'necessary evils' of nature.

Furthermore, these storms also have other advantages in addition to helping to maintain an energy balance for the Earth, and that is, they provide much needed rainfall to many parched areas of the Earth. A typical hurricane usually brings about 10 to 15 inches or greater of rainfall to much of the areas affected and in the process produces over 200 billion tons of rainwater each day, an amount equal to the average annual flow of the Colorado River. Although rainfall is often a major cause of damage associated with hurricanes, the effects are not always undesirable. Over a six month hurricane season of June-November, tropical systems generally account for 45% to 60% of the seasonal rainfall in the Caribbean. Hurricanes often provide this much-needed rain to drought-stricken coastlines.

Their ocean interactions can flush bays of pollutants, restoring the ecosystem's vitality. After the record rainfall from Hurricane Claudette in 1979 in Texas, fish were being caught in the northern industrialized reaches of Galveston Bay that had vanished for several years. Finally, in cruel Darwinian fashion, weak sea life and plants perish during a hurricane, leaving only the strong to survive and reproduce. In this same manner, sometimes hurricanes 'correct' humanity's mistakes. For example, in the early 1900's, non-native foliage, such as Australian pine trees, had been planted on the tip of Key Biscayne, Florida (now the Bill Baggs State Park). These non-native plants had very few natural enemies in their new environment and quickly dominated the plant life, resulting in a loss of the natural habitat of that area. However, these Australian non-native trees lacked the ability to withstand hurricane-force winds because of their shallow roots, and Hurricane Andrew came along and destroyed them all in 1992. It was only then that park officials seized the rare opportunity to replant the park with native foliage.

Virtually all literal use of the word 'hurricane' in literary works evokes violent wind. Yet some of the worst tropical cyclone catastrophes are caused not by winds, but by torrential rainfall (e.g. Hurricane Katrina in 2005). The rainfall associated with hurricanes is both beneficial and harmful.

Although the rains contribute to the water needs of the areas traversed by the hurricane, the rains are harmful when the amount is so large as to cause extensive flooding. There are about four factors that determine how much rain will fall in a given place: the amount of water vapour in the air, topography, the vertical extent and duration of the updraft. In fact, some of the most devastating floods are produced by tropical cyclones of sub-hurricane strength. The torrential rainfall that normally accompanies a hurricane can cause serious flooding. A recent and especially tragic example of this is Hurricane Mitch of 1998, the deadliest North Atlantic hurricane since the Great Hurricane of 1780. Floods produced by Mitch killed more than 11,000 people in Central America, and the President of Honduras declared that Mitch destroyed 50 years of progress in that country. Whereas, the storm surge and high winds are concentrated near the eye, the rain may extend outward for hundreds of miles away from the center and may last for several days, affecting areas well after the hurricane has diminished or passed over a particular area.

As stated earlier, an average of 10 to 15 inches of rain falls over coastal areas during the passage of a well-developed hurricane, but over 20 inches have been recorded, and rain may fall at the rate of one inch an hour. In twenty-four hours, a record of 32.67 inches of rain fell at Belize City in Belize from Hurricane Keith in 2000; for comparison, the average annual rainfall of Belize is about 74.4 inches. Furthermore, Hurricane Camille dumped over 760 millimeters (30 inches) of rainfall over Central Virginia, drowning 109 persons in the process with flash flooding. For comparison, the average annual rainfall of Central Virginia is about 45.22 inches. The Cedar Key Hurricane of September, 1950, poured nearly 39 inches of rain in 24 hours on Yankeetown, Florida, off the Gulf Coast. This 9-day hurricane traced an unusual double loop in the Cedar Keys area, and the coast from Sarasota northward suffered extensive wind and flood damage. The coastal areas inland from Yankeetown to Tampa were flooded for several weeks. In the 1963 Pacific hurricane season, Typhoon Gloria dumped 49.13 inches of rainfall in Baxin, Taiwan. While in the 1967 Pacific typhoon season 65.83 inches fell at Xinliao in Taiwan during a 24-hour period from Typhoon Carla. For comparison, the average annual rainfall of Xinliao, Taiwan, is about 85 inches. However, Tropical Cyclone Denise in Foc-Foc in the La Reunion Island on January 7th and 8th of

1966 holds a world record of 45 inches in just 12 hours and 71.80 inches of rainfall in 24 hours in the same location for the total amount of rainfall over a particular location from a tropical cyclone.

Of all the tropical cyclone damaging agents, strong winds are perhaps the best understood of all of them. Damaging winds will accompany any hurricane, no matter what category it is. A hurricane by definition has winds of at least 74 miles per hour. This wind speed alone is enough to cause great damage to poorly constructed signage and knock over some of the sturdiest trees and other vegetation. Obviously, the stronger the hurricane (higher winds), the more potential there is for wind damage to exists. The fierce winds that blow in an anti-clockwise direction around the center of the central calm in the northern hemisphere may reach 100 to 200 mph. Wind speeds are the greatest near the surface around the central calm or eye. However, whenever a hurricane touches a landmass, its wind speed is significantly reduced. The strongest winds (one minute sustained winds) reported in the Caribbean during the passage of a hurricane were Hurricane Camille in 1969 (190mph), Hurricane Allen in 1980 (190mph), Hurricane Wilma of 2005(185mph), and Hurricane Gilbert of 1988 (185mph).

Once a hurricane makes landfall, there is a significant drop in the surface and upper level winds. Two factors accounts for this abrupt drop in wind speeds once a hurricane makes landfall. Over land, a hurricane is no longer in contact with its energy source of warm ocean water. Furthermore, the increased surface roughness over land weakens the system. The land surface is rougher than the sea surface, so when a hurricane moves over land, its surface winds are slowed and blow at a greater angle across the isobars and toward the storm center. This wind shift causes the storm to begin to fill, that is, the central pressure rises, the horizontal pressure gradient weakens, and the winds slacken.

The energy released in a normal hurricane is great. An average hurricane's winds are so great that it is equipped with some 1.5 trillion watts of power in its winds, which if converted to electricity, would be equivalent to about half of the world's entire electrical generating capacity. In fact, in a single day a hurricane can release the amount of energy necessary to supply all of the United States' electrical needs for about six months. One second of a hurricane's energy is equivalent to about ten Hiroshima atomic bombs, and in total, a single hurricane during its lifetime can dissipate more energy than that contained in thirty thousand atomic bombs. The hurricane that hit Galveston, Texas, in September, 1900, during its lifespan had sufficient energy to drive all the power stations in the world for over four years. A large hurricane stirs up more than a million miles of atmosphere every second.

The force of the wind can quickly decimate the tree population, tear down power lines and utility poles, knock over signs, and may be strong enough to destroy some homes and buildings. Flying debris can also cause damage, and in some cases where people are caught outdoors, injuries and death can prevail. When a hurricane first makes landfall, it is common for tornadoes to form, which can cause severe localized wind damage. In most cases, however, wind is a secondary cause of damage. Storm surge is normally the primary cause. The right front quadrant is the strongest side of the hurricane; this is the area where there is positive convergence. In this quadrant, the winds are typically the strongest, the storm surge is highest, and the possibility of tornadoes is the greatest. The right side of a hurricane is the strongest side because the wind speed and the hurricane speed-of-motion are complementary there; meaning, on this side the wind blows in the same direction as the storm's forward motion.

On the left side, the hurricane's speed of motion subtracts from the wind speed because the main bulk of the storm is moving away from it. The storm's angle of attack is a key factor in its impact. Just as in an automobile accident, the highest level of destruction is caused by a hurricane hitting the coastline head-on. If a storm travels up the coast, with its left side brushing the seashore, the most dangerous part of the storm stays offshore, and the net effect will be much less damage. The worst-case scenario would be a hurricane arriving onshore at high or spring tide. With the ocean level already at its highest point of the day, the storm surge from a Category 4 or 5 hurricane can add another 15 to 20 feet of water, with abnormally large waves breaking on top of that. Water weighs around 1,700 pounds per cubic yard, and there are very few structures that can stand up to the force a high storm surge can produce.

Violent hurricane winds may produce storm surges of up to 45 feet high at sea, and storm surges of over twenty feet may crash against the shores at speeds of up to 40 mph. Long swells may move outwards from the eye of a hurricane for more than 1,000 miles. These long swells are often the first visible signs of an approaching hurricane and are known as the storm surge. A storm surge, also called a hurricane surge, is the abnormal rise in the sea level caused by wind and pressure forces of a hurricane. It can be extremely devastating, and is in fact a major cause of damage and danger to life during the passage of a hurricane. It is estimated that 75% of all hurricane related deaths and injuries are caused by the storm surge, and the remaining 20% to 25% are simply caused by negligence. For example, persons out of curiosity venturing out into the peak of the storm and being killed by flying debris or stepping on a live wire and getting electrocuted before the 'all-clear' is given.

The storm surge isn't just another wave pushed ahead of a storm; it acts like a gigantic bulldozer that can destroy anything in its path. Think of the storm surge as a moving wall of water weighing millions of tons. The storm surge itself is caused by the wind and pressure 'pushing' the water into the continental shelf and onto the coastline caused by a hurricane. The height of the storm surge is the difference between the observed level of sea surface and its level in the absence of the storm. In other words, the storm surge is estimated by subtracting the normal or astronomical tide from the observed or estimated storm tide. The astronomical tide is the result of the gravitational interactions between the Earth, moon, and sun, generally producing two high and two low oceanic tides per day. Should the storm surge coincide with the high astronomical tide, several additional feet could be added to the water level, especially when the sun and moon are aligned, which produces the highest oceanic tides (known as syzygy).

Hurricanes have a vacuum effect on the ocean. The water is pulled toward the hurricane, causing it to 'pile up' like a small mountain. A mound of water forms under the center of a hurricane as the intensely low pressure draws water up. The shape of the shoreline and the ocean bottom has a great deal to do with a storm surge's magnitude. Over the ocean, this mound of water is barely noticeable, but it builds up as the storm approaches land. The surge's height as it reaches land depends upon the slope of the ocean floor at the coast. The more gradual the slope, the less volume of sea there is in which the surge can dissipate, and further inland the water is displaced. This is why Hurricane Katrina did so much damage in 2005 and why areas like New Orleans in the United States will continue to remain vulnerable to future hurricanes. This dome of water can be up to 40 to 60 miles long as it moves onto the shoreline near the landfall point of the eye. A cubic yard of sea water weighs approximately 1,700 pounds, and this water is constantly slamming into shoreline structures, even well-built structures get quickly demolished because this water acts like a battering ram on these vulnerable shoreline structures.

The highest storm surge ever recorded was produced by the 1899 Cyclone Mahina, which caused a storm surge of over 13 meters (43 feet) at Bathurst Bay, Australia. This value was derived from reanalysis of debris sightings and eyewitness reports; as a result, it is controversial within the meteorological community, but clearly a phenomenal storm surge occurred. In the United States, the greatest recorded storm surge was generated by 2005's Hurricane Katrina, which produced a massive storm surge of approximately 9 meters (30 feet) high in the town of Bay St. Louis, Mississippi, and in the surrounding coastal counties. Hurricane Camille came in second with 24 feet of water in 1969.

The worst storm surge, in terms of loss of life, was the 1970 Bhola Cyclone, which occurred in the area of the Bay of Bengal. This area is particularly prone to tidal surges and is often referred to as the 'storm surge capital of the world', which produced 142 moderate to severe storm surge events from 1582 to 1991. These surges, some in excess of eight meters (26 feet), have killed hundreds of thousands of people, primarily in Bangladesh. The Caribbean Islands have endured many devastating surges as well. Unfortunately, the records for storm surge effects in the Caribbean are sadly lacking or virtually non-existent. These powerful hurricanes listed above caused very high storm surge. However, worldwide storm surge data is sparse. Hurricanes and the accompanying storm surge they produce can even affect the very depths of the ocean. In 1975, some meteorological and oceanographic instruments were dropped from a research reconnaissance airplane in the Gulf of Mexico, which showed that Hurricane Eloise disturbed the ocean hundreds of feet down and created underwater waves that persisted for weeks.

In the North Atlantic, the Saffir-Simpson Hurricane Wind Scale is use to classify hurricanes according to their strength and intensity. The practical usefulness of the Saffir-Simpson Hurricane Wind Scale is that it relates properties of the hurricane to previously observed damage. Until the Saffir-Simpson Hurricane Wind Scale was developed, hurricanes were referred to as, Great (or Extreme) Hurricanes, Severe Hurricanes, or Minor, Minimal or Major Hurricanes. A Minor Hurricane had maximum winds of 74 mph and a minimum central pressure of 29.40 inches. A Minimal hurricane had maximum winds of between 75 to 100 mph and a minimum central pressure of between 29.03 to 29.39 inches. A Major hurricane had winds between 101 to 135 mph and a minimal central pressure of 28.01 to 29.02 inches. An Extreme or Great hurricane had winds of 136 mph or over and a minimum central pressure of 28.00 inches or less. However, these terms are no longer used but may appear in historical materials now and then. It is important to note that when dealing with narrative descriptions of historical events, these determinations are somewhat subjective and can mean different things to different people. For the purposes of this book, these categories will be any storm causing devastating damage through either wind action or storm surge. Some authors over the years have used the word or terminology 'extreme' very loosely to describe the worst of these events, but I will refrain from using that terminology. The word 'extreme' in my opinion would imply the 'peak' or 'maximum' of a very powerful and destructive storm. For this book, I prefer to use the more acceptable and more appropriate word of 'Great' to label these very destructive and powerful storms, but I will mention it when it is only necessary. It is important to note that tropical storms are named but are not assigned a Saffir-Simpson category number.

CHAPTER THREE

The History behind the word 'Hurricane' and other Tropical Cyclone Names

What is a hurricane? Simply put, it is a large, violent storm that originates in a tropical region and features extremely high winds-by definition, in excess of 74 miles per hour that blow anti-clockwise about the center in the northern hemisphere. It also brings drenching rains and has the ability to spin off tornadoes. Hurricanes are storms that form between the tropics of Cancer and Capricorn in the Atlantic, Pacific and Indian Oceans. They have different names, depending on where they are formed and located throughout the world. In the Atlantic they are called hurricanes, in the north-west Pacific typhoons, in the Indian Ocean they are known as tropical cyclones, while north of Australia they are sometimes called Willy Willies. However, by any name, they are impressive to behold. To form, hurricanes need sea surface temperatures of 26.5°C or greater, abundant moisture and light winds in the upper atmosphere. The hurricane season in the North Atlantic lasts from June 1st to November 30th. Around 80 tropical storms form each year, with most of them occurring in the south or south-east of Asia. The North Atlantic region accounts for only a mere 12 percent of the worldwide total of tropical cyclones. These storms are enormous creatures of nature, often between 100 and 500 miles in diameter. They may last from a few days to a week or more, and their tracks are notoriously unpredictable.

A tropical cyclone is a powerful storm system characterized by a low pressure center and numerous severe thunderstorms that produce strong winds and flooding rainfall. A tropical cyclone feeds on the heat released (latent heat) when moist air rises and the water vapour it contains condenses. They are fueled by a different heat mechanism than other cyclonic windstorms such as nor'easters, European windstorms, and polar lows, leading to their classification as "warm core" storm systems. The term 'tropical' simply refers to both the geographic origin of these systems, which forms almost exclusively in tropical regions of the Earth, and their formation in maritime tropical air masses. The term "cyclone" refers to a family of such storms' cyclonic nature, with anti-clockwise rotation in the northern hemisphere and clockwise rotation in the southern hemisphere. Depending on their location and strength, tropical cyclones are referred to by other names, such as hurricanes, typhoons, tropical storms, cyclonic storms, tropical depressions and simply cyclones, which all have low atmospheric pressure at their center. A hurricane consists of a mass of organized thunderstorms that spiral in towards the extreme low pressure of the storm's eye or center. The most intense thunderstorms will have the heaviest rainfall, and the highest winds occurring outside the eye, in the region known as the eyewall. In the eye itself, the air is warm, winds are light, and skies are generally clear and rain-free but can also be cloudy to overcast.

Captain George Nares, a nineteenth century Scottish naval officer and polar explorer, was always on the lookout for hurricanes. "June-too soon," he wrote. "July-stand by; August-look out you must; September-remember; October-all over." Whatever you think about the dynamics of hurricanes-two things can be said about them, and that is they are very unpredictable and extremely destructive. The forces of nature, such as deadly hurricanes, have shaped the lives of people from the earliest times. Indeed, the first 'meteorologists' were priests and shamans of ancient communities. Whatever lifestyles these ancient people followed, they all developed beliefs about the world around them. These beliefs helped them to explain how the world began, what happens in the future, or what happened after a person died. The world of spirits was very important. Those people, who became noted for their skills at interpreting signs in the world around them, became spiritual leaders in their communities. All religions and different races of people recognized the power of the weather elements, and most scriptures contain tales about or prophecies foretelling great natural disasters sometimes visited upon a community because of the sins of its citizens. Ancient peoples often reacted to the weather in a fearful, superstitious manner. They believed that mythological gods controlled the weather elements, such as winds, rain and sun, which governed their existence. When weather conditions were favorable, there would be plenty of game to hunt, fish to catch, and bountiful harvests. But their livelihood was at the mercy of the wild weather because fierce hurricanes could damage villages of flimsy huts, destroy crops and generate vast floodwaters that could sweep away livestock.

In times of hurricanes, food shortages and starvation were constant threats, as crops failed and game animals became scarce when their food supplies dried up due to a hurricane. These ancient tribes, as you will see later, believed that their weather fortunes were inextricably linked with the moods and actions of their gods. For this reason, they spent a great deal of time and effort appeasing these mythological weather gods. Many of these ancient tribes tried to remain on favorable terms with their deities through a mixture of prayers, rituals, dances and sometimes even human sacrifices. In some cultures, such as the Aztecs of Central America, they would offer up human sacrifices to appease their rain-god Tláloc. In addition, Quetzalcoatl, the all-powerful and mighty deity in the ancient Aztec society whose name means 'Precious Feathered Serpent,' played a critical role; he was the creator of life and controlled devastating hurricanes. The Egyptians celebrated Ra, the Sun god. Thor was the Norse god of thunder and lightning, a god to please so that calm waters would grace their seafaring expeditions. The Greeks had many weather gods; however, it was Zeus who was the most powerful of them all.

The actual origin of the word 'hurricane' and other tropical cyclone names were based on the many religions, cultures, myths, and races of people. In modern cultures, 'myth' has come to mean a story or an idea that is not true. The word 'myth' comes directly from the Greek word 'mythos'(μύθος), whose many meanings include, 'word', 'saying', 'story', and 'fiction.' Today, the word 'myth' is used any and everywhere, and people now speak of myths about how to catch or cure the common cold. But the age-old myths about hurricanes in this book were an important part of these people's religions, cultures, and everyday lives. Often times, they were both deeply spiritual and culturally entertaining and significant. For many of these ancient races, their mythology was their history, and there was often little, if any, distinction between the two. Some myths were actually based on historical events, such as devastating hurricanes or even wars, but myths often offer us a treasure trove of dramatic tales. The active beings in myths are generally gods and goddesses, heroes and heroines, or animals. Most myths are set in a timeless past before recorded and critical history began. A myth is a sacred narrative in the sense that it holds religious or spiritual significance for those who tell it, and it contributes to and expresses systems of thoughts and values. It is a traditional story, typically involving supernatural beings or forces or creatures, which embodies and provides an explanation, aetiology (origin myths), or justification for something such as the early history of a society, a religious belief or ritual, or a natural phenomenon.

The United Nation's sub-body, the World Meteorological Organization estimates that in an average year, about 80 of these tropical cyclones kills up to 15,000 people worldwide and cause an estimate of several billion dollars' worth of property damage alone. Meteorologists have estimated that between 1600 to today, hurricanes have caused well over 200,000 deaths in this region alone and over 8 million deaths worldwide. Hurricanes, typhoons and cyclones are all the same kind of violent storms originating over warm tropical ocean waters and are called by different names all over the world. From the Timor Sea to as far as northwestern Australia, they are called cyclones or by the Australian colloquial term of 'Willy-Willies', from an old Aboriginal word (derived from whirlwind). In the Bay of Bengal and the Indian Ocean, they are simply called Cyclones (an English name based on a Greek word meaning "coil" as in "coil of a snake" because the winds that spiral within them resemble the coils of a snake) and are not named even to this day.

They are called Hurricanes (derived from a Carib, Mayan or Taínos/Arawak Indian word) in the Gulf of Mexico, Central and North America, the Caribbean and Eastern North Pacific Oceans (east of the International Dateline). A Hurricane is the name given to these intense storms of tropical origin, with sustained winds exceeding 64 knots (74 miles per hour). In the Indian Ocean all the way to Mauritius and along the Arabian Coasts they are known as 'Asifa-t.' In Mexico and Central America, hurricanes are also known as El Cordonazo, and in Haiti they are known as Tainos. While they are called Typhoons [originating from the Chinese word 'Ty-Fung' (going back to as far as the Song (960-1278) and Yuan (1260-1341) dynasties) translated to mean 'Big or Great Wind' . . .], in the Western North Pacific and in the Philippines and the South China Sea (west of the International Dateline) they are known as 'Baguios' or 'Chubasco'(or simply a Typhoon). The word Baguio was derived from the Philippine city of Baguio, which was inundated in July, 1911, with over 46 inches of rain in a 24-hour period. Also, in the scientific literature of the 1600s, including the book 'Geographia Naturalis' by geographer Bernhardus Varenius, the term whirlwind was used, but this term never achieved regional or worldwide acceptance as a name for a hurricane.

In Japan, they are known as 'Repus,' or by the more revered name of a Typhoon. The word "taifū" (台風) in Japanese means Typhoon; the first character meaning "pedestal" or "stand"; the second character meaning wind. The Japanese term for "divine wind" is Kamikaze (神風). The Kamikaze, were a pair or series of typhoons that were said to have saved Japan from two Mongol invasion fleets under Kublai Khan, who attacked Japan in 1274 and again in 1281. The latter is said to have been the largest attempted naval invasion in history, whose scale was only recently eclipsed in modern times by the D-Day invasion by the allied forces into Normandy in 1944. This was the term that was given to the typhoon winds that came up and blew the Mongol invasion fleet off course and destroyed it as it was poised to attack Japan.

On October 29, 1274, the first invasion began. Some 40,000 men, including about 25,000 Mongolians, 8,000 Korean troops, and 7,000 Chinese seamen, set sail from Korea in about 900 ships to attack Japan. With fewer troops and inferior weapons, the Japanese were far outmatched and overwhelmed and were sure to be defeated. But at nightfall, just as they were attacking the Japanese coastal forces, the Korean sailors sensed an approaching typhoon and begged their reluctant Mongol commanders to put the invasion force back at sea or else it would be trapped on the coast and its ships destroyed at anchor by this typhoon. The next morning, the Japanese were surprised and delighted to see the Mongol fleet struggling to regain the open ocean in the midst of a great typhoon. The ships, sadly, were no match for this great storm, and many foundered or were simply dashed to bits and pieces on the rocky coast. Nearly 13,000 men perished in this storm, mostly by drowning. This Mongol fleet had been decimated by a powerful typhoon as it was poised to attack Japan.

With the second storm, even as Kublai Khan was mounting his second Japanese offensive, he was waging a bitter war of conquest against southern China, whose people had resisted him for 40 years. But finally, in 1279, the last of the southern providences, Canton, fell to the Mongol forces, and China was united under one ruler for the first time in three hundred years. Buoyed by success, Kublai again tried to bully Japan into submission by sending his emissaries to the Japanese, asking them to surrender to his forces. But this time the Japanese executed his emissaries, enraging him even further and thereby paving the way for a second invasion. Knowing this was inevitable; the Japanese went to work building coastal fortifications, including a massive dike around Hakozaki Bay, which encompasses the site of the first invasion.

The second Mongol invasion of Japan assumed staggering proportions. One armada consisted of 40,000 Mongols, Koreans, and Chinese, who were to set sail from Korea, while a second, larger force of some 100,000 men were to set out from various ports in south China. The invasion plan called for the two armadas to join forces in the spring before the summer typhoon season, but unfortunately the southern force was late, delaying the invasion until late June 1281. The Japanese defenders held back the invading forces for six weeks until on the fifteenth and sixteenth of August, history then repeated itself when a gigantic typhoon decimated the Mongol fleet poised to attack Japan again.

As a direct result of these famous storms, the Japanese came to think of the typhoon as a 'divine wind' or 'kamikaze' sent by their gods to deliver their land from the evil invaders. Because they needed another intervention to drive away the Allied forces in WWII, they gave this name to their Japanese suicide pilots as nationalist propaganda. In the Japanese Shinto religion, many forces of nature are worshipped as gods, known as 'kami', and are represented as human figures. The Japanese god of thunder is often depicted as a strong man beating his drum. The Japanese called it Kamikaze, and the Mongols never ever returned to attack Japan again because of their personal experiences with these two great storms. In popular Japanese myths at the time, the god Raijin was the god who turned the storms against the Mongols. Other variations say that the god

Fūjin or Ryūjin caused the destructive kamikaze. This use of *kamikaze* has come to be the common meaning of the word in English.[1]

Whatever name they are known by in different regions of the world, they refer to the same weather phenomena a 'tropical cyclone.' They are all the same severe tropical storms that share the same fundamental characteristics, aside from the fact that they rotate clockwise in the southern hemisphere and counterclockwise in the northern hemisphere. However, by World Meteorological Organization International Agreement, the term tropical cyclone is the general term given to all hurricane-type storms that originate over tropical waters. The term cyclone, used by meteorologists, refers to an area of low pressure in which winds move counterclockwise in the northern hemisphere around the low pressure center and are usually associated with bad weather, heavy rainfall and strong wind speeds. Whereas, a tropical cyclone was the name first given to these intense circular storms by Englishman Captain Henry Piddington (1797-1848), who was keenly interested in storms affecting India and spent many years collecting information on ships caught in severe storms in the Indian Ocean. He would later become the President of the Marine Courts of Inquiry in Calcutta, India. He used the term tropical cyclone to refer to a tropical storm that blew the freighter 'Charles Heddles' in circles for nearly a week in Mauritius in February of 1845. In his book *'Sailor's Hornbook for the Laws of Storms in All Parts of the World,'* published in 1855, he called these storms cyclones, from the Greek word for coil of a snake. He called these storms tropical cyclones because it expressed sufficiently what he described as the 'tendency to move in a circular motion.'

The word cyclone is from the Greek word 'κύκλος', meaning 'circle' or Kyklos meaning 'coils of the snake', describing the rotating movement of the storm. An Egyptian word 'Cykline' meaning to 'to spin' has also been cited as a possible origin. In Greek mythology, Typhoeus or Typhōn was the son of Tartarus and Gaia. He was a monster with many heads, a man's body, and a coiled snake's tail. The king of the gods and god of the sky and weather, Zeus, fought a great battle with Typhoeus and finally buried him under Mount Etna. According to legend, he was the source of the powerful storm winds that caused widespread devastation, the loss of

---

[1] Emanuel, K.(2005) *Divine Wind-The History and Science of Hurricanes*, Oxford University Press, pgs 3-5.

many lives and numerous shipwrecks. The Greek word 'typhōn' meaning 'whirlwind', comes from this legend, another possible source for the origin of the English word 'typhoon.' The term is most often used for cyclones occurring in the Western Pacific Ocean and Indian Ocean. In addition, the word is an alteration of the Arabic word, tūfān, meaning hurricane, and the Greek word, typhōn, meaning violent storm and an Egyptian word 'Cykline' meaning to 'to spin.'

The history of the word 'typhoon' presents a perfect example of the long journey that many words made in coming to the English Language vocabulary. It travelled from Greece to Arabia to India and also arose independently in China before assuming its current form in our language. The Greek word typhōn, used both as the name of the father of the winds and a common noun meaning 'whirlwind, typhoon,' was borrowed into Arabic during the Middle Ages, when Arabic learning both preserved and expanded the classical heritage and passed it on to Europe and other parts of the world. In the Arabic version of the Greek word, it was passed into languages spoken in India, where Arabic-speaking Muslim invaders had settled in the eleventh century. Thus, the descendant of the Arabic word, passing into English through an Indian language and appearing in English in forms such as touffon and tūfān, originally referred specifically to a severe storm in India.

The modern form of typhoon was also influenced by a borrowing from the Cantonese variety of Chinese, namely the word 'Ty-Fung', and respelled to make it look more like Greek. 'Ty-Fung', meaning literally 'great wind', was coincidentally similar to the Arabic borrowing and is first recorded in English guise as tuffoon in 1699. The Cantonese tai-fung and the Mandarin ta-feng are derived from the word jufeng. It is also believed to have originated from the Chinese word 'jufeng.' 'Ju' can mean either 'a wind coming from four directions' or 'scary'; 'feng' is the generic word for wind. Arguably, the first scientific description of a tropical cyclone and the first appearance of the word jufeng in the literature are contained in a Chinese book called *'Nan Yue Zhi* (Book of the Southern Yue Region)', written around A.D. 470. In that book, it is stated that *"Many Jufeng occur around Xi'n County. Ju is a wind (or storm) that comes in all four directions. Another meaning for Jufeng is that it is a scary wind. It frequently occurs in the sixth and seventh month (of the Chinese lunar calendar; roughly July and*

August of the Gregorian calendar). Before it comes, it is said that chickens and dogs are silent for three days. Major ones may last up to seven days, and minor ones last one or two days. These are called heifeng (meaning black storms/winds) in foreign countries."[2]

European travellers to China in the sixteenth century took note of a word sounding like typhoon being used to denote severe coastal windstorms. On the other hand, typhoon was used in European texts and literature around 1500, long before systematic contact with China was established. It is possible that the European use of this word was derived from Typhon, the draconian Earth demon of Greek Legend. The various forms of the word from these different countries coalesced and finally became typhoon, a spelling that officially first appeared in 1819 in Percy Bysshe Shelley's play 'Prometheus Unbound.' This play was concerned with the torments of the Greek mythological figure Prometheus and his suffering at the hands of Zeus. By the early eighteenth century, typhon and typhoon were in common use in European literature, as in the famous poem 'Summer' by Scottish poet James Thomson (1700-1748):

> *"Beneath the radiant line that grits the globe,*
> *The circling Typhon, whirled from point to point.*
> *Exhausting all the rage of all the sky,*
> *And dire Ecnephia, reign."*[3]

In Yoruba mythology, Oya, the female warrior, was the goddess of fire, wind and thunder. When she became angry, she created tornadoes and hurricanes. Additionally, to ward off violent and tropical downpours, Yoruba priests in southwestern Nigeria held ceremonies around images of the thunder and lightning god Sango to protect them from the powerful winds of hurricanes. In ancient Egyptian legend, Set was regarded as the god of storms. He was associated with natural calamities like hurricanes, thunderstorms, lightning, earthquakes and eclipses. In Iroquois mythology, Ga-oh was the wind giant whose house was guarded by several animals,

---

[2]   Emanuel, K.(2005) *Divine Wind-The History and Science of Hurricanes*, Oxford University Press, pgs 18-21.

[3]   Emanuel, K.(2005) *Divine Wind-The History and Science of Hurricanes*, Oxford University Press, pg 21.

each representing a specific type of wind. The Bear was the north wind, who brought winter hurricanes, and he was also capable of crushing the world with his storms or destroying it with his cold air. In Babylonian mythology, Marduk, the god of gods, defeated the bad tempered dragon goddess Tiamat with the help of a hurricane. When the other gods learned about Tiamat's plans to destroy them, they turned to Marduk for help. Armed with a bow and an arrow, strong winds and a powerful hurricane, Marduk captured Tiamat and let the hurricane winds fill her jaws and stomach. Then he shot an arrow into her belly and killed her and then became the lord of all the gods.

The Meso-American and Caribbean Indians worshipped many gods. They had similar religions based on the worship of mainly agricultural and natural elements gods, even though the gods' names and the symbols for them were a bit different. People asked their gods for good weather, lack of hurricanes, abundant crops and good health or for welfare. The main Inca god was the creator god Viracocha. His assistants were the gods of the Earth and the sea. As farming occupied such an important place in the region, the 'Earth mother' or 'Earth goddess' was particularly important. The Aztecs, Mayas, Taínos and other Indians adopted many gods from other civilizations. As with the Mayans, Aztecs and Taínos, each god was connected with some aspects of nature or natural forces, and in each of these religions, hurricanes or the fear of them and the respect for them played a vital part of their worship. The destructive power of storms like hurricanes inspires both fear and fascination, and it is no surprise that humans throughout time have tried to control these storms. Ancient tribes were known to make offerings to the weather gods to appease them. People in ancient times believed that these violent storms were brought on by angry weather gods. In some cultures, the word for hurricane means 'storm god', 'evil spirit', 'devil' or 'god of thunder and lightning.'

The word 'hurricane' comes to us via the early Spanish explorers of the New World, who were told by the Indians of this region of an evil god capable of inflicting strong winds and great destruction on their lives and possessions. The natives of the Caribbean and Central America had a healthy respect for hurricanes and an uncanny understanding of nature. In the legends of the Mayan civilizations of Central America and the Taínos of the Caribbean, these gods played an important role in their Creation. According to their beliefs and myths, the wicked gods Huracán, Hurrikán, Hunraken, and Jurakan annually victimized and savagely ravaged their homes, inflicting them with destructive winds, torrential rainfall and deadly floods. These natives were terrified whenever these gods made an appearance. They would beat drums, blew conch shells, shouted curses, engage in bizarre rituals and did everything possible to thwart these gods and drive them away. Sometimes they felt they were successful in frightening them off, and at other times their fury could not be withstood and they suffered the consequences from an angry weather god. Some of these natives depicted these fearsome deities on primitive carvings as a hideous creature with swirling arms, ready to release his winds and claim its prey.

There are several theories about the origin of the word 'hurricane'; some people believe it originated from the Caribbean Taíno-Arawak speaking Indians. It is believed that these Indians named their storm god 'Huracán', and over time it eventually evolved into the English word 'hurricane.' Others believed that it originated from the fierce group of cannibalistic Indians called the Caribs, but according to some historians this seems like the least likely source of this word. Native people throughout the Caribbean Basin linked hurricanes to supernatural forces and had a word for these storms, which often had similar spellings, but they all signified death and destruction by some evil spirit, and the early European colonial explorers to the New World picked up the native names. Actually, one early historian noted that the local Caribbean Indians, in preparation for these storms, often tied themselves to trees to keep from being blown away from the winds of these storms. According to one early seventeenth-century English account, Indians on St. Christopher viewed 'Hurry-Cano' as a "tempestuous spirit." These ancient Indians of this region personalized the hurricane, believing that it was bearing down on them as punishment by the gods for something they had done-or not done. These days, there is more science and less superstition to these powerful storms of nature called hurricanes. Yet we humanize hurricanes with familiar names, and the big ones become folkloric and iconic characters, their rampages woven into the histories of the Caribbean, North and Central American coastal towns and cities.

Another popular theory about the hurricane's origin is that it came from the Mayan Indians of Mexico, who had an ancient word for these storms, called 'Hurrikán' (or 'Huracán'). Hurrikán was the Mayan god of the storm. He was present at all three attempts to create humanity, in which he did most of the actual work of creating human beings under the direction of Kukulkán (known by the Aztec name Quetzalcoatl) and Tepeu. Unlike the other Creators, Hurrikán was not heavily personified by the Mayans and was generally considered to be more like the winds and the storms themselves. In the Mayan language, his name means "one-legged." The word hurricane is derived from Hurrikán's name. Hurrikán is similar to the Aztec god Tlaloc. In Mayan mythology, 'Hurrikán' ("one legged") was a wind, storm and fire god and one of the creator deities who participated in all three attempts of creating humanity. 'Hurrikán' was the Mayan god of big wind, and his image was chiseled into the walls of the Mayan temples. He was one of the three most powerful forces in the pantheon of deities, along with Cabrakán (earthquakes) and Chirakán (volcanoes). He also caused the Great Flood after the first humans angered the gods. He supposedly lived in the windy mists above the floodwaters and repeated "Earth" until land came up from the seas. In appearance, he has one leg, the other being transformed into a serpent, a zoomorphic snout or long-nose, and a smoking object such as a cigar, torch holder or axe head, which pierces a mirror on his forehead.

Actually, the first human historical record of hurricanes can be found in the ancient Mayan hieroglyphics. A powerful and deadly hurricane struck the Northern Yucatán in 1464, wiping out most of the Mayan Indian population of that area. According to Mayan mythology, the Mayan rain and wind god Chac sent rain for the crops. But he also sent hurricanes, which destroyed crops and flooded villages. The Mayans hoped that if they made offerings to Chac (including human sacrifices), the rains would continue to fall, but the hurricanes would cease. Every year, the Mayans threw a young woman into the sea as a sacrifice to appease the god Hurrikán, and a warrior was also sacrificed to lead the girl to Hurrikán's underwater kingdom. Also, one of the sacrifices in honour of this god was to drown children in wells. In some Maya regions, Chac, the god of rain and wind, was so important that the facades of their buildings were covered with the masks of Chac. In actual fact, at its peak it was one of the most densely populated and culturally dynamic societies in the world, but still they always built their homes far away from the hurricane-prone coast.

By customarily building their major settlements away from the hurricane-prone coastline, the Mayan Indians practiced a method of disaster mitigation that, if rigorously applied today, would reduce the potential for devastation along coastal areas. The only Mayan port city discovered to date is the small-to-medium sized city of Tulum, on the east coast of the Yucatán Peninsula south of Cancun. Tulum remained occupied when the Spaniards first arrived in the sixteenth century, and its citizens were more prepared for the storms than for the Spaniards. As the many visitors to these ruins can see, the ceremonial buildings and grounds of the city were so skillfully constructed that many remain today and withstand many hurricanes. The Indians of Guatemala called the god of stormy weather 'Hunrakán.' Of course, the Indians did not observe in what period of the year these hurricanes could strike their country; they believed that the devil or the evil spirits sent them whenever they pleased. Their gods were the uncontrollable forces of nature on which their lives were wholly dependent, the sun, the stars, the rains and the storms.

The Taínos were generally considered to be part of the Taíno-Arawak Indians, who travelled from the Orinoco-Amazon region of South America to Venezuela and then into the Caribbean Islands of the Dominican Republic, Haiti, the Bahamas, Jamaica, Puerto Rico, and as far west as Cuba. Christopher Columbus called these inhabitants of the western hemisphere 'Indians' because he mistakenly thought he had reached the islands on the eastern side of the Indian Ocean. The word 'Taíno' comes directly from Christopher Columbus because they were the indigenous set of people he encountered on his first voyage to the Caribbean, and they called themselves 'Taíno', meaning 'good' or 'noble', to differentiate themselves from their fierce enemies-the Carib Indians. This name applied to all the Island Taínos, including those in the Lesser Antilles. These so-called Indians were divided into innumerable small ethnic groups, each with its own combination of linguistic, cultural, and biological traits.

Locally, the Taínos referred to themselves by the name of their location. For example, those in Puerto Rico referred to themselves as Boricua, which means 'people from the island of the valiant noble lords.' Their island was called Borike'n, meaning 'great land of the valiant noble lord.' Those occupying the Bahamas called themselves 'Lucayo' or 'Lucayans', meaning 'small islands.' Another important consequence of their navigation skills and their canoes was the fact that the Taínos had contact with other indigenous groups of the Americas, including the Mayas of Mexico and Guatemala. What is the evidence to suggest that the Taínos had contact with the Mayan culture? There are many similarities between the Mayan god 'Hurrikán' and Taíno god 'Huracán', also similarities in their ballgames and similarities in their social structure and social stratification. Furthermore, the Meso-Indians of Mexico also flattened the heads of their infants in a similar fashion to the Island based Taínos and their relatives.

The Taíno Indians believed in two supreme gods, one male and the other female. They also believed that man had a soul and that after death he would go to a paradise called 'Coyaba', where the natural weather elements such as droughts and hurricanes would be forgotten in an eternity of feasting and dancing. In the Taíno Indians culture, they believed in a female zemi (spirit) named Guabancex, who controlled hurricanes, among other things-but when angered, she sent out her herald Guataba to order all the other zemis to lend her their winds, and with this great power she made the winds and the waters move and cast houses to the ground and uprooted trees. Representations of Guabancex portrayed her head as the eye of the storm, with twisting arms symbolizing the swirling winds. The international symbol that we use today for hurricanes was derived from this zemi. The various likenesses of this god invariably consist of a head of an indeterminate gender with no torso, two distinctive arms spiraling out from its sides. Most of these images exhibit cyclonic (counterclockwise) spirals. The Cuban ethnologist Fernando Ortiz believes that they were inspired by the tropical hurricanes that have always plagued the Caribbean. If so, the Taínos discovered the cyclonic or vortical nature of hurricanes many hundreds of years before the descendents of European settlers did. How they may have made this deduction remains a mystery to this day.

The spiral rain bands so well known to us from satellites and radars were not officially 'discovered' until the meteorological radar was developed during World War II, and they are far too big to be discerned by eye from the ground. It is speculated that these ancient people surveyed the damage done by the hurricane, and based on the direction by which the trees fell, concluded that the damage could only have been done by rotating winds.

Or perhaps they witnessed tornadoes or waterspouts, which are much smaller phenomena whose rotation is readily apparent, and came to believe that all destructive winds are rotary. They also believed that sickness or misfortunes such as devastating hurricanes were the works of malignant or highly displeased zemis, and good fortune was a sign that the zemis were pleased. To keep the zemis pleased, great public festivals were held to propitiate the tribal zemis, or simply in their honour. On these occasions, everyone would be well-dressed in elaborate outfits, and the cacique would lead a parade beating a wooden drum. Gifts of the finest cassava were offered to the zemis in hopes that the zemis would protect them against the four chief scourges of the Taínos' existence: fire, sickness, the Caribs, and most importantly devastating hurricanes.

The language of the Taínos was not a written one, and written works from them are very scarce. Some documentation of their lifestyles may be found in the writings of Spanish priests, such as Bartholomew de Las Casas in Puerto Rico and the Dominican Republic during the early 16th century. Some of the Taíno origin words were borrowed by the Spanish and subsequently found their way into the English Language and are modern day reminders of this once proud and vigorous race of people. These words include: avocado, potato, buccaneer, cay, manatee, maize, guava, barbacoa (barbecue), cacique (chief), jamaca (hammock), Tabacú (tobacco), caniba (cannibal), canoa (canoe), Iguana (lizard), and huracán or huruká (hurricane).

Interestingly, two of the islands here in the Bahamas, Inagua and Mayaguana both derived their names from the Lucayan word 'Iguana.' Bimini (meaning "two small islands" in English), another island here in the Bahamas, also got its name from these Indians; however, most of the other islands here in the Bahamas and the rest of the Caribbean were also given Indian names, but they have been changed over the many years and centuries by various groups of people who settled or passed through the Bahamas or other Caribbean islands. For example, in the Bahamas the Lucayans called the island of Exuma-Yuma, San Salvador was called Guanahani, Long Island was called Samana, Cat Island was called Guanima, Abaco was called Lucayoneque, Eleuthera was called Cigateo, Rum Cay was called Manigua and Crooked Island was called Saomere. Christopher Columbus, when he came to the Bahamas and landed on

Guanahani, renamed it San Salvador, Manigua, he renamed it Santa Maria de la Concepcion, Yuma, he renamed it Fernandina, Saomete, he renamed it Isabella, and the Ragged Island chain he renamed Islas de Arenas.[4] However, for the early Spanish explorers, the islands of the Bahamas were of no particular economic value, so therefore they established only temporary settlements, mainly to transport the peaceful Indians to be used as their slaves in East Hispaniola and Cuba to mine the valuable deposits of gold and silver and to dive for pearls.

Jurakán is the phonetic name given by the Spanish settlers to the god of chaos and disorder that the Taíno Indians in Puerto Rico (and also the Carib and Arawak Indians elsewhere in the Caribbean) believed controlled the weather, particularly hurricanes. From this we derive the Spanish word huracán, and eventually the English word hurricane. As the spelling and pronunciation varied across various indigenous groups, there were many alternative names along the way. For example, many West Indian historians and indigenous Indians called them by the various names, including Juracán, furacan, furican, haurachan, herycano, hurachano, hurricano, and so on. The term makes an early appearance in William Shakespeare's King Lear (Act 3, Scene 2). Being the easternmost of the Greater Antilles, Puerto Rico is often in the path of many of the North Atlantic tropical storms and hurricanes that tend to come ashore on the east coast of the island. The Taínos believed that Juracán lived at the top of a rainforest peak called El Yunque (literally, the anvil, but truly derived from the name of the Taíno god of order and creation, Yuquiyú), from where he stirred the winds and caused the waves to smash against the shore.

In the Taíno culture, it was said that when the hurricane was upon them, these people would shut themselves up in their leaky huts and shouted and banged drums and blew shell trumpets to keep the evil spirits of the hurricane from killing them or destroying their homes and crops. According to Taíno legend, the goddess Atabei first created the Earth, the sky, and all the celestial bodies. The metaphor of the sacred waters was included because the Taínos attributed religious and mythical qualities to water. For example, the goddess Atabei was associated with water. She was also the goddess of water. Yocahú, the supreme deity, was also associated

---

[4]   Barratt, P.(2006) *Bahamas Saga-The Epic Story of the Bahama Islands*, Author House, pg 51.

with water. Both of these deities are called Bagua, which is water, the source of life. This image of water as a sacred entity was central to their beliefs. They were at the mercy of water for their farming. Without rain, they would not be able to farm their conucos.

These Indians prayed to the twin gods of rain and fair weather so that they would be pleased and prayed to these gods to keep the evil hurricane away from their farms and homes. To continue her (Atabei) work, she bore two sons, Yucaju and Guacar. Yucaju created the sun and moon to give light and then made plants and animals to populate the Earth. Seeing the beautiful fruits of Yucaju's work, Guacar became jealous and began to tear up the Earth with powerful winds, renaming himself Jurakan, the god of destruction. Yucaju then created Locuo, a being intermediate between a god and a man, to live in peaceful harmony with the world. Locuo, in turn, created the first man and woman, Guaguyona and Yaya. All three continued to suffer from the powerful winds and floods inflicted by the evil god Jurakán. It was said that the god Jurakán was perpetually angry and ruled the power of the hurricane. He became known as the god of strong winds, hence the name today of hurricane. He was feared and revered, and when the hurricanes blew, the Taínos thought they had displeased Jurakán. Jurakán would later become Huracán in Spanish and Hurricane in English.

The origin of the name "Bahamas" is unclear in the history of these islands. Some historians believe it may have been derived from the Spanish word baja mar, meaning lands of the 'shallow seas', or the Lucayan Indian word for the island of Grand Bahama, ba-ha-ma meaning 'large upper middle land.'[5] The seafaring Taíno people moved into the uninhabited Southeastern Bahamas from the islands of Hispaniola and Cuba sometime around 1000-800 A.D. These people came to be known as the Lucayans. According to various historians, there were estimated reports of well over 20,000 to 30,000+ Lucayans living in the Bahamas at the time of world famous Spanish explorer Christopher Columbus's arrival in 1492. Christopher Columbus' first landfall in the New World was on an island called San Salvador, which is generally accepted to be present-day San Salvador (also known as Watlings Island) in the Southeastern Bahamas.

---

[5]   Saunders, A.(2006) *History of Bimini Volume 2*, New World Press, pgs 5-9.

The Lucayans called this island Guanahaní, but Columbus renamed it San Salvador (Spanish for "Holy Saviour").[6] However, Columbus discovery of this island of San Salvador is a very controversial and debatable topic among historians, scientists and lay-people alike. Even to this day, some of them still suggest that Columbus made his landfall in some other islands in the Bahamas, such as Rum Cay, Samana Cay, Cat Island, and some even suggested he landed as far south as the Turks and Caicos Islands. However, it still remains a matter of great debate and mystery within the archeological and scientific community. Regrettably, that question may never be solved, as Columbus' original log book has been lost for centuries, and the only evidence is in the edited abstracts made by Father Bartholomew Las Casas.

In the Bahamas, Columbus made first contact with the Lucayans and exchanged goods with them. The Lucayans-a word that meant 'meal-eaters' in their own language, from their dependence upon cassava flour made from the bitter manioc root as their staple starch food. They were sub-Taínos of the Bahamas and believed that all of their islands were once part of the mainland of America but had been cut off by the howling winds and waves of the hurricanes, and they referred to these storms as huruká. The Lucayans (the Bahamas being known then as the Lucayan Islands) were sub-Taínos who lived in the Bahamas at the time of Christopher Columbus landfall on October 12, 1492. Sometime between 1000-800 A.D., the Taínos of Hispaniola, pressured by over-population and trading concerns, migrated into the southeastern islands of the Bahamas. The Taínos of Cuba moved into the northwestern Bahamas shortly afterwards. They are widely thought to be the first Amerindians encountered by the Spanish.

Early historical accounts describe them as a peaceful set of people, and they referred to themselves as 'Lucayos,' 'Lukku Kairi' or 'Lukku-Cairi', meaning 'small islands' or 'island people' because they referred to themselves by the name of their location. The Lucayans spoke the Ciboney dialect of the Taíno language. This assumption was made from the only piece of speech that was recorded phonetically and has been passed down to us. Las Casas informs us that the Taíno Indians of the Greater Antilles and Lucayans were unable to understand one another,

---

6   Saunders, A.(2006) *History of Bimini Volume 2*, New World Press, pgs 6-9.

'*here*'(in Hispaniola), he wrote *"they do not call gold 'caona' as in the main part of the island, nor 'nozay' as on the islet of Guanahani(San Salvador) but tuob."*[7] This brief hint of language difference tends to reinforce the theory that these Bahamian Islands were first settled by people coming from eastern Cuba of the sub-Taíno culture.

Before Columbus arrived in the Bahamas, there were about 20,000 to 30,000+ Lucayans living there, but because of slavery, diseases such as smallpox and yellow fever (to which they had no immunity), and other hardships brought on by the arrival of the Europeans, by 1517 they were virtually non-existent. As a matter of fact, when Spanish Conquistador Ponce de Leon visited those islands in 1513 in search of the magical 'Fountain of Youth,' he found no trace of these Lucayan Indians, with the exception of one elderly Indian woman. These Indians of the Caribbean and Central America lived in one of the most hurricane prone areas of the Earth; as a result, most of them built their temples, huts, pyramids and houses well away from the hurricane prone coastline because of the great fear and respect that they had for hurricanes.

Many early colonists in the Caribbean took solace by displaying a Cord of Saint Francis of Assisi, a short length of rope with three knots with three turns apiece, in their boats, churches and homes as a protective talisman during the hurricane season. Various legends and lore soon developed regarding Saint Francis and his connection with nature, including tropical weather and hurricanes. According to tradition, if these residents untied the first knot of the cord, winds would pick up, but only moderately. Winds of 'half a gale' resulted from untying the second knot. If all three knots were untied, winds of hurricane strength were produced. Today, some descendants of African slaves in the West Indies still tie knots in the leaves of certain trees and hang them in their homes to ward off hurricanes.

Similar accounts also emerged from encounters with the Carib Indians. In old historical accounts, these Indians were referred to by various names, such as, 'Caribs,' 'Charaibes,' 'Charibees' and 'Caribbees', and they were a mysterious set of people who migrated from the Amazon jungles of South America.[8] They were a tribe of warlike and cannibalistic Indians who

---

[7] Barratt, P.(2006) *Bahamas Saga-The Epic Story of the Bahama Islands*, Author House, pg 51

[8] Saunders, A.(2006) *History of Bimini Volume 2*, New World Press, pg 14.

migrated northwards into the Caribbean in their canoes, overcoming and dominating an earlier race of peaceful people called the Arawaks. While Columbus explored all parts of the West Indies, his successors colonized only those parts inhabited by the Arawak or Taíno Indians, avoiding the Carib inhabited islands because they lacked gold, but most importantly because the Carib Indians were too difficult to subjugate. Ironically, the region became known as the Caribbean, named after these fierce Indians.

Their practice of eating their enemies so captured the imagination of the Europeans that the Caribbean Sea was also named after these Indians. The English word 'cannibal' is derived from the term 'Caniba', used by the Arawaks to refer to the Caribs eating the flesh of their enemies. Their raids were made over long distances in large canoes and had as one of their main objectives to take the Arawak women as their captives, wives and slaves. While on the other hand, the captured Arawak men were tortured and killed and then barbecued and eaten during an elaborate ceremony because it was believed that if they did this, they would obtain their enemies' personal power and control their spirits. The French traveller Charles de Rochefort wrote that when these Caribs Indians heard the thunder clap, they would *"make all the haste they can to their little houses and sit down on low stools about the fire, covering their faces and resting their heads on their hands and knees, and in that posture they fall a weeping and say . . . Maboya is very angry with them: and they say the same when there happens a Hurricane."*[9]

The Caribs were terrified of spilling fresh water into the sea because they believed that it aroused the anger of hurricanes. They had no small stone gods but believed in good and powerful bad spirits called 'Maboya', which caused all the misfortunes of their lives. They even wore carved amulets and employed medicine men to drive the evil Maboya away. When a great and powerful storm began to rise out of the sea, the Caribs blew frantically into the air to chase it away and chewed manioc bread and spat it into the wind for the same purpose. When that was no use, they gave way to panic and crouched in their communal houses, moaning with their arms held over their heads. They felt that they were reasonably safe there because they fortified their houses with corner posts dug deep into the

---

[9] Mulcahy, M. (2006) *Hurricanes and Society in the British Greater Caribbean, 1624-1783*, The John Hopkins Uni versity Press, pg 35.

ground. They also believed that beyond the Maboya were great spirits, the male sun and the female moon. They believed that the spirits of the stars controlled the weather. They also believed in a bird named Savacou, which was sent out by the angry Maboya to call up the hurricane, and after this task was finished, this bird would then be transformed into a star.

According to noted English Historian John Oldmixon of the late 1600's and early 1700's, he reported that the Carib Indians excelled in forecasting hurricanes. Writing about a hurricane that occurred in 1740 on the island of St. Christopher he said:- *"Hurricanes are still frequent here, and it was some time since the custom of both the English and French inhabitants in this and the other Charibbees-Islands, to send about the month of June, to the native Charibbees of Dominica and St. Vincent, to know whether there would be any hurricanes that year; and about 10 or 12 Days before the hurricane came they constantly sent them word, and it was rarely failed."* According to Carib Indians 'Signs or Prognosticks,' a hurricane comes *"on the day of the full change, or quarters of the moon. If it will come on the full moon, you being in the change, then observe these signs. That day you will see the skies very turbulent, the sun more red than at other times, a great calm, and the hills clear of clouds or fogs over them, which in the high-lands are seldom so. In the hollows of the Earth or wells, there will be great noise, as if you were in a great storm; the stars at night will look very big with Burs about them, the north-west sky smelling stronger than at other times, as it usually does in violent storms; and sometimes that day for an hour or two, the winds blows very hard westerly, out of its usual course. On the full moon you have the same signs, but a great Bur about the moon, and many about the moon, and many about the sun. The like signs must be taken notice of on the quarter-days of the moon."*[10]

According to several elderly Carib Indians, hurricanes had become more frequent in the recent years following the arrival of the Europeans to the Caribbean, which they viewed as punishment for their interactions with them. In fact, as early as the 1630s, English colonists reported that Carib Indians knew when storms would strike by the number of rings that appeared around the moon: three rings meant the storm would arrive in three days, two rings meant two days and one ring meant the storm

---

[10] *An Early Colonial Historian: John Oldmixon and the British Empire in America-Journal of American Studies Vol.3 (August, 1973)*, pgs 113-123 . . . Cambridge University Press.

would arrive in one day. Of course, the connection between such signs and the onset of hurricanes was indeed a very unreliable way to predict the onset of hurricanes. The Carib Indians, while raiding islands in the Caribbean, would kill off the Arawak men and take the Arawak women as wives and mothers to their children. Actually, when the Europeans came to the Caribbean, they surprisingly found that many Carib women spoke the Taíno language because of the large number of female Taíno captives among them. So, it is speculated that a word like 'hurricane' was passed into the Carib speech, and this was how these fierce people learned about the terror of these savage storms. Native Indians of the West Indies often engaged in ritual purifications and sacrifices and offered songs and dances to help ward off hurricanes.

An Aztec myth tells that when the gods created the world, it was dark and cold. The youngest of the gods sacrificed himself to create a sun. But it was like him, weak, dim and feeble. Only when more powerful gods offered themselves did the sun blaze into life and shine brightly on them. However, there was one disadvantage, and that was that these gods needed constant fuel, human lives and the Aztecs obliged. They offered tens of thousands of human sacrifices a year just to make sure that the sun rose each morning and to prevent natural disasters such as devastating hurricanes from destroying their communities and villages. Tlaloc was an important deity in Aztec religion, a god of rain, fertility, and water. He was a beneficent god who gave life and sustenance, but he was also feared for his ability to send hurricanes, hail, thunder and lightning and for being the lord of the powerful element of water. In Aztec iconography, he is usually depicted with goggle eyes and fangs. He was associated with caves, springs and mountains. He is known for having demanded child sacrifices.

The Aztec god Tezcatlipoca (meaning Lord of the Hurricane) was believed to have special powers over the hurricane winds, as did the Palenque god Tahil (Obsidian Mirror) and the Quiché Maya sky god Huracán. The Aztec god Tezcatlipoca was feared for his capricious nature and the Aztecs called him Yaotl (meaning 'Adversary'). Tonatiuh was the Aztec Sun god, and the Aztecs saw the sun as a divinity that controlled the weather, including hurricanes and consequently, all human life forms. The Aztecs of Mexico, in particular, built vast temples to the sun god Tonatiuh and made bloody sacrifices of both human and animal to persuade him to shine brightly on them and in particular not send any destructive hurricanes their way and to allow prosperity for their crops. When they built these temples, they were constructed according to the Earth's alignment with the sun, but most importantly they were always constructed with hurricanes in mind and away from the hurricane-prone coastline.

The Aztec people considered Tonatiuh the leader of Tollán, their heaven. He was also known as the fifth sun because the Aztecs believed that he was the sun that took over when the fourth sun was expelled from the sky. Mesoamerican creation narratives proposed that before the current world age began, there were a number of previous creations. The Aztecs' account of the five suns or world ages revealed that in each of the five creations, the Earth's inhabitants found a more satisfactory staple food than eaten by their predecessors. In the era of the first sun, which was governed by Black Tezcatlipoca, the world was inhabited by a race of giants who lived on acorns. The second sun, whose presiding god was a serpent god called Quetzatzalcóatl, was believed to be the creator of life and in control of the vital rain-bearing winds, and he saw the emergence of a race of primitive humans who lived on the seeds of the mesquite tree.

After the third age, which was ruled by Tláloc, in which people lived on plants that grew on water, such as the water lily, people returned to a diet of wild seeds in the fourth age of Chalchiúhtlicue. It was only in the fifth and current age, an age subject to the sun god Tonatiuh that the people of Mesoamerica learned how to plant and harvest maize. According to their cosmology, each sun was a god with its own cosmic era. The Aztecs believed they were still in Tonatiuh's era, and according to their creation mythology, this god demanded human sacrifices as a tribute, and without it he would refuse to move through the sky, hold back on the rainfall for their crops and would send destructive hurricanes their way. It is said that some 20,000 people were sacrificed each year to Tonatiuh and other gods, though this number, however, is thought to be highly inflated either by the Aztecs, who wanted to inspire fear in their enemies, or the Spaniards, who wanted to speak-ill of the Aztecs. The Aztecs were fascinated by the sun, so they worshiped and carefully observed it and had a solar calendar second only in accuracy to the Mayans.

It was Captain Fernando de Oviedo who gave these storms their modern name when he wrote *"So when the devil wishes to terrify them, he promises them the 'Huracan,' which means tempest.*"[11] The Portuguese word for them is Huracao, which is believed to have originated from the original Taíno word Huracán. The Native American Indians had a word for these powerful storms, which they called 'Hurucane', meaning 'evil spirit of the wind.' When a hurricane approached the Florida coast, the medicine men of the North American Indians worked frantic incantations to drive the evil hurricane away. The Seminole Indians of Florida were actually the first to flee from a storm, citing the blooming of the Florida Everglades sawgrass. They believed that only 'an atmospheric condition' such as a major hurricane would cause the pollen to bloom on the sawgrass several days before a hurricane's arrival, giving the native Indians an advanced warning of the impending storm.

Many other sub-culture Indians had similar words for these powerful storms, which they all feared and respected greatly. For example, the Galibi Indians called these hurricanes Yuracan and Hyroacan. The Quiche people of Guatemala believed in the god Huraken, for their god of thunder and lightning. Giuana Indians called them Yarukka, and other similar Indian names were Hyrorokan, aracan, urican, huiranvucan, Yurakon, Yuruk or Yoroko. As hurricanes were becoming more frequent in the Caribbean, many of the colonists and natives of this region had various words and spellings, all sounding phonetically similar for these powerful storms. The English called them 'Hurricanes', 'Haurachana', 'Uracan', 'Herocano', 'Harrycane', 'Tempest', and 'Hyrracano.' The Spanish called them 'Huracán'and 'Furicane', and the Portuguese called them 'Huracao', and 'Furicane.' The French had for a long time adapted the Indian word called 'Ouragan', and the Dutch referred to them as 'Orkan.' These various spellings were used until the word 'hurricane' was finally settled on in the English Language. Among the Caribbean, Central and North American peoples, the word 'hurricane' seems to have always been associated with evil spirits and violence.

After his first voyage to the New World, Columbus returned to Isabella in Hispaniola with seventeen ships. Columbus' settlers built houses, storerooms, a Roman Catholic Church, and a large house for Columbus. He brought more than a thousand men, including sailors,

---

[11]   http://hrsbstaff.ednet.ns.ca/primetl/school/juan/hurricanesheets.html.

soldiers, carpenters, stonemasons, and other workers. Priests and nobles came as well. The Spaniards brought pigs, horses, wheat, sugarcane, and guns. Rats and microbes came with them as well. The settlement took up more than two hectares. At the time, some estimated the Taíno Indian population in Hispaniola to be as high as one million persons. They lived on fish and staples such as pineapple, which they introduced to the Spaniards. The food that they provided was important to the Spaniards. Describing these Indians, Columbus said that there were no finer people in the world. In March 1494, Columbus' men began to search, with Taíno Indians, in the mountains of Hispaniola for gold, and small amounts were found. In June 1495, a large storm that the Taíno Indians called a hurricane hit the island. The Indians retreated to the mountains, while the Spaniards remained in the colony. Several ships were sunk, including the flagship, the 'Marie-Galante.'

Christopher Columbus, on his first voyage, managed to avoid encountering any hurricanes but it wasn't until some of his later voyages that he encountered several hurricanes that disrupted these voyages to the New World. Based on his first voyage before encountering any hurricanes, Columbus concluded that the weather in the New World was benign: *"In all the Indies, I have always found May-like weather,"* he commented. Although sailing through hurricane-prone waters during the most dangerous months, he did not have any serious hurricane encounters on his early voyage. However, on his final voyages, Christopher Columbus himself weathered at least three of these dangerous storms. The town of La Isabella was struck by two of the earliest North Atlantic hurricanes observed by Europeans in 1494 and 1495. Columbus provided the earliest account of a hurricane in a letter written to Queen Isabella in 1494. In this letter, he wrote, *"The tempest arose and worried me so that I knew not where to turn; Eyes never behold the seas so high, angry and covered by foam. We were forced to keep out in this bloody ocean, seething like a pot of hot fire. Never did the sky look more terrible; for one whole day and night it blazed like a furnace. The flashes came with such fury and frightfulness that we all thought the ships would be blasted. All this time the water never ceased to fall from the sky . . . The people were so worn out, that they longed for death to end their terrible suffering."*[12]

The extensive shallow banks and coral reefs in the vicinity of most Caribbean islands present hazards to navigation that were immediately appreciated by the Spanish explorers. These dangers were compounded by violent tropical storms and hurricanes that appeared without sufficient warning and by the unseaworthy character of vessels that had spent months cruising in shipworm-infested waters. Despite the explorers' exercising what must have seemed like due caution, there is an extensive list of shipwrecks. Columbus himself lost nine ships: Santa María, which was wrecked near Haiti on Christmas Eve on his first voyage; Niña and three other vessels at La Isabella in 1495; and the entire fleet of his fourth voyage-Vizcaina and Gallega off the coast of Central America in 1503, and Capitana and Santiago in Puerto Santa Gloria, Jamaica, 1504. However, as early as June of 1494, the small town of Isabella, founded by Columbus on Hispaniola, became the first European settlement destroyed by a hurricane. The Spaniards who accompanied Columbus on his four voyages to the New World took back to Europe with them a new concept of what a severe storm could be, and naturally, a new word of Indian origin. It seems that the Indian word was pronounced 'Furacán' or 'Furacánes' during the early years of discovery and colonization of America. Peter Martyr, one of the earliest historians of the New World, said that they were called by the natives 'Furacanes,' although the plural is obviously Spanish. The Rev. P. du Tertre, (1667) in his great work during the middle of the seventeenth century, wrote first 'ouragan', and later 'houragan.'

After 1474, some changes in the Spanish language were made. For instance, words beginning with 'h' were pronounced using the 'f consonant.' The kingdoms of Aragon and Castile were united in 1474, before the discovery of America, and after that time some changes in the Spanish language were made. One of them involved words beginning with the letter 'h.' In Aragon, they pronounced such words as 'f'. As Menéndez Pidal said, "Aragon was the land of the 'f', but the old Castilian lost the sound or pronunciation," so that Spanish Scholar Nebrija (Nebrija wrote a grammar of the Castilian language and is credited as the first published grammar of any Romance language) wrote, instead of the lost 'f', an aspirated 'h.' Menéndez wrote concerning the pronunciation of the word 'hurricane' and its language used by Fernando Colón, son of Christopher Columbus, "Vacillation between 'f' and 'h' is very marked predominance of the 'h.' And so, the 'h' became in Spanish a silent letter, as it still is today."

Father Bartholomew de Las Casas, referring to one of these storms, wrote: *"At this time the four vessels brought by Juan Aguado were destroyed in the port (of Isabella) by a great tempest, called by the Indians in their language 'Furacán.' Now we call them hurricanes, something that almost all of us have experienced at sea or on land . . ."*[13] Las Casas, outraged by the brutal treatment of the Indians on Hispaniola, declared that the wrath of the hurricane that struck Hispaniola was the judgment of God on the city and the men who had committed such sins against humanity. All other European languages coined a word for the tropical cyclone, based on the Spanish 'Huracán.' Gonzalo Fernandez de Oviedo (Oviedo y Valdes, 1851, Book VI, Ch. III) is more explicit in his writings concerning the origin of the word 'hurricane.' He says: *"Hurricane, in the language of this island, properly means an excessively severe storm or tempest; because, in fact, it is only a very great wind and a very great and excessive rainfall, both together or either these two things by themselves."* Oviedo further noted that the winds of the *'Huracán'* were so *"fierce that they topple houses and uproot many large trees."*[14]

Even in the English Language, the word 'hurricane' evolved through several variations. For example, William Shakespeare mentioned it in his play 'King Lear', where he wrote *"Blow, winds, and crack your cheeks! Rage! Blow! You catracts and hurricanes, spout till you have drench'd out steeples, drown'd the cocks!"* Girolamo Benzoni, in 1565 in his Book *History of the New World,* mentioned his encounter with a hurricane in Hispaniola, which at the time he referred to as *'Furacanum.' "In those days a wondrous*

[13] Millas, C.J. (1968) *Hurricanes of The Caribbean and Adjacent Regions 1492-1800,* Edward Brothers Inc/ Academy of Arts and Sciences of the Americas Miami, Florida. Pg xi.

[14] Millas, C.J. (1968) *Hurricanes of The Caribbean and Adjacent Regions 1492-1800,* Edward Brothers Inc/ Academy of Arts and Sciences of the Americas Miami, Florida. Pg xi.

and terrible disaster occurred in this country. At sunrise such a horrible, strong wind began that the inhabitants of the island thought they had never seen or heard anything like it before. The raging storm wind (which the Spaniards called Furacanum) came with great violence, as if it wanted to spit heaven and Earth apart from one another, and hurl everything to the ground . . . The people were as a whole so despairing because of their great fear that they run here and there, as if they were senseless and mad, and did not know what they did . . . The strong and frightful wind threw some entire houses and capitals including the people from the capital, tore them apart in the air and threw them down to the ground in pieces. This awful weather did such noticeable damage in such a short time that not three ships stood secure in the sea harbour or came through the storm undamaged. For the anchors, even if they were yet strong, were broken apart through the strong force of the wind and all the masts, despite their being new, were crumpled. The ships were blown around by the wind, so that all the people in them were drowned. For the most part the Indians had crawled away and hidden themselves in holes in order to escape such disaster."[15]

As stated earlier, Christopher Columbus did not learn on his first voyage, the voyage of discovery, of the existence of such terrible 'tempests' or 'storms.' He had the exceptional good fortune of not being struck by any of them during this voyage. The Indians, while enjoying pleasant weather, had no reason to speak about these storms to a group of strangers who spoke a language that they could not understand. Naturally, Columbus did not say one word about these awful storms in his much celebrated letter "The letter of Columbus on the Discovery of America." However, on his second voyage things were quite different. After arriving on November 3, 1493, at an island in the Lesser Antilles that he named Dominica, Columbus sailed northward and later westward, to Isabella Hispaniola, the first city in the New World, at the end of January 1494. Then in June of that year, 1494, Isabella was struck by a hurricane, the first time that European men had seen such a terrible storm. Surely, for the first time they heard the Taíno Indians, very much excited, extending their arms raised upward into the air and shouting, "Furacán! Furacán!" when the storm commenced. We can indeed say that it was that moment in history when

---

[15]   Benzon, G. (1837) *History of the New World Vol. 21*, Hakluyt Society.

the word 'hurricane' suddenly appeared to the Europeans. Columbus was not at that time in Isabella because he was sailing near the Isle of Pines, Cuba. So, his companions of the ships 'Marigalante' and 'Gallega' were the first white men to hear these words, which were of Indian origin and about a phenomenon of the New World. Knowledge of 'Furacanes,' both the word and the terrifying storms it described, remained limited to Spanish speakers until 1555, when Richard Eden translated Columbus' ship report and other Spanish accounts of the New World, making it the first time it appeared in the English vocabulary.

In October of 1495, probably in the second half of the month, another hurricane struck Isabella, which was much stronger than the first. It finally gave Columbus, who was there at the time, the opportunity of knowing what a hurricane was and of its destructive abilities. It also gave him the opportunity of hearing the Indians shouting the same word with fear and anxiety on their faces, on the account of these terrible storms of the tropics, which they believed were caused by evil spirits. Christopher Columbus would later declare that *"nothing but the service of God and the extension of the monarchy would induce him to expose himself to such danger from these storms ever again."*[16] 'The Niña' was the only vessel that was the smallest, oldest and the most fragile at the time, but amazingly it withstood that hurricane. The other two ships of Columbus, 'The San Juan' and 'The Cordera,' were in the harbour and were lost or badly damaged by this hurricane. Columbus gave orders to have one repaired and another ship known as 'India' constructed out of the wreck of the ones that had been destroyed, making it the first ship to be built in the Caribbean by Europeans.

In 1502, during his fourth voyage, Columbus warned the Governor Don Nicolas de Orvando of Santo Domingo of an approaching hurricane, but he was ignored; as a result, a Spanish treasure fleet set sailed and lost 21 of 30 ships with 500 men. Columbus had a serious disagreement with the bureaucrats appointed by Spain to govern the fledgling colonies in the Caribbean to extract gold, pearl and other precious commodities from the native Indians. Among the more unfriendly of these exploiters was Don Nicolas de Orvando, the Governor of Hispaniola, with whom Columbus

[16] Tannehill, I.(1950) *Hurricanes-Their Nature and History*, Princeton University Press, pg 141.

had been forbidden to have any contact by the request of his Spanish sovereigns. But as Columbus approached Santa Domingo, he recognized the early signs of an approaching hurricane, such as large ocean swells and a veil of cirrostratus clouds overhead. Concerned for the safety of his men and ships, he sent a message to Governor Orvando, begging him to be allowed to seek refuge in Santa Domingo Harbour. Columbus had observed that the Governor was preparing a large fleet of ships to set sail for Spain, carrying large quantities of gold and slaves, and warned him to delay the trip until the hurricane had passed. Refusing both the request and the advice, Orvando read Columbus' note out loud to the crew and residents, who roared with laughter at Columbus' advice. Unfortunately, the laughter was very short-lived, and Orvando's ships left port only to their own demise when 21 of the 30 ships were lost in a hurricane between Hispaniola and Puerto Rico. An additional four of them were badly damaged, but fortunately they were able to return to port, where they, too, eventually sunk. Only one ship, the *Aguja*, made it to Spain, and that one, no doubt to Orvando's intense distress, was carrying what little remained of Columbus' own gold.

Meanwhile, Columbus, anticipating strong winds from the north from this hurricane, positioned his fleet in a harbour on the south side of Hispaniola. On June 13, the storm hit with ferocious northeast winds. Even with the protection of the mountainous terrain to the windward side, the fleet struggled. In Columbus' own words, *"The storm was terrible and on that night the ships were parted from me. Each one of them was reduced to an extremity, expecting nothing save death; each one of them was certain the others were lost."*[17] The anchors held only on Columbus' ship; the others were dragged out to sea, where their crews fought for their lives. Nevertheless, the fleet survived with only minimal damage. Almost 18 months later, Columbus returned to Santo Domingo, only to discover that it had been largely destroyed by the hurricane.

When the Europeans first attempted to create settlements in the Caribbean and the Americas, they quickly learned about these storms. As time passed and these settlers learned more about their new homeland, they experienced these storms on such a regular basis that they became

---

[17]   National Geographic Magazine, November 1986-*A Columbus Casebook-A Supplement to "Where Columbus Found the New World."*

accustomed to them. Eventually, they began calling them equinoctial storms, as the storms would normally hit in the weeks around the period of the fall equinox, which in the northern hemisphere occurs in late September.

English explorers and privateers soon contributed their own accounts of encounters with these storms. In 1513, Juan Ponce de León completed the first recorded cruise along the Florida coast and came ashore near present-day St. Augustine to claim Florida for Spain. Famous for his unsuccessful search for the magical 'Fountain of Youth,' he might have discovered Florida earlier had it not been for the ravages of hurricanes. In August of 1508, he was struck by two hurricanes within two weeks. The first drove his ship onto the rocks near the Port of Yuna, Hispaniola, and the second left his ship aground on the southwest coast of Puerto Rico. Soon after Hernando Cortés found treasures of gold and silver in the newly discovered lands of the West, expeditions to retrieve the riches of the New World for Spain began in earnest. In 1525, Cortés lost the first ship he sent to Mexico in a severe hurricane, along with its crew of over seventy persons. Famous English explorer Sir John Hawkins wrote his own encounters with these storms. Sir John Hawkins wrote that he left Cartagena in late July 1568 *"Hoping to have escaped the time of their stormes . . . which they call Furicanos."*[18] Hawkins did not leave soon enough, and he and his ships were bashed by an "extreme storme", as he referred to it, lasting several days.

English Explorer Sir Francis Drake encountered several major hurricanes while sailing the dangerous seas of the Americas and the Atlantic Ocean, and in most cases these encounters changed the course of West Indian and American history. Sir Francis Drake, who travelled the seas of the globe in quest of glory and valuable loot, nearly lost his ships in the fleet on the Outer Banks of Carolina. One of his most famous encounters was with a major hurricane that occurred while he was anchored near the ill-fated Roanoke colony in present day North Carolina in June of 1586. His ships were anchored just off the banks while he checked on the progress of Sir Walter Raleigh's colonists on Roanoke Island. The hurricane lasted for three days, scattering Drake's fleet and nearly destroying many of his ships. There was no greater thorn in the side of the Spaniards than Francis

---

[18] Mulcahy, M. (2006) *Hurricanes and Society in the British Greater Caribbean, 1624-1783*, The John Hopkins Uni versity Press, pgs 14-15.

Drake. His exploits were legendary, making him a hero to the English but a simple pirate to the Spaniards, and for good reasons because he often robbed them of their valuable treasures. To the Spanish, he was known as El Draque, "the Dragon"; "Draque" is the Spanish pronunciation of "Drake." As a talented sea captain and navigator, he attacked their fleets and took their ships and treasures. He raided their settlements in America and played a major role in the defeat of the greatest fleet ever assembled, the "Spanish Armada."

No other English seaman brought home more wealth or had a bigger impact on English history than Drake. At the age of 28, he was trapped in a Mexican port by Spanish war ships. He had gone there for repairs after an encounter with one of his first major hurricanes at sea. Drake escaped but some of the sailors left behind were so badly treated by the Spanish that he swore revenge. He returned to the area in 1572 with two ships and 73 men. Over the next fifteen months, he raided Spanish towns and their all-important Silver train across the isthmus from Panama. Other English accounts reported ships damaged or lost in storms characterized by extreme wind and rain, some of which were definitely hurricanes. The English (including Drake and Hawkins) had a great respect for hurricanes, to such an extent that as the hurricane season was understood to be approaching, more and more pirates went home or laid up their ships in some sheltered harbour until the last hurricane had passed and was replaced by the cool air of old man winter.

Probably those that first discovered the period of the year in which hurricanes developed were Spanish priests, officers of the navy or army, or civilians that had lived for a long time in the Caribbean. By the end of the sixteenth century, they should have already known the approximate period that these hurricanes occurred. The Roman Catholic Church knew early on that the hurricane season extended at least from August to October because the hierarchy ordered that all of the churches in the Caribbean say a special prayer to protect them from these deadly hurricanes. The prayer that had to be said was: 'Ad repellendas tempestates,' translated to mean 'for the repelling of the hurricanes or tempests.' It was also ordered that the prayer should be said in Puerto Rico during August and September and in Cuba in September and October. This indicates that it was known that hurricanes were more frequent in those islands during the months mentioned. Eventually, West Indian colonists, through first-hand experiences with these storms, gradually learned that hurricanes struck the Caribbean within a well-defined season. Initially, those early colonists believed that hurricanes could strike at any time of the year, but by the middle of the seventeenth century most of them recognized that there was a distinct hurricane season. This was because the hurricanes simply occurred too frequent within a particular time period for them to remain strange and unusual in their eyes. Numerous letters and reports written by colonists specifically discussed the period between July and October as the 'time of hurricanes.'

The geography of hurricanes challenged the concept of these storms as 'national judgments or divine favor' by which God spoke to a specific group of people or country. Individual storms routinely struck various islands colonized by different European powers. For example, in 1707 a hurricane devastated the English Leeward Islands, the Dutch Islands of Saba and St. Eustatius, and the French Island of Guadeloupe. In 1674, a Dutch attack on the French Islands was thwarted by a hurricane, which also caused significant damage in the English Leeward Islands and in Barbados. The presence of hurricanes made colonists question their ability to transform the hostile environment of the Caribbean, and by extension their ability to establish successful and stable societies here. But hurricanes raised other questions as well: What caused them? What forces gave rise to such powerful and dangerous storms? For some-probably a significant majority during the first several decades of the seventeenth century-they believed that these storms came directly from the hands of God. They interpreted hurricanes as 'wondrous events' or 'divine judgments' for human sins. Others linked hurricanes to various natural processes, including shifting wind patterns. The explosion of various natural processes, including shifting wind patterns, the explosion of various chemicals in the atmosphere, and the celestial movement of the planets and stars.

CHAPTER FOUR

The Naming of Hurricanes

North Atlantic Tropical Cyclone Names

2013	2014	2015	2016	2017	2018
Andrea	Arthur	Ana	Alex	Arlene	Alberto
Barry	Bertha	Bill	Bonnie	Bret	Beryl
Chantal	Cristobal	Claudette	Colin	Cindy	Chris
Dorian	Dolly	Danny	Danielle	Don	Debby
Erin	Edouard	Erika	Earl	Emily	Ernesto
Fernand	Fay	Fred	Fiona	Franklin	Florence
Gabrielle	Gustav	Grace	Gaston	Gert	Gordon
Humberto	Hanna	Henri	Hermine	Harvey	Helene
Ingrid	Ike	Ida	Ian	Irma	Isaac
Jerry	Josephine	Joaquin	Julia	Jose	Joyce
Karen	Kyle	Kate	Karl	Katia	Kirk
Lorenzo	Laura	Larry	Lisa	Lee	Leslie
Melissa	Marco	Mindy	Matthew	Maria	Michael
Nestor	Nana	Nicholas	Nicole	Nate	Nadine
Olga	Omar	Odette	Otto	Ophelia	Oscar
Pablo	Paulette	Peter	Paula	Philippe	Patty
Rebekah	Rene	Rose	Richard	Rina	Rafael
Sebastien	Sally	Sam	Shary	Sean	Sara
Tanya	Teddy	Teresa	Tobias	Tammy	Tony
Van	Vicky	Victor	Virginie	Vince	Valerie
Wendy	Wilfred	Wanda	Walter	Whitney	William

Information Courtesy of NOAA.

For as long as people have been tracking and reporting hurricanes, also known as tropical cyclones, they've been struggling to find ways to identify them. Until well into the 20th century, newspapers and forecasters in the Caribbean and the Americas devised names for storms that referenced their time period, geographic location or intensity or some other distinguishing factor. It's a funny thing, this naming of storms. We don't name tornadoes, blizzards, or frontal systems. It would seem silly, but we do name our hurricanes. On the opposite corners of our stormy planet, meteorologists name their cyclones too (although with sometimes more meaningful or symbolic names). Hurricanes are the only weather disasters that have been given their own iconic names, such as Hurricanes Sandy, Andrew, Gilbert, Katrina, Camille or Mitch. No two hurricanes are the same, but like people, they share similar characteristics; yet, still they have their own unique stories to tell. The naming of storms or hurricanes has undergone various stages of development and transformation. Initially, the word 'Hurricane' accompanied by the year of occurrence was used. For example, 'the Great Hurricane of 1780', which killed over 22,000 persons in Martinique, Barbados and St. Eustatius. Another example was 'the Great Storm of 1703', whose incredible damage of the British Isles was expertly detailed by Robinson Crusoe's author, Daniel Defoe. The naming scheme was later substituted by a numbering system (e.g. Hurricane #1, #2, #3 of 1833 etc . . .); however, this became too cumbersome and confusing, especially when disseminating information about two or more storms within the same geographical area or location.

For the major hurricanes of this region, they were often named after the particular country or city they devastated. This was especially true for severe hurricanes, which made their landing somewhere in the Caribbean. Three notable examples were: first, 'the Dominican Republic Hurricane of 1930', which killed over 8,000 persons in the Dominican Republic. The 1930 Dominican Republic Hurricane, also known as 'Hurricane San Zenon', is the fifth deadliest North Atlantic hurricane on record. The second of only two known tropical cyclones in the very quiet 1930 North Atlantic hurricane season, the hurricane was first observed on August 29 to the east of the Lesser Antilles. The cyclone was a small but intense Category 4 hurricane.

Next was 'the Pointe-à-Pitre Hurricane of 1776', which devastated the country of Guadeloupe and killed over 6,000 persons and devastated its largest city and economic capital of Pointe-à-Pitre. The 1776 Pointe-à-Pitre hurricane was at one point the deadliest North Atlantic on record. Although its intensity and complete track is unknown, it is known that the storm struck Guadeloupe on September 6, 1776, near Pointe-à-Pitre, which is currently the largest city on the island. At least 6,000 fatalities occurred on Guadeloupe, which was a higher death toll than any other known hurricane before it to hit that country. The storm struck a large convoy of French and Dutch merchant ships, sinking or running aground 60% of the vessels. The ships were transporting goods to Europe.

Finally, 'the Great Nassau Hurricane of 1926', which devastated the city of Nassau in the Bahamas during the 1926 North Atlantic hurricane season. The Great Nassau Hurricane of 1926, also known as 'the Bahamas-Florida Hurricane of July 1926' and 'Hurricane San Liborio,' was a destructive Category 4 hurricane that affected the Bahamas at peak intensity. Although it weakened considerably before its Florida landfall, it was reported as one of the most severe storms to affect Nassau in the Bahamas in several years until the Great Lake Okeechobee Hurricane of 1928, which occurred just two years later. Approximately 268 persons died in this storm in the Bahamas.

In some cases, they were even named after the holiday on which they occurred, for example, 'the Great Labour Day Hurricane of 1935.' The Great Labour Day Hurricane of 1935 was the strongest tropical cyclone during the 1935 North Atlantic hurricane season. This compact and intense hurricane caused extensive damage in the Bahamas and the upper Florida Keys. To this day, the Great Labour Day Hurricane of 1935 is the strongest and most intense hurricane on record to ever have struck the United States in terms of barometric pressure. The Great Labour Day Hurricane of 1935 was one of the strongest recorded hurricane landfalls worldwide. It was the only hurricane known to have made landfall in the United States with a minimum central pressure below 900 Mbar; only two others have struck the United States with winds of Category 5 strength on the Saffir-Simpson Scale. It remains the third-strongest North Atlantic hurricane on record, and it was only surpassed by Hurricane Gilbert (888Mbar) in 1988 and Hurricane Wilma (882Mbar) in 2005. In total, at least 408 people were killed by this hurricane.

In some cases they were named after the ship that experienced that particular storm. Two notable examples were: - 'the Racer's Storm of 1837' and 'the Sea Venture Hurricane of 1609.' The 1837 Racer's Storm was a very powerful and destructive hurricane in the 19th century, causing 105 deaths and heavy damage to many cities on its 2,000+ mile path. The Racer's Storm was the 10th known tropical storm in the 1837 North Atlantic hurricane season. The Racer's Storm was named after the British war ship HMS Racer, which encountered the storm in the extreme northwest

Caribbean on September 28th. Another example was 'the Sea Venture Hurricane of 1609.' On July 28th of 1609, a fleet of seven tall ships, with two pinnaces in tow carrying 150 settlers and supplies from Plymouth, England, to Virginia to relieve the starving Jamestown colonists, was struck by a hurricane while en route there. They had been sent by the Virginia Company of London to fortify the Jamestown settlement. Sir George Somers' mission was to resupply the six hundred or so pioneers who a year before had settled in the infant British colonial settlement of King James' Town, sited in one of the estuaries south of the Potomac River.

The ship 'Sea Venture' was grounded at Bermuda, which for some time was called Somers Island after the ship's captain, Admiral Sir George Somers. After being struck by this hurricane, the Sea Venture sprung a leak and everyone on board worked frantically to save this ship and their lives by trying to pump the water out of the hull of the ship. They tried to stem the flow of water coming into the ship by stuffing salt beef and anything else they could find to fit into the leaks of the ship. After this proved futile, most of the crew simply gave up hope, falling asleep where they could, exhausted and aching from their relentless but futile efforts. But just as they were about to give up and face the grim reality that they would be lost to the unforgiving Atlantic Ocean, they spotted the island of Bermuda. Somers skillfully navigated the floundering Sea Venture onto a reef about half a mile to the leeward side of Bermuda. They used the ship's long boat to ferry the crew and passengers ashore.

The passengers of the shipwrecked Sea Venture became Bermuda's first inhabitants, and their stories helped inspire William Shakespeare's writing of his final play 'The Tempest', making it perhaps the most famous hurricane in early American history. *"And another storm brewing,"* William Shakespeare wrote in 'The Tempest.' *"I hear it sing in the wind."*[19] Most of those venturing to the New World had no knowledge of the word or the actual storm. The lead ship, the three-hundred-ton Sea Venture, was the largest in the fleet and carried Sir Thomas Gates, the newly appointed governor of the colony, and Sir Georges Somers, admiral of the Virginia Company. It is interesting to note that Shakespeare did not name his play 'The Hurricane.' He actually did know the word "hurricano" because it

---

[19]   http://www.william-shakespeare.info/shakespeare-play-the-tempest.html.

appears in two earlier plays, King Lear and Troilus and Cressida. Maybe he recognized that such a title would be confusing and unfamiliar to most of his audience, so he chose a more familiar word 'The Tempest', instead. Though the island was uninhabited, Spaniards had visited Bermuda earlier and set ashore wild pigs. The shipwrecked passengers fed on those wild pigs, fish, berries and other plentiful game on the island. Although they yearned to stay on that island paradise, they managed to make two vessels 'Patience' and 'Deliverance' out of what was left of the Sea Venture, and ten months later they set sail for Jamestown. However, some persons remained on the island and became the first colonists of that island, including Admiral Sir George Somers, who initially left with the other Jamestown passengers but eventually returned and died on that island. To this day, Bermuda still celebrates 'Somers' Day' as a public holiday.

In some instances, hurricanes were named after important persons within this region; one such storm was the 'Willoughby Gale of 1666.' The word 'gale' during these colonial times was often interchanged with the word 'hurricane', but they often meant the same thing-a hurricane, and not the official term we now use today for the definition of a 'meteorological gale.' This storm was named after the British Governor of Barbados, Lord Francis Willoughby, who lost his life aboard the flagship 'Hope' along with over 2,000 of his troops in his fleet in this hurricane. He was appointed Governor of Barbados by Charles II in May of 1650 and attempted to negotiate the strained politics of that island, which also experienced a division between the Royalists and Parliamentarians. His last act on behalf of the English Crown came in July 1666, when having learned of the recent French seizure of St. Kitts, he formed a relief force of two Royal Navy Frigates, twelve other large vessels (including commandeered merchant ships), a fire ship, and a ketch, bearing over 2,000 men.

Lord Willoughby had planned to proceed north to Nevis, Montserrat, and Antigua to gather further reinforcements before descending on the French. Leaving Barbados on July 28th, his fleet waited for the French just off the coast of Martinique and Guadeloupe, where he sent a frigate to assault the harbour and ended up capturing two French merchant vessels on August 4th. This success could not be exploited, however, as that night most of his force was destroyed by a strong hurricane, including the flagship Hope, from which Willoughby drowned during the storm. This hurricane occurred in 1666 and was a very intense storm which struck the islands of St. Kitts, Guadeloupe, and Martinique. The fleet was actually caught by surprise by this hurricane after leaving Barbados en-route to St. Kitts and Nevis to aid the colonists there to help battle against the French attacks. After the storm, only two vessels from this fleet were ever heard from again, and the French captured some of these survivors. All of the vessels and boats on the coast of Guadeloupe were dashed to pieces. For a period in the late seventeenth century, some colonists referred to especially powerful and deadly hurricanes as "Willoughby Gales."

Personal names were also used elsewhere in this region, for example, 'Saxby's Gale' which occurred in Canada in 1869 and was named after a naval officer who was thought to have predicted it. The Saxby Gale was the name given to a tropical cyclone that struck eastern Canada's Bay of Fundy region on the night of October 4–5, 1869. The storm was named for Lieutenant Stephen Martin Saxby, a naval instructor and amateur astronomer who, based on his astronomical studies, had predicted extremely high tides in the North Atlantic Ocean on October 5, 1869, which would produce storm surges in the event of a storm. The hurricane caused extensive destruction to port facilities and communities along the Bay of Fundy coast in both New Brunswick and Nova Scotia, as well as Maine, particularly Calais, St. Andrews, St. George, St. John, Moncton, Sackville, Amherst, Windsor and Truro. Much of the devastation was attributed to a 2-metre storm surge created by the storm, which coincided with a perigean spring tide; the Bay of Fundy having one of the highest tidal ranges in the world. The Saxby Gale storm surge produced a water level that gave Burntcoat Head, Nova Scotia, the honor of having the highest tidal range ever recorded. It is also thought to have formed the long gravel beach that connects Partridge Island, Nova Scotia, to the mainland.

The storm (which pre-dated the practice of naming hurricanes) was given the name 'Saxby' in honor of Lieutenant Stephen Martin Saxby, Royal Navy, who was a naval instructor and amateur astronomer. Lt. Saxby had written a letter of warning, published December 25, 1868, in London's 'The Standard' newspaper, in which he notes the astronomical forces predicted for October 5, 1869, which would produce extremely high tides in the North Atlantic Ocean during the height of hurricane season. Lt. Saxby followed this warning with a reminder published on

September 16, 1869, to 'The Standard', in which he also warns of a major 'atmospheric disturbance' that would coincide with the high water level at an undetermined location. Many newspapers took up Saxby's warning in the coming days. In a monthly weather column published October 1, 1869, in Halifax's 'The Evening Express,' amateur meteorologist Frederick Allison relayed Lt. Saxby's warning for a devastating storm the following week. Despite the warning, many readers throughout the United Kingdom, Canada, Newfoundland and the United States dismissed Saxby since there were frequent gales and hurricanes during the month of October. The fact that the high tides occurred throughout the North Atlantic basin was unremarkable and astronomically predictable, except for their coinciding with the hurricane that struck the Gulf of Maine and Bay of Fundy to produce the devastating storm surge. Lt. Saxby's predictions were considered quite lunatic at the time. Some believed that his predictions were founded upon astrology, which was not the case.

Another example was 'the Daniel Defoe Hurricane of 1703', which occurred in November of 1703 and moved from the Atlantic across to southern England. It was made famous by an obscure political pamphleteer, Daniel Defoe. It was six years before he wrote the world famous book *'Robinson Crusoe.'* At the time the hurricane struck, he needed money, so the storm gave him the idea of collecting eye-witness accounts of the storm and publishing them in a pamphlet. He printed and sold this pamphlet under the very strange and exceptionally long title of *'The storm or collection of the Most Remarkable Casualties and Disasters which happened in the late Dreadful Tempest both by Sea and Land.'* In total, around 8,000 sailors lost their lives, untold numbers perished in the floods on shore, and 14,000 homes, 400 windmills and 16,000 sheep were destroyed. Some of the windmills burned down because they turned so fast in the fierce winds that friction generated enough heat to set them on fire. The damage in London alone was estimated to have cost £2 million (at 18th century prices).

An additional example was 'the Benjamin Franklin Hurricane of October 1743,' which affected the Northeastern United States and New England, brought gusty winds and rainy conditions as far as Philadelphia, and produced extensive flooding in Boston. This was the first hurricane to be measured accurately by scientific instruments. John Winthrop, a professor of natural philosophy at Harvard College, measured the pressure and tides during the storm passage. This storm, wasn't particularly powerful, but it was memorable because it garnered the interest of future patriot and one of the founders of the United States, Benjamin Franklin, who believed the storm was coming in from Boston. He was wrong because it was actually going to Boston. From this information, he surmised that the storm was travelling in a clockwise manner from the southwest to northeast. Putting two and two together, Franklin concluded that the low pressure system was causing the storm to move in this manner.

One aspect of the Earth's general circulation is that storms are not stationary; they move, and in somewhat predictable ways. Until the mid-eighteenth century, it had been generally assumed that storms were born, played out, and died in a single location and that they did not move across the Earth's surface. Benjamin Franklin had planned to study a lunar eclipse one evening in September 1743, but the remnants of this hurricane ruined his evening. This was a big disappointment to him because he had been looking forward to the lunar eclipse that this storm had obscured. His curiosity aroused, Franklin gathered additional details about the storm by reading the Boston newspapers and learned that the storm had moved up the Atlantic seaboard and against the surface winds. He learned that this hurricane struck Boston a day later, sending flood tides sweeping over the docks, destroying boats, and submerging waterfront streets. In the succeeding months, he collected additional reports from travellers and newspapers from Georgia to Nova Scotia and satisfied himself that at least in this part of the world, storms have a tendency to take a northeasterly path up the Atlantic Coast. Thus science took the first step toward a basic understanding of hurricanes and their movements.

Benjamin Franklin is also popularly known for his off-the-wall weather experiment years later, where during a thunderstorm, in 1752, he carried out a dangerous experiment to demonstrate that a thunderstorm generates electricity. He flew a kite, with metal objects attached to its string, high in the sky into a thunderstorm cloud (Cumulonimbus). The metal items produced sparks, proving that electricity had passed along the wet string. After discovering that bolts of lightning were in fact electricity, with this knowledge Franklin developed the lightning rod to allow the lightning bolt to travel along the rod and safely into the ground. This discovery by Franklin is still used even to this day all over the world. A year later, after

Benjamin Franklin's famous kite flight, Swedish physicist G.W. Richmann conducted a similar experiment following Franklin's instructions to the letter, and as fate would have it, he was struck by lightning, which killed him instantly. Sailing home from France on the fifth of September, 1789, after his great years as a U.S. Ambassador, Benjamin Franklin experienced a storm that may have been the same storm that devastated Dominica. He was eighty years old and suffering from "the Stone" but was busy observing the temperatures of the sea water, which would eventually lead to his discovery of the Gulf Stream.

Finally, there was the 'Alexander Hamilton Hurricane of 1772,' which he experienced growing up as a boy living in the Caribbean on the island of St. Kitts in the Leeward Islands. This was an extremely powerful and deadly hurricane. He later on in life became the confidential aide to George Washington, and his greatness rests on his Federalist influence on the American Constitution as much as on his financial genius as the first United States Secretary of the Treasury. Today he is featured on the United States ten dollar bill and he is one of two non-presidents featured on currently issued United States bills. The other is Benjamin Franklin, who is found on the United States $100 bill. A westward moving hurricane hit Puerto Rico on August 28. It continued through the Caribbean, hitting Hispaniola on August 30 and later on Jamaica. It moved northwestward through the Gulf of Mexico and hit just west of Mobile, Alabama, on September 4th. Many ships were destroyed in the Mobile area, and its death toll was very severe. In Pensacola, it destroyed most of the wharves. The most devastation occurred in the vicinity of Mobile and the Pasca Oocola River. All shipping at the Mouth of the Mississippi was driven into the marshes; this included the ship 'El Principe de Orange', from which only 6 persons survived.

This storm was famously described by Alexander Hamilton, who was living on the island of St. Croix at the time and wrote a letter about it to his father in St. Kitts. The letter was so dramatic and moving that it was published in newspapers locally on the island and first in New York, and then in other states (please see my book- *'Rediscovering Hurricanes'* for a complete copy of this letter), and the locals on St. Kitts raised enough money to have him brought to America to receive a formal education to make good use of his intellectual abilities. This was because this letter created such a sensation that some planters of St. Kitts, in the midst of the hurricane devastation, took up a collection to send him to America for better schooling because they saw in him great potential. By 1774, he was a student at King's College, now Columbia University, in New York. On St. Kitts, the damage was considerable, and once again many houses were flattened, and there were several fatalities and many more injuries. Total damage from this storm alone was estimated at £500,000 on St. Kitts. The second storm struck just three days later, causing even more significant damage to the few remaining houses on this island already battered and weakened by the previous storm in 1772.

Several claimants have been put forth as the originators of the modern tropical cyclone 'naming' system. However, it was forecaster Clement Lindley Wragge, an Australian meteorologist who in 1887 began giving women's names, names from history and mythology and male names, especially names of politicians who offended him, to these storms before the end of the 19th century. He was a colourful and controversial meteorologist in charge of the Brisbane, Australia, Government weather office. He initially named the storms after mythological figures but later named them after politicians he didn't like. For example, Wragge named some of these storms using biblical names, such as Ram, Raken, Talmon, and Uphaz, or the ancient names of Xerxes and Hannibal. Wragge even nicknamed one storm Eline, a name that he thought was reminiscent of "dusty maidens with liquid eyes and bewitching manners." Most ingeniously, he gained a measure of personal revenge by naming some of the nastiest storms with politicians' names, such as Drake, Barton, and Deakin. By properly naming a hurricane, he was able to publicly describe a politician (perhaps a politician who was not too generous with the weather bureau appropriations) as "causing great distress" or "wandering aimlessly about the Pacific." By naming these storms after these hated politicians, he could get a degree of revenge on them without suffering any repercussions from them. During his last days in office, he fought with the Australian Government over the right to issue national forecasts, and he lost and was fired in 1902.

For a while, hurricanes in the West Indies were often named after the particular Saint's Day on which the hurricane occurred. As Christianity took hold in the West Indies, the naming system of storms here in the

Caribbean was based on the Catholic tradition of naming these storms with the 'Saint' of the day (e.g. San Ciprian on September 26th). This system for naming them was haphazard and not really a system at all. Powerful hurricanes hitting especially the Spanish speaking islands of the Caribbean got Catholic Saints' names. According to Historian Alejandro Tapia, the first hurricane to be named with the Saint of the day was the 'Hurricane of San Bartolomé' which devastated Puerto Rico and the Dominican Republic on August 24th and 25th of 1568. The earlier tropical cyclones were simply designated by historians years later after their passages.

One example of a great storm named after a Saint of the day was 'Hurricane San Felipe', which struck Puerto Rico on September 13, 1876. Another example was 'Hurricane San Felipe the Second', which occurred, strangely enough, on the very same date 52 years later on September 13, 1928, and was responsible for well over 3,433 deaths. Another hurricane, which was named the 'Hurricane of Santa Elena', struck Puerto Rico on August 18, 1851, and caused massive casualties. Then there was the 'Hurricane of Santa Ana' (in English, Saint Anne), which struck Puerto Rico and Guadeloupe on July 26, 1825, the date of the feast in honor of the Mother of the Blessed Virgin, which killed over 1,300 persons. In addition, there was the 'Hurricane of San Ciriaco', which killed 3,369 persons in Puerto Rico on August 8, 1899, (feast day of Saint Cyriacus) and remains one of the longest duration tropical storms (28 days) to hit the Caribbean or anywhere in the world.

The tradition of naming storms after the Saint of the day officially ended with Hurricane Betsy in 1956, which is still remembered as the 'Hurricane of Santa Clara.' However, years later with the passage of Hurricane Donna in 1960, the storm was recognized as the 'Hurricane of San Lorenzo.' At this time, only the major hurricanes were given names, so most storms, especially the minor storms before 1950 in the North Atlantic, never received any kind of special designation. This is why this hurricane in 1929 was never named but was simply referred to as 'the Great Bahamas Hurricane of 1929.' The word 'Great' simply meant that the hurricane was a powerful storm and that it had sustained winds of 136 mph or greater and a minimum central pressure of 28.00 inches or less.

Later, latitude-longitude positions were used. At first, they listed these storms by the latitude and longitude positions where they were first reported. This was cumbersome, slow, open to errors and confusing. For example, a name like 'Hurricane 12.8ºN latitude and 54.7ºW longitude' was very difficult to remember, and it would be easy to confuse this storm with another that was seen two months later but almost at the same location. In addition, this posed another significant problem in the 1940's, when meteorologists began airborne studies of tropical cyclones and ships and aircrafts communicated mainly in Morse code. This was fine for the letters of the alphabet, but it was awkward at dealing with numbers because it was slow and caused confusion among its users.

In this region, these early storms were often referred to as Gales, Severe Gales, Equinoctial Storms, or Line Storms. The latter two names referred to the time of the year and the location from which these storms were born (referring to the Equatorial line). Gauging the strength and fury of a seventeenth or eighteenth-century storm was quite a difficult task because at the time these colonists had no means of measuring the wind speeds of a hurricane. Contemporaries recognized a hierarchy of winds ranging from 'a stark calm' to 'a small Gale' to 'a Top-Sail Gale' to 'a fret of wind' and 'a Tempest.' These terms were later replaced by the word 'hurricane', but such terms offered little help in interpreting the power of hurricanes or differentiating lesser tropical storms from hurricanes. Furthermore, increased development of the built environment over time meant that the potential for damage, even from minor storms, increased as well, making damage estimates a questionable foundation for judging the power of storms.

Experience has shown that using distinctive names in communications is quicker and less subject to error than the cumbersome latitude-longitude identification methods. The idea was that the names should be short, familiar to users, easy to remember, and that their use would facilitate communications with millions of people of different ethnic races threatened by the storm. This was because a hurricane can last for a week or more and there can be more than one storm at a given time, so weather forecasters starting naming these storms so that there would be absolutely no confusion when talking about a particular storm. Names are easier to use and facilitate better communications among individuals and meteorologists with language barriers within the same geographical region, such as within the Caribbean, Central America and North America.

The first U.S. named hurricane (unofficially named) was Hurricane George, which was the fifth storm in 1947 season. George had top winds of 155 mph as it came ashore around mid-day on September 17th, between Pompano Beach and Delray Beach. The second hurricane unofficially named was Hurricane Bess (named for the outspoken First Lady of the USA, Bess Truman, in 1949). The third storm was nicknamed by the news media 'Hurricane Harry', after the then President of the United States Harry Truman. United States Navy and Air Force meteorologists working in the Pacific Ocean began naming tropical cyclones during World War II, when they often had to track multiple storms. They gave each storm a distinctive name in order to distinguish the cyclones more quickly than listing their positions when issuing warnings.

Towards the end of World War II, two separate United States fleets in the Pacific lacking sufficient weather information about these storms were twice badly damaged when they sailed directly into them, resulting in massive causalities. Three ships were sunk, twenty-one were badly damaged, 146 planes were blown overboard, and 763 men were lost. One of the results that came out of these tragedies was the fact that all U.S. Army and Navy planes were then ordered to start tracking and studying these deadly storms so as to prevent similar disasters like those ones from occurring again. During World War II, this naming practice became widespread in weather map discussions among forecasters, especially Air Force and Navy meteorologists, who plotted the movements of these storms over the wide expanses of the Pacific Ocean. Using the convention of applying 'she' to inanimate objects such as vehicles, these military meteorologists, beginning in 1945 in the Northwest Pacific, started naming these storms after their wives and girlfriends. However, this practice didn't last too long, for whatever reason, but my guess is that those women rejected or took offense to being named after something that was responsible for so much damage and destruction. Another theory was that this practice was started by a radio operator who sang "Every little breeze seems to whisper Louise" when issuing a hurricane warning. From that point on, that particular hurricane and future hurricanes were referred to as Louise and the use of female names for hurricanes became standard practice.

An early example of the use of a woman's name for a storm was in the best selling pocketbook novel *"Storm"*, by George R. Stewart, published by Random House in 1941, which has since been made into a major motion picture by Walt Disney, further promoting the idea of naming storms. It involved a young meteorologist working in the San Francisco Weather Bureau Office tracking a storm, which he called 'Maria,' from its birth as a disturbance in the North Pacific to its death over North America many days later. The focus of the book is a storm named Maria, but pronounced 'Ma-Rye-Ah.' Yes, the song in the famous Broadway show 'Paint Your Wagon' named "They Call the Wind Maria" was inspired by this fictional storm. He gave it a name because he said that he could easily say 'Hurricane Maria' rather than *the low pressure center which at 6pm yesterday was located at latitude one-seventy four degrees east and longitude forty-three degrees north'*, which he considered too long and cumbersome. As Stewart detailed in his novel, *'Not since at any price would the Junior Meteorologist have revealed to the Chief that he was bestowing names-and girls' names-upon those great moving low-pressure areas.'* He unofficially gave the storms in his book women names such as Lucy, Katherine and Ruth, after some girls he knew because he said that they each had a unique personality. It is not known whether George Stewart was indeed the inspiration for the trend toward naming hurricanes, which came along later in the decade, but it seems likely.[20]

In 1950, military alphabet names (e.g. Able, Baker, Charley, Dog, Easy, Fox etc . . .) were adopted by the World Meteorological Organization (WMO), and the first named Atlantic hurricane was Able in 1950. The Joint Army/Navy (JAN) Phonetic Alphabet was developed in 1941 and was used by all branches of the United States military until the promulgation of the NATO phonetic alphabet in 1956, which replaced it. Before the JAN phonetic alphabet, each branch of the armed forces used its own phonetic alphabet, leading to difficulties in inter-branch communications. This naming method was not very popular and caused a lot of confusion because officials soon realized that this naming convention would cause more problems in the history books if more than one powerful Hurricane Able made landfall and caused extensive damage and death to warrant

---

[20]   Stewart, George R. (1941) *STORM*, University of Nebraska Press.

retirement. This was because hurricanes that have a severe impact on the lives or the economy of a country or region are remembered for generations after the devastation they caused, and some go into weather history, so distinguishing one storm name from another is essential for the history books.

The modern naming convention came about in response to the need for unambiguous radio communications with ships and aircrafts. As air and sea transportation started to increase and meteorological observations improved in number and quality, several typhoons, hurricanes or cyclones might have to be tracked at any given time. To help in their identification, in 1953 the systematic use of only regular women names were used in alphabetical order, and this lasted until 1978. The 1953's Alice was the first real human-named storm. At the time, they named them after women because these meteorologists reasoned that people might pay more attention to a storm if they envisioned it as a tangible entity, a character, rather than just a bundle of wind. But the use of only women names eventually was rejected as sexist, and forecasters finally went with both male and female names. Beginning in 1960, four semi-permanent sets of names were established, to be re-cycled after four years. This list was expanded to ten sets in 1971, but before making it through the list even once, these sets were replaced by the now familiar 6 sets of men and women names.

This naming practice started in the Eastern Pacific in 1959 and in 1960 for the remainder of the North Pacific. It is interesting to note that in the Northwest Pacific Basin, the names, by and large, are not personal names. While there are a few men and women names, the majority of the Northwest Pacific tropical cyclone names generally reflect Pacific culture, and the names consists of flowers, animals, birds, trees, or even foods, while some are just descriptive adjectives. In addition, the names are not allotted in alphabetical order but are arranged by the contributing nation, with the countries being alphabetized. For example, the Cambodians have contributed Naki (a flower), Krovanh (a tree) and Damrey (an elephant). China has submitted names such as Yutu (a mythological rabbit), Longwang (the dragon king and god of rain in Chinese mythology), and Dainmu (the mother of lightning and the goddess in charge of thunder). Micronesian typhoon names include Sinlaku (a legendary Kosrae goddess) and Ewiniar (the Chuuk Storm god). Hurricanes in the central Pacific have name lists for only four years and use Hawaiian names.

In the North Atlantic Basin in 1979, gender equality finally reached the naming process of hurricanes when thousands of sexism complaints written to the WMO and feminists groups in the USA and worldwide urged the WMO to add men's names; hence, both men and women names were used alternately, and this practice is still in use today. That year would also herald the practice of drawing up a list of names in advance of the hurricane season, and today an alphabetical list of 21 names is used. Hurricane Bob was the first North Atlantic storm named after a man in the 1979 hurricane season; however, it was not retired (it would eventually be retired in the 1991 hurricane season). Hurricane David was the second storm named after a man and it was the first male storm to be retired in the North Atlantic Region. This was due to the great death toll and substantial damage it inflicted to the countries of Dominica, the Dominican Republic and the Bahamas during the last week of August and the first week of September in 1979.

Since 1979, the naming list now includes names from non-English speaking countries within this region, such as Dutch, French and Spanish names, which also have a large presence here in the Caribbean. This is done to reflect the diversity of the different ethnic languages of the various countries in this region, so the names of Spanish, French, Dutch, and English persons are used in the naming process. The names of storms are now selected by a select committee from member countries of the World Meteorological Organization that falls within that particular region of the world, and we here in the Caribbean come under Region IV for classification purposes. This committee meets once a year after the hurricane season has passed and before the beginning of the new hurricane season to decide on which names to be retired and to replace those names with a new set of names when and where necessary.

The practice of giving different names to storms in different hurricane basins has also led to a few rare circumstances of name-changing storms. For example, in October of 1988, after Atlantic Hurricane Joan devastated Central America, it proceeded to move into the Pacific and became Pacific tropical storm Miriam. Hurricane Joan was a powerful hurricane that caused death and destruction in over a dozen countries in the Caribbean and Central America. Another example was Hurricane Hattie, which was a powerful Category 5 hurricane that pounded Central America on Halloween during the 1961 North Atlantic hurricane season. It caused $370 million in damages and killed around 275 persons. Hattie is the only hurricane on record to have earned three names (Hattie, Simone, Inga) while crossing into different basins twice. Hattie swept across the Caribbean and came ashore in the town of Belize City, British Honduras (now called Belize), on October 31st. It was a strong Category 4 hurricane at landfall, having weakened from a Category 5 hurricane just offshore. After making landfall, its remnants crossed over into the Pacific and attained tropical storm status again under the name Simone. In a remarkable turn of events, after Simone itself made landfall, its remnants crossed back over to the Gulf of Mexico, where the storm became Tropical Storm Inga before dissipating. However, it is debatable whether Inga in fact formed from the remnants of Simone at all.

It is interesting to note here that the letters Q, U, X, Y, and Z are not included in the hurricane list because of the scarcity of names beginning with those letters. However, in other regions of the world, some of these letters are used; for example, only "Q" and "U" are omitted in the Northeastern Pacific Basin. When a storm causes tremendous damage and death, the name is taken out of circulation and retired for reasons of sensitivity. It is then replaced with a name of the same letter and of the same gender, and if possible, the same language as the name being retired (e.g. neither Hurricane Irene in 2011 nor Hurricane Katrina in 2005 will ever be used again). The list includes one tropical storm, Allison of 2001, which caused billions in damage from its heavy rains.

The name used the most, at least with the same spelling, is Arlene (seven times), while Frances and Florence have been used seven and six times, respectively. However, considering different spellings of the same name, Debbie/Debby has been used seven times, and Anna/Ana has been used eight times. The first name to be called into use five times was Edith, but that name hasn't been used since 1971. After the 1996 season, Lilly has the distinction of being the first 'L' name to be used three times, while Marco is the first 'M' name to be used more than once. The name Kendra was assigned to a system in the 1966 hurricane season, but in post-season analysis it was decided it had not been a bona fide tropical storm. This storm marked the birth of reclassification of storms in the post-hurricane season (Hurricane Andrew was a storm that was reclassified from a Category four hurricane to a Category five hurricane in the off season).

In only five years (2005, 1995, 2010, 2011,2012) have names beginning with the letter 'O' and beyond been used, but there have been several other years in which more than 14 storms have been tracked, such as: 1887-19 storms, 1933-21 storms, 1936-16 storms, 1969-18 storms, 1995-19 storms, 2005-28 storms, 2010-19 storms, 2011-19 storms and 2012-19 storms. The 2010 Atlantic hurricane season has been extremely active, being the most active season since 2005. It must be noted that the 2010, 2011 and 2012 seasons ties the record with the 1995 North Atlantic hurricane season and the 1887 North Atlantic hurricane season for the third most named storms (19). Furthermore, 2010 also ties the record with the 1969 North Atlantic hurricane season and 1887 for the second most hurricanes (12). The 2012 Atlantic hurricane season was the third most active season, tied with 1887, 1995, 2010, and 2011. It was an above average season in which 19 tropical cyclones formed. All nineteen depressions attained tropical storm status, and ten of these became hurricanes. Two hurricanes further intensified into major hurricanes. The first three of these years were well before the naming of storms began, but 1969 requires an explanation. This was early in the era of complete satellite coverage, and forecasters were still studying the evolution of non-tropical systems (sub-tropical) into warm-core, tropical-type storms. Several systems that year were not named as tropical because they began at higher latitudes and were initially cold-cored.

Formal classification of subtropical (hybrid type) cyclones and public advisories on them began in 1972, and a few years later a review was made of satellite imagery from the late 60's and early 70's, and several of these systems were included as tropical storms. In fact, two of the storms added in 1969 were hurricanes, so 1969 now stands as having 12 hurricanes. Today, subtropical storms are named using the same list as tropical storms and hurricanes. This makes sense because subtropical cyclones often take on tropical characteristics. Imagine how confusing it would be if the system got a new name just because it underwent internal changes. There is no subtropical classification equivalent to a hurricane. The assumption is that once a storm got that strong, it would have acquired tropical characteristics and therefore be called a hurricane, or it would have merged with an extratropical system in the North Atlantic and lost its name altogether. For example, on October 24, 1979, a subtropical storm briefly reached hurricane strength as it neared Newfoundland, Canada. It quickly combined with another low-pressure system, but it was never named.

Whenever a hurricane has had a major impact, any country affected by the storm can request that the name of the hurricane be 'retired' by agreement of the World Meteorological Organization (WMO). Prior to 1969, officially, retiring a storm name actually meant that it cannot be reused for at least 10 years, to facilitate historic references, legal actions, insurance claim activities, etc . . . and to avoid public confusion with another storm of the same name. But today these storms are retired indefinitely, and if that happens, it is replaced with a storm's name with the same gender because the retired storm often becomes a household name in the regions or countries it affected. When that list of names is exhausted, the Greek Alphabet (Alpha, Beta, Gamma, Delta, Epsilon, Zeta, Eta, Theta, Iota, Kappa and Lambda) is used. It must be noted that so far this list has only been used once in either the Pacific or the Atlantic Basins, which was in the North Atlantic hurricane season of 2005. It is important to note here that there were a few subtropical storms that used the Greek Alphabet in the 1970's, but they were really not truly tropical in nature.

If a storm forms in the off-season, it will take the next name on the list based on the current calendar date. For example, if a tropical cyclone formed on December 29th, it would take the name from the previous season's list of names. If a storm formed in February, it would be named from the subsequent season's list of names. Theoretically, a hurricane or tropical storm of any strength can have its name retired; retirement is based entirely on the level of damage and death caused by a storm. However, up until 1972 (Hurricane Agnes), there was no Category 1 hurricane that had its name retired, and no named tropical storm had its name retired until 2001 (Tropical Storm Allison). Allison is the only tropical storm to have its name retired without ever having reached hurricane strength. This is at least partially due to the fact that weaker storms tend to cause less damage, and the few weak storms that have had their names retired caused most of their destruction through heavy rainfall rather than winds.

While no request for retirement has ever been turned down, some storms such as Hurricane Gordon in 1994 caused a great deal of death and destruction but nonetheless was not retired, as the main country affected-Haiti-did not request retirement. Hurricane Gordon in 1994 killed 1,122 persons in Haiti, and 23 deaths in other nations. Damage in the United States was estimated at $400 million, and damages in Haiti and Cuba were severe. Despite the tremendous damage caused, the name 'Gordon' was not retired and was reused in both the 2000 and 2006 North Atlantic hurricane seasons. Since 1950, 77 storms have had their names retired. Of these, two (Carol and Edna) were reused after the storm for which they were retired but were later retroactively retired, and two others (Hilda and Janet) were included on later lists of storm names but were not reused before being retroactively retired. Before 1979, when the first permanent six-year storm names list began, some storm names were simply not used anymore. For example, in 1966, 'Fern' was substituted for 'Frieda,' and no reason was cited.

In the North Atlantic Basin, in most cases, a tropical cyclone retains its name throughout its life. However, a tropical cyclone may be renamed in several situations. First, when a tropical storm crosses from the Atlantic into the Pacific, or vice versa, before 2001 it was the policy of National Hurricane Center (NHC) to rename a tropical storm that crossed from the Atlantic into the Pacific, or vice versa. Examples included Hurricane Cesar-Douglas in 1996 and Hurricane Joan-Miriam in 1988. In 2001, when Iris moved across Central America, NHC mentioned that Iris would retain its name if it regenerated in the Pacific. However, the Pacific tropical depression developed from the remnants of Iris was called Fifteen-E instead. The depression later became Tropical Storm Manuel. NHC explained that Iris had dissipated as a tropical cyclone prior to entering the eastern North Pacific Basin; the new depression was properly named Fifteen-E, rather than Iris. In 2003, when Larry was about to move across Mexico, NHC attempted to provide greater clarity: *Should Larry remain a tropical cyclone during its passage over Mexico into the Pacific, it would retain its name. However, a new name would be given if the surface circulation dissipates and then regenerates in the Pacific.*[21] Up to now, it is extremely rare for a

---

[21]   www.nhc.noaa.gov/archice/2003/dis/al172003.discus.016.shtml.

tropical cyclone to retain its name during the passage from the Atlantic to the Pacific, or vice versa.

Second, storms are renamed in situations where there are uncertainties of the continuation of storms. When the remnants of a tropical cyclone redevelop, the redeveloping system will be treated as a new tropical cyclone if there are uncertainties of the continuation, even though the original system may contribute to the forming of the new system. One example is the remnants of Tropical Depression #10 reforming into Tropical Depression #12 from the 2005 season, which went on to become the powerful and deadly Hurricane Katrina. Another example was a storm that had the most names, as stated earlier; in 1961, there was one tropical storm that had three lives and three names. Tropical Storm Hattie developed off the Caribbean Coast of Nicaragua on October 28, 1961, and drifted north and west before crossing Central America at Guatemala. It re-emerged into the Pacific Ocean on November 1st and was re-christened Simone. Two days later, it recurved back towards the coastline of Central America and crossed over into the Atlantic via Mexico, re-emerging into the Gulf of Mexico as Inga.

CHAPTER FIVE

The Sponging Industry during the Great Bahamas Hurricane of 1929

Sketches of the various stages within the Sponging Industry (from the harvesting of the sponges to the shipping of the sponges) here in the Bahamas (Courtesy of the Bahamas National Archives, Nassau, Bahamas).

In the Bahamas in the 1800s, the sea itself was by no means unproductive, yet little of its abundance could be exported with ease. The exceptions were turtle shells, ambergris, and an occasional pearl. On land, the sisal industry developed in the late 1880's and 1890's and also became an important industry in the Bahamas. Unfortunately, the acquisition of the Philippine Islands by the United States led to the decline of the Bahamian sisal industry. This privileged access to the American market by the Philippines meant that the Bahamas was unable to compete on an equal footing and was therefore left at a distinct disadvantage. The large Bahamian estates, many of them badly located on unsuitable and nutrient lacking soils with an insufficient labour force, fell into bankruptcy, and the mills closed. Produced uneconomically on smallholdings and beaten crudely by hand in salt water, the quality and price of the Bahamian Fibre declined even further. The government ordinances supervising the production and grading the sisal became a dead letter, and the Bahamian product became far inferior to those grown in vast quantities in the Philippines, India and East Africa. By the 1920's, the sisal industry in the Bahamas was dead. Worldwide, by the late 1930's it came to an end with the introduction of synthetic nylon, which was much cheaper to produce and more versatile than the natural sisal plant. This opened the door to the more lucrative sponge trade.

Workers clipping and sorting sponges in preparation for export at the sponge exchange warehouse in Nassau, Bahamas

(Courtesy of the Jonathan Ramsey-Balmain Antiques, Nassau, Bahamas).

Many Bahamian men accustomed to making their living on boats or on land turned their attention from sisal production more fully to marine resource extraction, in particular the sea sponge industry. In the late 1800's and early 1900's, farming, fishing, sponging, sisal production and wrecking and salvaging were the five main ways most Bahamians supported their families. Throughout the 17th and 18th centuries, products from the sea, such as conch shells, turtle shells, and turtle meat, had been exported from the Bahamas, but on a much lesser scale; however, it was sponging that was the first industry that was profitable enough to employ thousands of men for nearly a century.

From 1841 to 1910, exports grew exponentially, reaching a peak of 1.5 million metric tons. The sponging industry began as early as 1841, when a Frenchman named M. Gustave Renouard was shipwrecked here in the Bahamas. He exported parcels of prized Bahamian sponges to Paris, where the varieties from 'wool' to 'velvet' found in the Bahamas were highly favoured over sponges from the Mediterranean (prior to this time, sponges were imported from the Mediterranean). The export trade was greatly expanded by Mr. Edward Brown, Renouard's son-in-law, and the Great Bahama Bank was opened up to full scale development. This large extensive area offshore from the island of Andros was called 'The Mud' and was about 140 miles long and 10 to 40 miles wide and was one of the greatest sponge beds in the world. The seabed was shallow and the water very clear, enabling the sponge fishermen to easily harvest the sponges from the seabed with little effort or diving equipment as compared to other areas of the world. This trade eventually encompassed, Jamaica, Honduras, Nicaragua, and Mexico; however, the Bahamas, Cuba, and Florida were always the largest producers.

Workers at a sponge warehouse in Nassau preparing sponges for export (Courtesy of the Department of Archives, Nassau, Bahamas).

Before the Second World War, well over 47 million pounds of live sponges were harvested annually from our waters and employed thousands of people and hundreds of ships here in the Bahamas. Although marine sponges have been a highly sought after product since ancient times, industrialization created a growing worldwide demand for them in cleaning, ceramics, shoe-finishing, and printing industries, in addition to household, bathing, and medical uses, which generated a lucrative international trade. As Bahamian sponges became highly favored on the world market, further beds were opened on the Little Bahama Bank, off southern Eleuthera and in Acklins.

A Sponge Exchange was opened in Nassau, and many Greeks familiar with the trade emigrated from Greece, bringing with them their families, language, religion and customs, which are still proudly maintained in the Bahamas today. In fact, the Vouvalis Company brought in the first Greek sponge experts in 1887. Vouvalis established his sponge warehouse on West Bay Street between the now Mayfair Hotel and the now defunct Ocean Spray Restaurant and Hotel. He then sent Aristide Daminanos and his brother George here to manage his business. The Damianos brothers would eventually sent up their own business at the top of Fredrick Street steps. In the 1920s, Christodoulos Esfakis established an operation on Market Street, and many other Greeks sponge merchants opened similar operations in or near the Downtown area. James Mosko was brought in to rebuild the Vouvalis operation after the 'Nassau Hurricane of 1926' devastated his sponge warehouse, and his son would eventually establish Mosko's Construction Company. Over time, the Greeks were more or less assimilated, and the second, third and fourth generations still now form a close-knit community of more than 300 professionals and business owners scattered throughout the Bahamas.

Sponging was a great benefit to shipbuilding. More boats were launched than at the peak of the wrecking industry. In 1901, at the peak of the Bahamian sponge industry, there were 265 schooners of up to 43 tons burden, 322 sloops of up to 16 tons, and 2,808 open boats engaged in the sponging trade. It was 5,967 men and boys, or roughly one-third of the available labour force, were employed in this trade.[22] Approximately, 258 men and women were also employed in sorting, clipping and packing on shore. But the money earned benefited every class and found its way into almost every Bahamian pocket. The sponge fishermen were all Bahamians; it was illegal for non-Bahamians to engage directly in harvesting the sponge. Before a vessel went out on a sponge fishing trip, the 'outfitter', as he was called, furnished the consumable goods and services to the sponge fishermen. This was done entirely on a credit basis and he was not reimbursed until the catch was marketed at the end of the voyage. The goods were booked at cost, plus a considerable margin of profit. These 'personal advances' to members of the crew, often including food for their families, were recovered at high rates of interest, making it almost impossible for the sponge fishermen to make any economic profit. Often he was left in debt, seldom breaking even. It was very rare for a fisherman to even make three hundred dollars a year. The outfitters, however, felt justified in their high rates, as they themselves took considerable risks. Their vessels were not insured, and there were risks of bad weather, such as hurricanes in the summer and gales in the winter, which affected the size of the catch, mismanagement and unscrupulous behavior on the part of the crew, theft from kraals, and damage to the catch during transit to Nassau.

---

[22] Craton, M. (1986) *A History of the Bahamas, 3rd Edition*, San Salvador Press, pg 239.

Workers sorting sponges in straw baskets in preparation for auction and export at the sponge exchange warehouse in Nassau, Bahamas (Courtesy of Old Bahamas.com, Nassau, Bahamas).

The sponging trips usually lasted from five to eight weeks. Each sponging schooner or sloop carried about five dinghies, which were used for gathering the sponge. The value of the catch was almost wholly dependent upon the skill of the fishermen and the fickle luck of the Bahamian weather. At the sponge beds, the water was very clear and shallow, only between eight to twenty-four feet deep, making it very easy to harvest the sponges. Once the sponges were harvested, they would be placed in large storage and cleaning containments called 'kraals' filled with salt water, which allowed the animal matter to die because the sponge is really the skeleton of a soft coral. The sponge kraal was an enclosed pen, fenced in by sticks of wood or mangrove to allow a free circulation of the ebb and tidal flow of the sea water. Here, the sponges were soaked and washed for four to six days by the action of the sea water. The sponge vessels visited the kraal once a week to land the sponge load. The sponges were then taken out and beaten with sticks until the decayed outer coverings had been entirely removed. After the sponges were beaten and gelatinous tissue removed, they were scraped to remove excess coral, sand or rock. After the dead animal was washed out, they would then be clipped, graded and strung in the boat rigging to dry.

They then took the sponges to Nassau, where the sponges were sold by auction to the Greeks merchants, who were agents for houses in New York, London and Paris. Once at the exchange, men and women, usually women, sat on boxes clipping the sponges using sheep-shearing shears. During the clipping of the sponges, the women often smoked their clay tobacco pipes and sang spirituals and other religious hymns to keep themselves occupied. The roots were cut off and the sponges trimmed, retaining the symmetry of the sponge as much as possible. Once trimmed and the pieces of rock removed, the sponges were thrown into large native straw baskets. A full basket was removed and handed over to the 'sorters', who in turn trimmed the sponges further if necessary and examined them for elasticity, size and texture. They were then placed in pens, packaged and prepared for shipping.

A sponge yard in Downtown Nassau, which shows sponges laid out in lots, sized and graded in preparation for an upcoming auction. If you look real close you will see the sponge vessels in the background (Courtesy of Old Bahamas.com).

Until the disastrous visitation of a microscopic fungus, which devastated up to about 90 percent of all the West Atlantic sponges and all the Bahamian 'velvet' variety in November and December of 1938, sponge continued to be the major item in the Bahamian economy. In

December 1938, spongers found that instead of pulling up intact sponges, hooks came to the surface with only slivers and strings; and the rest of the sponge skeleton at the bottom of the seafloor had disintegrated due to this deadly fungus. Within two months from the time it was first observed, the disease (fatal only to sponge) had reached epidemic proportions and had wiped out ninety-nine percent of the sponge; as a result, thousands of Bahamians lost their livelihood because of this disaster. The sponge disease appeared in Florida about three months after it had struck the beds in the Bahamas. It was believed to have been transmitted to the Florida sponge beds by means of the ocean currents.

In addition to the fungus, which destroyed the sponge beds, hurricanes, the introduction of synthetic sponges and over-sponging also led to a great decline in the trade. Sea sponge is a very slow growing sea animal, and whenever the sponges were harvested; the entire sponge was removed from the sea bottom, thereby not allowing re-growth by the sponge. In addition, the sponges in the area of the Mud was a finite resource, so gradually the sponges in the late 1920's and early 1930's were already starting to see a drastic decline in the industry even before the fungus attacked the sponges. As a result of this decline, the demand for sponge at this time was high, and so was consequently the price, due to the scarcity of it. Up to 1925 it must have seemed that sponge-fishing would endure forever and get better and better. At that time, the total annual income earned by sponge fishermen soared to over £200,000, and the local song, 'Sponger Money Never Done,' commemorated both the durability and prosperity of the sponge trade.

The series of severe hurricanes (hurricanes of 1866, 1899, 1926, 1928, 1929, 1932 and 1933), which began in 1866, did much damage to the sponge beds and schooners, but apart from this, there developed an unmistakable evidence of over-sponging. The deadly 1899 Hurricane, the three hurricanes in 1926 (plus a tropical storm), the 1929 Hurricane and a series of other hurricanes in the late 1920's and 1930's devastated the sponge beds. In addition, these hurricanes, especially the three powerful hurricanes in 1926, one in 1929, one in 1932, and a series of other powerful hurricanes in the 1930's (1933 had four hurricanes and one tropical storm, which hit the Bahamas) destroyed the sponging infrastructures, such as the warehouses and the sponging schooners and sloops.[23] For example, H. & F. Pritchard were among the most important Bahamian sponge merchants, and in 1899 a powerful hurricane struck the Bahamas and totally destroyed both their ships and the sponges. Another hurricane struck the Bahamas in 1883, totally wiping out the sponge beds in Eleuthera. After the three hurricanes of 1926, the sponge industry was crippled and sponge cultivation diminished considerably in spite of efforts on the part of sponge businessmen Mr. H.C. Christie, father of the late Sir Harold Christie, to encourage artificial sponge cultivation.

A Sponge Yard in Downtown Nassau, which shows sponges laid out in lots, sized and graded in preparation for an upcoming auction (Courtesy of Old Bahamas.com).

Although sponge planting produced encouraging results, output still diminished considerably, largely due to over-sponging of the beds, and the practice of hooking the younger and not-quite matured sponges. This abuse led to the Agricultural and Marine Products Board Sponge Amendment Rules of 1937, which forbade the fishing of sponge under a certain size and imposed a closed season. In 1929, a powerful and deadly hurricane known as 'The Great Bahamas Hurricane of 1929' devastated the sponging infrastructures in Nassau and wiped out many of the sponging

---

[23]   Neely, W (2006) *The Major Hurricanes to Affect the Bahamas*, Author House.

schooners on some of the Family Islands, especially on the islands of Andros, Eleuthera and Abaco, further crippling the industry. In fact, from 1926 to 1940 at least two storms a year devastated the Bahamas and the sponge beds (except for 1930, when there was none, and 1931, when there was only one). So, these storms changed the economy of the Bahamas, and it can be argued that hurricanes played a minor if not a major role in the decline of the sponging industry.

When the first signs of disease appeared in 1938, the industry and sponge population were already severely stressed from devastating hurricanes, over-sponging and only a few reserve populations remained. This disease ultimately reduced the remaining commercial sponge populations by up to 99%. Over-sponging, the introduction of synthetic sponges, hurricanes and sponge disease caused a drastic decline in the sponging industry in the 1930s. By the 1940s, the economic situation in the Bahamas was again so desperate that the British (the Bahamas was still a colony of England at the time) and Bahamian officials began in earnest to develop export and subsistence fisheries to support the local population. In 1935, the Bahamas export in sponges ranked third in quantity but seventh in value. Sponge output had been diminishing for a little while due to over-sponging of the beds. For example, the total weight of the sponge exported in 1940 was 70,848 lbs, and the total value was 13,986 ($41,958), as compared to 164,000($492,000) in 1917. This shows the tremendous decline in the total sponge exports brought about by over-sponging and the disease of 1938.[24] The low output was also attributed to a poorer quality of sponge being fished from the beds. Probably with diminishing output, the sponge fishermen were not conscientious of the quality of the sponges they removed.

---

[24] *The Sponging Industry Booklet*, the Department of Archives-18-22 Feb. 1974.

Numerous sponging schooners in Nassau Harbour (Courtesy of the Department of Archives Nassau, Bahamas).

The sponging industry received a devastating blow from the Great Bahamas Hurricane of 1929. As a result of this hurricane, a fleet of approximately 336 vessels were destroyed, with twice that amount being badly damaged. If this hurricane did not hit the Bahamas, the vessels would have been used to harvest the sponges. It was estimated that during the Great Bahamas Hurricane of 1929, at least well over 70% of the sponging vessels throughout the Bahamas were destroyed. In addition to the losses of the sponging vessels and the schooners, which were owned by the sponge brokers and merchants, they also had to absorb the loss of outfitting the fishermen and schooners, including stores and advances to the crewmen and their families during the lying up period. After this storm was over, well over 134 persons died and over 5,000 were left homeless, or a similar amount of men that were left unemployed as a result of the destroyed sponging vessels at Andros, Nassau and Exuma. Many remained unemployed for well over a year after the storm, further exacerbating the economic hardships that these residents throughout the Bahamas faced. In addition, these men had families to support, so this storm affected them in a negative way as well, and many women became instant widows and had to fend for themselves after their husbands were killed in this hurricane. This sponger money was vital because it circulated throughout the country and kept the industry and the Bahamian economy going and helped sustained the majority of Bahamian families. As a result, many persons especially on the Family Islands found it very difficult to make ends meet, and many Bahamians went to bed hungry with little or no food for many months to follow.

Four sponging schooners in Nassau Harbour with a cargo of sponges onboard (Courtesy of the Department of Archives Nassau, Bahamas).

Today in the Bahamas, the sponge industry has almost come to a complete halt, with the more commercially viable industries of tourism, agriculture, sports and commercial fishing, and banking and finance providing sustainable economic growth for the Bahamian economy. However, it is important to note that today sponging is still harvested and exported from the Bahamas, but on a much lesser scale than during its heyday, such as in Mangrove Cay and Red Bays, Andros. Some of it is sold locally in the tourism market, mainly for souvenir sales, and the rest is exported. Aside from its cultural fascination, the history of the Bahamas sponge industry has important lessons for the future of other valuable marine resources, like conch, lobster and grouper. That is that these resources are not limitless and requires careful management lest we risk losing them, just like we did with the sponging industry. The era of sponge fishing lasted less than a century, but it left its mark on the culture and economy of the Bahamas and the ecology of the reefs that will never ever be forgotten.

Three sponging Dinghy Boats off-loading their sponges into the Sponge Kraals (Courtesy of Old Bahamas.com Nassau, Bahamas).

CHAPTER SIX

Run Come See Jerusalem-Blake (Blind Blake) Alphonso Higgs

Birth Name:	Blake Alphonso Higgs
Other Name:	Blind Blake
Born:	1915
Birth Place:	Matthew Town, Inagua
Died:	1986
Genres:	Goombay, Calypso
Instruments Played:	Banjo, Guitar, Ukulele
His Most Popular Songs:	1} Run Come See Jerusalem, 2} John B. Sail {Wreck of The Sloop John B.}, 3} Love, Love Alone, 4} J. P. Morgan, 5} Yes, Yes, Yes, 6} Gin And Coconut Water, 7} Jones (Oh Jones), 8} Hold Him Joe/Jump In The Line/Wheel And Turn Me, 9} Watermelon Spoilin On The Vine, 10} Peas And Rice, and 11} Conch Ain't Got No Bone.

Blind Blake Biography (Courtesy of the Department of Archives Nassau, Bahamas).

B lake Alphonso Higgs, who is considered the father of Bahamian goombay music, was born in 1915 in Matthew Town, Inagua, and died in 1986 at age 71. He was better known by his stage name "Blind Blake" (not to be confused with the American Blues singer/guitarist of the same nickname) and was the best-known performer of goombay and calypso in the Bahamas from the 1930s to the 1970s. Goombay is a popular form of Bahamian music, and a goat skin drum is used to create it. The goombay name has also evolved to become synonymous with local African-Bahamian music related to calypso. In the Bahamas, its most famous practitioner in modern times was Blake Alphonso Higgs, who performed at the Nassau International Airport for many years.

Blind Blake was one of those rare gems of an artist whose output stands alone in the annals of Bahamian sound recording history. He is one of the foremost musical exports of the Bahamas during this era. Between the 1930s and 1960s, he was the band leader at Nassau's Royal Victoria Hotel and established singular oeuvre compositing old island songs with American folk ballads and calypso. This extensive collection demonstrates the full richness of Blake's career, including a particularly interesting rendition of 'John B. Sail', one of the oldest songs in the Bahamian canon, and the inspiration for the Beach Boys' 'Sloop John B' from Pet Sounds. Blind Blake was adept at string instruments - ukulele, banjo, tenor banjo, six-string guitar, and he also played the piano. He lost his eyesight at the age of sixteen and kept pursuing the goal of a career in music and a unique style, a blend of folksong, calypso and early jazz. His recognition grew from 1935, when he recorded for Philco Radio some of his own songs on the political and social life of the Bahamas.

Blake Higgs has no doubt left an indelible mark on the landscape of Bahamian music. He started developing his skills at an early age with the influence of his mother and older brother, who played the guitar. Progressing from playing on a piece of wood with a string stretched across it to the ukulele, he continued to master just about every stringed instrument until settling on the banjo. Blind Blake came to be a permanent fixture at the Nassau International Airport later in his life, but earlier his career placed him in the company of kings and some of the most wealthy and powerful people in the world.

Alexander Maillis, a well-known Nassau lawyer and businessman of Greek origins claims to have given Blake Higgs, his childhood friend, his first break in the music business upon returning home from World War II. Maillis recalls that Blind Blake was not blind as a child and further states that Blake suffered his fate from staring at the sun for extended periods. After serving time in the armed services, Maillis arrived at the seaport of Downtown Nassau, where Blind Blake was playing for pennies. Maillis recalls saying to him, "What you doin' out here with this can, playin for pennies? Come with me and play at our hotel" (Maillis 2004). That very evening, Blind Blake showed up with his ukulele at the Imperial Hotel, which was owned and operated by the Maillis family, but he was rejected by the small combo that was employed there at the time. The combo even threatened to quit if Blind Blake was given a job at the Imperial. However, taken aback at Maillis' advice that they were free to leave, in the final analysis they remained but took every opportunity to ridicule Blind Blake whenever he made any mistakes during his performances with them. After a short time, Blind Blake became quite popular, says Maillis. Tourists came to the Bahamas seeking out the man they referred to as "the Blind Minstrel."[25]

In addition to playing for pennies in the 'Over-The-Hill' areas of Nassau, Blind Blake would perform in other clubs and popular venues, such as Dirty Dick's, Blackbeard's Tavern, St. Mary's Schoolroom, the Orthodox Hall, and the Archer Club on East Street. But life as a musician wasn't always easy. It was not until 1933 that he found steady employment at the Royal Victoria Hotel, where he spent 30 years performing and entertaining tourists. Back then, the peak season for tourism visits were between the months of December to April (and not year round, as it is today), which provided only a small window of opportunity for musicians and others who relied on the tourism industry to make a living. During these segregated times in the 30's, Blacks were still not welcomed with open arms in the hotels and clubs in the downtown Nassau. However, Blind Blake was not treated like the average Black man because he had a charm that kept him floating during the off-season in lodge halls and at private functions. It is said that the wealthy folks that frequented these islands were so pleased with Blind Blake that for years he collected his salary at the end of the season, living off the handsome tips he received.

---

[25] *www.bahamasentertainers.com/ . . ./BlindBlake/blake_bio.html*

Legendary Bahamian Folk Singer Blind Blake (Courtesy of Old Bahamas.com).

When tourism finally became a year-round experience, locals were only exposed to this giant through his recordings. Out of these many recordings, it is not believed that Blind Blake gained any reward other than some degree of added publicity. In fact, persons like Harry Belafonte, Joan Crawford, and Acker Bilk recorded his songs. However, for much of his stellar career, Blind Blake was based at the Royal Victoria Hotel in Downtown Nassau. Included in his wide repertoire was one of his most popular songs, 'Love, Love Alone' (a song originally sung by a Trinidadian calypsonian called Caresser), about the abdication of Edward VIII. Blind Blake's version of this calypso is said to have been enjoyed by the former king himself, who as the Duke of Windsor served as Governor of the Bahamas during World War II. Initially he was forbidden to play the song upon the arrival of the Duke and Duchess of Windsor to the Colony but was invited to play the song by the Duke at Government House where he received a standing ovation by the Duke and his party.

In 1936, a major constitutional crisis developed within the British Empire and was caused by King-Emperor Edward VIII's proposal to marry his love interest Wallis Simpson. She was an American socialite who was divorced from her first husband and was pursuing a divorce from her second husband. It created a great uproar because the marriage was vehemently opposed by the government of the United Kingdom and the autonomous Dominions of the British Commonwealth. Religious, legal, political, and moral objections were also raised. As British monarch, Edward was the nominal head of the Church of England, which did not allow divorced people to remarry if their ex-spouses were still alive; so it was widely believed that Edward could not marry Wallis Simpson and remain on the throne. Mrs. Simpson was perceived to be politically and socially unsuitable as a wife because of her two failed marriages. It was widely assumed by the Establishment that she was driven by love of money or position rather than true love for the King. Despite the opposition, Edward declared that he loved Simpson and intended to marry her whether his government or anyone else approved it or not. The widespread unwillingness to accept Simpson as the King's consort, and Edward's refusal to give her up, led to his abdication in December 1936. He remains the only British monarch to have voluntarily renounced the throne since the Anglo-Saxon period. He was succeeded by his brother Albert, who took the regnal name George VI. Edward was given the title 'His Royal Highness the Duke of Windsor' following his abdication, and he married Wallis Simpson the following year. They remained married until his death 35 years later.

In contrast to the mentioned international artists who credited Blake, however, there were many foreign producers, managers and related professionals who preyed on artists all over the Caribbean, taking ownership of their songs. Some of them ended up making ever-so-slight changes and registering them as their own with no credit to or arrangement with the true composers. Copyright laws were virtually nonexistent at the time. Blake wrote many songs over his colourful career. Songs like "Conch Ain' Gat No Bone", "Love Alone", "Pretty Boy", "Yes, Yes, Yes", "Watermelon Spoilin on the Vine" and the most popular and recognized of them all, "Run Come See Jerusalem."

Legendary Bahamian Folk Singer Blind Blake with his band mates at the Royal Victoria Gardens.

Higgs played banjo and sang, releasing 4 albums during his tenure at the Royal Victoria Hotel, one with singer Lou Adams and several other lesser albums towards the end of his career. His first four albums were released on Floridian label Art, including a 10" with Lou Adams. Although never famous in his own right, his music has been covered by the likes of Dave Van Ronk "Yes, Yes, Yes", although the original is actually called "The Duck's Yas-Yas-Yas." A 1929 hit by blues pianist-singer James "Stump" Johnson was also successfully recorded by Oliver Cobb that same year. Pete Seeger ("Foolish Frog"), Lord Mouse and the Kalypso Katz ("Tomatoes"), the Percentie Brothers ("Goombay Drums"). Perhaps most famous was The Beach Boys, who covered his 1952 recording of the Caribbean folk song "John B Sail" ("Wreck of the John B") and called it "Sloop John B." His style was a mix of Dixieland, calypso/goombay, and American folk, probably because of the close proximity the Bahamas has to the USA. For several decades, he was arguably the most important figure in the Bahamian tourist entertainment industry. One of his most famous songs, the medley "Little Nassau/Peas and Rice", written during the U.S. prohibition era, is about the easy access to alcoholic beverages in Nassau, then complaining of the locals' frustration with a diet of just peas and rice. Here is a list of his recorded albums:

- *Blind Blake and the Royal Victoria Hotel "Calypso" Orchestra: A Group of Bahamian Songs* (1951)
- *Blind Blake and the Royal Victoria Hotel "Calypso" Orchestra: A Second Album of Bahamian Songs* (1952)
- *Blind Blake and the Royal Victoria Hotel "Calypso" Orchestra: A Third Album of Bahamian Songs* (1952)
- *Lou Adams Plays Bahamiana Calypso featuring vocals by Blind Blake* (1952)
- *Blind Blake and the Royal Victoria Hotel "Calypso" Orchestra: A Fifth Album of Bahamian Songs* (1952)
- *A Cultural Experience* (with Pandora Gibson) (1976)
- *Blind Blake & The Royal Victoria Hotel Calypsos: Bahamian Songs* (2009)
- *Bahamas Goombay 1951-1959*, a vintage Bahamas music anthology (Frémeaux et Associés 2011)
- *Calypso - The Dance Master Classics 1944 - 1958*, an international calypso anthology featuring Blind Blake's rare *A Conch Ain't Got No Bones* and other songs of his. (Frémeaux et Associés 2011)[26]

Legendary Bahamian Folk Singer Blind Blake singing 'Love Alone' July 1980 (Courtesy of Old Bahamas.com).

---

[26] *www.bahamasentertainers.com/ . . ./BlindBlake/blake_bio.html*

A singer and leader of the house band at the Royal Victoria Hotel in Nassau, Bahamas, Blind Blake's music was a strange mix of old island classics, more recent calypso compositions and American ballads. Blake performed for many Heads of State and Royalty, such as United States President John F. Kennedy and British Prime Minister Harold Macmillan. He performed for tourists at the Royal Victoria Hotel, Dirty Dicks, Blackbeard's and many other Bahaman hotels and clubs. He gave performances in several major American cities. Over the years, many visiting celebrities, such as, Mahalia Jackson, Louis Armstrong and Duke Ellington praised Blind Blake for his Bahamian style and his originality.

In the 70s and early 80s, Blind Blake's band was employed by the Ministry of Tourism to play at the Nassau International Airport, giving a musical welcome to arriving visitors. He died in 1986. His musicians combined jazz guitar licks with vocal harmonies and West Indian rhythms, with the result that his recordings have an easy humour and swing that few musicians from any continent can match. He was adept at string instruments - ukulele, banjo, tenor banjo, six-string guitar-and also played the piano. It must be noted that even though he lost his eyesight at the tender age of sixteen, he kept pursuing the goal of a career in music and a unique style, a blend of folksong, calypso and early jazz. The traditional song 'Peas and Rice', featured on his album (almost a Bahaman national anthem), originated during the First World War when the scarcity of imported cooking fats forced the substitution of local coconut oil. And one of the oldest Bahamian songs is the tragi-comic ballad 'John B. Sail' (later adapted and performed by many artists, notoriously The Beach Boys as 'Sloop John B.' on their 'Pet Sounds' album). The 'John B.' was an old sponger boat whose crew members were in the habit of getting quite merry whenever they reached port. One of his most popular songs, 'Love, Love Alone' ("It was love, love alone, 'cause King Edward to leave the throne") was based on the love affair of King Edward VIII with Wallis Simpson.

Blind Blake wrote about sixty Goombay songs, starting in the 1930s, including 'Run Come See Jerusalem', based on the devastating effects of the Great Bahamas Hurricane of 1929, 'Jones (Oh Jones)' and 'J.P. Morgan.' These albums were drawn from a series of recordings made in the early 1950s, when his band 'The Royal Victoria Hotel Calypsos' featured Dudley Butter (guitar, maracas), Chatfield Ward (guitar), Freddie Lewis (lead guitar), George Wilson (bass fiddle), and at times Lou Adams on trumpet. The band's popularity with tourists led to them being widely heard in the U.S., and they became an inspiration to many folk revival musicians. Josh White and Johnny Cash covered 'Delia', Pete Seeger 'Foolish Frog', Dave Van Ronk 'Yes, Yes, Yes', and 'Run, Come See Jerusalem' was done by dozens of groups.

In 1951, Blake recorded Run Come See Jerusalem with his band, -The Royal Victoria Hotel Calypso Orchestra, on a vinyl LP titled 'A Group of Bahamian Songs.' This record was a hit for years to come and featured popular tracks like 'Yes, Yes, Yes', 'Pretty Boy', 'Jones! Oh Jones', 'Watermelon Spoilin On The Vine', and the most recognized and perhaps most popular of them all, 'Run Come See Jerusalem.' Most people don't know that this song was based on the destruction caused by the Great Bahamas Hurricane of 1929, although it is one of the best-known Bahamian folk songs. The Ethel, the Myrtle and the Pretoria were actual vessels that sunk in the storm as they tried to sail from Nassau to Andros. Since it was written, this song has appeared in many movies, stage shows, plays and television programmes, but we seem to have lost the original message that Blind Blake so vividly recalled. Here is a list of some of Blind Blake's most popular songs:

1. Run Come See Jerusalem
2. John B. Sail (Wreck of The John B.)
3. Love, Love Alone
4. J. P. Morgan
5. Consumptive Sara Jane
6. Yes, Yes, Yes
7. Never Interfere With Man And Wife
8. Gin And Coconut Water
9. The Cigar Song
10. Jones (Oh Jones)
11. Bahama Lullaby
12. My Pigeon Got Wild
13. Delia Gone
14. Tanneray
15. Loose Goat

16. Lord Got Tomatoes
17. Bellamena
18. Hold Him Joe/Jump In The Line/Wheel And Turn Me
19. Go Down Emmanuel Road
20. Watermelon Spoilin On The Vine
21. Oh Look Misery
22. Foolish Frog
23. Peas And Rice
24. Eighteen Hundred And Ninety One
25. Monkey Song
26. On A Tropical Isle
27. Goombay Drum
28. Better Be Safe Than Sorry
29. Conch Ain't Got No Bone

The controversy surrounding the song "Pretty Boy" (which was also recorded by George Symonette, Joan Crawford, Andre Toussaint and many others) and was said to have been co-written with Eric Cash, a member of the Lou Adams Orchestra, has been put to rest by Mr. Eric Cash himself. In an interview, Mr. Cash himself, an accomplished musician, claims to have been approached by Blind Blake for a copy of the lyrics for the song. Soon thereafter, he heard a recording being played. This, of course, didn't sit well with Cash. But nonetheless, he did not further pursue the issue due to unclear copyright laws at the time.

Several versions of Blind Blake's 'Run Come See Jerusalem'

In 1929, the Bahamas was devastated by a hurricane with little or no advanced warning. Three boats bound for Andros, the *Ethel*, *Myrtle*, and *Pretoria*, were caught in the storm. The Pretoria sunk, and 27 lives were lost when it sunk at the entrance of Fresh Creek Harbour Channel. Unfortunately, only three lives were saved from this ship, and they were Yorick Newton of Blanket Sound, Victor Spence of Small Hope Bay and Henley Brown of Blanket Sound. These 'lucky three', as they were referred to at the time, were able to swim ashore after the Pretoria capsized. The Bahamian 43 foot schooner the Pretoria was one of the largest wooden sloops ever constructed by Jeremiah Duncan Lowe, Sr. of Marsh Harbour Abaco. It was a sloop built for use in the sponging era and as a Mailboat to transport people to and from Nassau and Andros and as a sponge boat. This song was written by Blake Higgs (he recorded it in 1951), a Bahamian calypso singer who was well known for entertaining tourists in Nassau. This song has been covered by many American folk singers, including The Weavers. It's about a devastating hurricane in the Bahamas in1929 that caught people unaware and destroyed many ships. Alan Lomax documented another song also about the same storm, called A Great Storm Pass Over, written by a Bahamian sponge fisherman called Tappy Joe; it was recorded in 1935. The first version below is how the Jolly Rogers perform it, but the words are somewhat shortened from the original. The second version is transcribed from Classic Maritime Music, Various Artists, and Smithsonian Folkways Album. It contains much more detail about the ships and places.

RUN COME SEE JERUSALEM Version 1

It was in nineteen hundred and twenty nine,
Run come see, run come see,
I remember that day very well
It was in nineteen hundred and twenty nine
Run come see, Jerusalem.

That day they were talkin' 'bout a storm on the islands
Run come see, run come see,
My God, it was a beautiful mornin'
Run come see, Jerusalem.

That day there were three ships leavin' out the harbour
Run come see, run come see,
It was the Ethel, the Myrtle and the Pretoria,
Run come see, Jerusalem.

These ships were bound for a neighboring island
Run come see, run come see,
With mothers and children on board
Run come see, Jerusalem.

Now when the Pretoria was out on the ocean,
Run come see, run come see,
Rocking from side to side
Yes, the Pretoria was out on the ocean,
Run come see, Jerusalem.

My God, when the first wave hit the Pretoria
Run come see, run come see,
The mothers grabbin hold unto the children
When the first wave hit the Pretoria
Run come see, Jerusalem.

My God, there were thirty-three souls in the water
Run come see, run come see,
They were swimming and praying to the good Lord
There were thirty-three souls in the water
Run come see, Jerusalem.

My God, now George Brown he was the captain
Run come see, run come see,
He shouted my children now come pray
He said, "Come now, witness your judgment"
Run come see, Jerusalem.

It was in nineteen hundred and twenty nine,
Run come see, run come see,
I remember that day very well
It was in nineteen hundred and twenty nine
Run come see, Jerusalem.

RUN COME SEE JERUSALEM-Version 2-Probably closer to the original:

It was nineteen hundred and twenty-nine (Run come see, run come see)
I remember that day pretty well
It was nineteen hundred and twenty-nine (Run come see Jerusalem)

There were three sail leavin' out the harbour (Run come see, run come see)
There was the Ethel and the Myrtle and the Pretoria
There were three sail leavin' out the harbour (Run come see Jerusalem)

There was the Ethel and the Myrtle and the Pretoria (Run come see, run come see)
My God what a beautiful morning
There was the Ethel and the Myrtle and the Pretoria (Run come see Jerusalem)

Well the Ethel was bound for Fresh Creek (Run come see, run come see)
With the mothers and the children on board
Well the Ethel was bound for Fresh Creek (Run come see Jerusalem)

Now the Myrtle was bound for Spanish Creek (Run come see, run come see)
My God what a beautiful morning
The Myrtle was bound for Spanish Creek (Run come see Jerusalem)

Pretoria was out on the ocean (Run come see, run come see)
She was dashin' from side to side
Pretoria was out on the ocean (Run come see Jerusalem)

Well a big storm built up in the northwest (Run come see, run come see)
The children come holdin' to their mothers
And a big storm built up in the northwest (Run come see Jerusalem)

Then the first sea hit the Pretoria (Run come see, run come see)
And the mothers came grabbin' for the children
And the first sea hit the Pretoria (Run come see Jerusalem)

That sail head down went to the bottom (Run come see, run come see)
The skipper came grabbin' for the tiller
That sail head down went to the bottom (Run come see Jerusalem)

There was thirty-three souls on the water (Run come see, run come see)
Just swimmin' and prayin' to Daniel, God
There was thirty-three souls on the water (Run come see Jerusalem)

Now George Brown he was the captain (Run come see, run come see)
He shouts, 'My children come pray'
George Brown he was the captain (Run come see Jerusalem)

Well come now witness your judgment (Run come see, run come see)
He shouts, 'My children come pray'
Well come now witness your judgment (Run come see Jerusalem)

Source: Various Artists 'Classic Maritime Music' Smithsonian Folkways SFW CD 40053

RUN COME SEE JERUSALEM-(Singout version) Version 3

It was nineteen-hundred and twenty-nine. (Run come see, run come see.)
Me see, I remember that day pretty well.
It was in nineteen-hundred and twenty-nine. (Run come see Jerusalem.)

That day, they were talking about a storm in the islands.
My God, what a beautiful morning!
They were talking about a storm in the islands.

That day, there were three ships a-leaving out the harbour,
the Ethel and the Myrtle and the Pretoria.
There were three ships a-leaving out the harbor.

These ships were bound for a neighboring island,
With mothers and children on board.
These ships were bound for a neighboring island.

The Pretoria was out on the ocean,
Rocking from side to side.
The Pretoria was out on the ocean.

Right then, it was a big sea built up in the northwest.
They were out on the perilous ocean.
Then it was a big sea built up in the northwest.

My God, when the first wave hit the Pretoria,
The mothers come a-holding onto the children.
My God, when the first wave hit the Pretoria.

My God, there were thirty-three souls on the water,
Swimming and praying to the good Lord God.
There were thirty-three souls on the water.

My God, now George Brown he was the captain.
He shouted, "My children, come pray."
My God, now George Brown he was the captain.

He said, "Come now, witness your judgment."
He shouted, "My children, come pray."
He said, "Come now, witness your judgment."

RUN COME SEE JERUSALEM-(Weaver's Songbook version) Version 4

It was nineteen-hundred and twenty-nine.
I remember that day pretty well.
Nineteen-hundred and twenty-nine.

My God, they were talkin' 'bout a storm in the island.
My God, what a beautiful morning!
They were talkin' 'bout a storm in the island.

My God, there were three sails leaving from the harbour,
With the mothers and children on board.
They were bound for the island of Andros.

My God, they were the Ethel and the Myrtle and the Pretoria,
And the Myrtle was bound for French Creek.
The Ethel was bound for Spanish Creek.

My God, the Pretoria was alone on the ocean,
Dashing from side to side in the waves.
The Pretoria was alone on the ocean.

My God, then a big sea built up on the starboard.
My God, what wind and waves!
Well, a big sea built up on the starboard.

My God, then the first sea hit the Pretoria,
And the children came a-grabbing for their mothers.
The first sea hit the Pretoria.

My God, well, it sent her head down to the bottom,
And the captain came a-running for the tiller.
It sent her head down to the bottom.

My God, there were thirty-three souls on the water,
Swimming and praying to their Daniel, God.
Thirty-three souls on the water.

My God, now George Brown he was the captain.
My God, he shouts, "Now children, come pray.
Come and witness your judgment."

Blake Alphonso Higgs was the other Blind Blake--I assume his nom de guerre was in emulation of the blues guitarist, but it may just be mere coincidence. For many years, he fronted the house band at the Royal Victoria Hotel in Nassau. His music was a unique mix of old islands favorites, more recent calypso compositions, and a quirky grab-bag of minstrel songs and ballads from the United States. Minstrelsy was an especially important element of Blake's work, evident both in his choice of the banjo and his popular songs like "Watermelon Spoilin' On the Vine," "You Shall Be Free," and "J.P. Morgan" ("My Name Is Morgan, But it Ain't J.P."). Blake has none of the self-conscious dialect and overdone comedy that was typical of the minstrel genre, though, and his sidemen combined the jazzy guitar licks and harmonies of groups like the Ink Spots with West Indian rhythms, with the result that his recordings have an easy humor and swing that few musicians from any continent can match or even duplicate.

Of course, Blake also played lots of island songs, which he performed in a style that falls somewhere between the string-band calypso of Wilmouth Houdini and Jamaican Mento, the slicker sound of tourist bands like the Bermuda Strollers, and the vocal group jive of American combos like the Cats and the Fiddle. They range from folk ballads like "Run, Come See Jerusalem" to upbeat tourist favorites like "Conch Ain't Got No Bone" and calypsos like "Love, Love Alone," the comic saga of King Edward's abdication to marry an American divorcee. There is also a Joseph Spence connection because Blake knew Spence and provided his contact information to Fritz Richmond when Richmond came to Nassau to record what became the 'Happy All the Time' album, and there are several overlapping numbers in their repertoires--which means that people who want to know what Spence was singing can often find out by listening to the Blake versions.

And then there are unique oddities like "Jones (Oh Jones)," a cheerful ditty of an impending murder: "I'm going to kill you dead and bury you/ Dig you up for fun/I'm gonna sit down and watch the buzzards pick the meat off your bones/I'm going to take my Wade & Butcher*/Chop you through and through/I'm going to chop you into pieces just big enough for stew/And when I get through, everybody's gonna moan, 'Jones, Oh Jones.'" (*Wade & Butcher was a very popular brand of straight razor). This album was drawn from a series of recordings made in the early 1950s whose popularity with tourists led to them being widely heard in the U.S. and imitated by many early folk revival musicians. Johnny Cash's notorious rewrite of "Delia," for example, almost certainly comes via Josh White's cover of Blake's recording, and he was also the source for Pete Seeger's "Foolish Frog," Dave Van Ronk's "Yas, Yas, Yas," Paul Geremia's "Jones (Oh Jones)," and "Run, Come See Jerusalem," which was done by dozens of groups--and that's not to mention his influence on Harry Belafonte. All of which being said, it is kind of silly to applaud Blake as a source for other artists, since none of them ever bettered his versions and few even came close.[27]

There is no denying, however, that Blind Blake is another one of our unsung Bahamian heroes, although it is claimed that he received a letter of commendation from Her Majesty Queen Elizabeth in his later years, Blind Blake was seen by many as the old man with the banjo singing at the airport. Many passed him by, not knowing the value of the many contributions that he made not only to this country, but also to younger musicians, opening doors that probably would have still been closed today.

---

[27] *The Bahamas Goombay 1951 - 1959* anthology (The English version of the detailed, very informative booklet with full Blind Blake biography by noted music historian Bruno Blum).

CHAPTER SEVEN

Meteorological History of the Great Bahamas Hurricane of 1929

Date Formed:	September 22, 1929
Date Dissipated:	October 4, 1929
Highest Sustained Winds:	140 mph
Lowest Central Pressure:	924 mbar (hPa); 27.29 inHg
Fatalities:	137 direct: Bahamas-134 Florida-3
Damage:	$676,000 in Florida (1929 USD) $8,954,552 in Florida (Today's USD) Bahamas Damage Unknown
Areas Affected:	Bahamas, Florida, Georgia & the Carolinas

Meteorological History of the Great
Bahamas Hurricane of 1929

Roof damage to St. Agnes Church after the Great Bahamas Hurricane of 1929. The cross of Jesus somehow withstood the storm's strong winds intact (Courtesy of the Charles Whelbell Collection-the Bahamas National Archives, Nassau, Bahamas).

In 1929, only three North Atlantic tropical storms were recorded, and all three reached hurricane strength. The storm we are discussing was the second of the season. The Great Bahamas Hurricane of 1929 (also known as the Great Andros Island Hurricane of 1929) was the second hurricane and the only major hurricane during the very inactive 1929 North Atlantic hurricane season. The hurricane was the only hurricane to cause any significant damage, resulting in $676,000 (1929 USD, $8.9 million 2012 USD) in damage in the United States alone, and an unknown amount in the Bahamas. [28] Only a year after the 1928 Great Lake Okeechobee Hurricane of 1928, the hurricane caused 134 deaths (mostly mariners and sponge fishermen) in the Bahamas and only three deaths in southern Florida, a low number due to well-executed warnings. The hurricane was much more severe in the Bahamas, where damage was near extreme due to the hurricane stalling over the area for three consecutive days.

A tropical wave moved off the coast of Africa on September 11th. September is the busiest month for hurricanes in the Atlantic basin. Since 1851, 317 hurricanes have formed in September in the Atlantic, Caribbean,

---

[28] *"1929 NOAA Report on the 1929 Hurricane"* (PDF). Retrieved 2009-10-09

or Gulf of Mexico. Other active months for hurricanes are August (216) and October (158). September is also the month when the most hurricanes have hit the Bahamas, with 100+ land falling hurricanes since 1851. The Atlantic hurricane season lasts from June through November. It moved across the Atlantic Ocean and passed the northern Leeward Islands before being detected as a tropical storm on the 22nd. The storm then moved westward and became a Category 1 hurricane on September 23rd. It continued to intensify, becoming a strong Category 4 hurricane on September 24th as it passed through the northwestern Bahamas.

Due to higher pressures and blocking action to the north, the hurricane drifted to the southwest, causing the hurricane to strike near Nassau on the 26th as it reached its peak winds of 140 mph. Had this storm continued on its west-northwest track, the Bahamas would have been spared, but this dramatic southwesterly turn put New Providence and Andros directly in its path. Several significant events then happened. First, the storm slowed to about 2 to 3 miles per hour while increasing in strength to a Category 4 hurricane as the eye passed over Nassau at 8pm on September 25th. The calm lasted for at least two hours. The lowest barometer reading at the time was 936.2 mbar, or 27.65 inches at Nassau, which meant that the hurricane was a Category 4 hurricane in today's standards. The eye of the storm moved over central Andros on September 26th, travelling very slowly and causing great flooding and wind damage. By the morning of the 27th, it was 60 miles west of the southern tip of Andros and then turned toward the northwest and increased its forward speed as it passed over the Florida Keys.[29]

---

[29] *"1929 NOAA Report on the 1929 Hurricane"* (PDF). Retrieved 2009-10-09

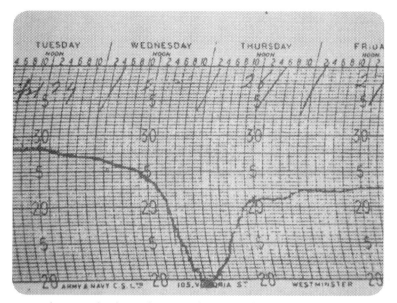

A barograph chart showing the steep drop in atmospheric pressure as the storm passed over Nassau (Courtesy of Andrew McKinney).

In the past, if a hurricane never made landfall on an island with a barometer, it would have been impossible to measure the barometric pressure of the storm. Today, such readings are easily obtained from barometers on Family Island weather stations, reconnaissance aircrafts, and automatic weather stations on land and at sea, as well as ship reports. The only way to measure the minimum central pressure in the eye of a hurricane is by flying a reconnaissance aircraft into the storm. This information is vital to determine the strength of a hurricane. Reconnaissance aircraft are operated by the U.S. military and weather services, but the data they gather are used by many countries. One of the ways this storm was unique is that it remained almost stationary over Nassau and Andros for more than three days. This had never happened before and has never happened since. By today's standards, this storm would be called a freak of nature or a 'once in a blue moon storm.'

This storm ranks with Hurricane Andrew in terms of strength and the amount of damage it caused. It was the first hurricane on record to approach the Bahamas from a northeasterly direction, which is significant. First, this meant that the island of New Providence and Andros experienced the strongest quadrant of the storm-the area where meteorologists say there is positive convergence. Since 1929, this has happened only five times: Hurricane #6 of 1935, Hurricane Able in 1951, Hurricane Betsy in 1965, Hurricane Arlene in 1987, and Hurricane Jeanne in 2004. Also, Tropical Storm #6 did it in 1938. Second, at the time most commerce took place along the coast while homes were inland. This usually meant that businesses felt the full impact of hurricane force winds and storm surge while residential areas were more protected. But this storm eliminated that advantage. In three days of pounding, this hurricane was able to weaken even the strongest buildings, no matter how far from the coast they were.

While slowly drifting westward through the Bahamas, the hurricane weakened and struck extreme southern Florida as a Category 3 hurricane on September 28th. The hurricane turned to the northwest and continued to weaken until making landfall in the Florida Panhandle as a tropical storm on September 30th. The storm turned to the northeast and became extratropical over South Carolina on October 2nd. The extratropical storm persisted for two more days, moving through the eastern United States before losing its identity over eastern New Brunswick.

Many boats were driven ashore and totally destroyed in the Great Bahamas Hurricane of 1929. Workmen walked amidst the wreckage to salvage pieces of wood (Courtesy of the Charles Whelbell Collection-the Bahamas National Archives, Nassau, Bahamas).

Fearing a repeat of the Great Lake Okeechobee Hurricane of 1928, which resulted in at least 2,500 fatalities in the United States and 18 fatalities in the Bahamas, weather officials issued early hurricane warnings in the Bahamas and South Florida as a precaution. On September 24th, hurricane warnings were issued for the Bahamas and areas from Florida to South Carolina. On the 25th, the warnings were extended to the Florida Keys as the storm turned to the southwest. More warnings were issued hours before the hurricane made landfall in South Florida. Even though weather warnings were issued for the Bahamas, many sponge fishermen and mariners on the islands of Andros and New Providence didn't know about this approaching storm and were caught out at sea in the sponging trade and succumbed to the storm. Weather officials also issued warnings for the Florida Panhandle before the storm made landfall as a tropical storm. In the state of Florida, the American Red Cross and local officials in South Florida took precautions while residents evacuated low lying areas in the Everglades.

Although a strong tropical cyclone, the hurricane caused little damage and only three deaths in Florida, a sharp contrast to the Okeechobee Hurricane a year earlier; by contrast, however, damage was very severe in the Bahamas and several persons died, mainly at sea in or near Nassau and Andros. In Cuba, the hurricane brought only rough seas and overcast skies. A weather station in Nassau recorded an unofficial pressure reading of 936.2 mbar (27.65 inHg). The weather station also recorded a wind gust of 164 mph. According to the Associated Press, the hurricane's 12 ft (3.7 meters) storm surge flooded a road and damaged a seawall, while property damage was severe. In total, there were 134 deaths in the Bahamas and three deaths in the United States.

On September 26th, in the settlement of Fresh Creek, the hurricane, while travelling slowly at about 2 to 3 mph, destroyed six houses and damaged ten others. It also damaged a communications station, disrupting telegraph service. Many deaths were reported on Andros, and according to press reports at least 24 persons were declared missing. Elsewhere in the Bahamas, the hurricane damaged or destroyed well over 63 homes and buildings and brought severe flooding that left Andros Island under 20 feet (6 meters) of water. On the island of Andros, many sponging schooners were wrecked including, 'the Governor Shea,' 'the Revive,' 'Income,' 'Trail' and 'the Repeat.' Offshore, a steamship run aground near the island of Abaco, killing 34 persons, while a tanker broke in two near the island of Andros. In one instance, eight sailors perished when their 18-foot schooner sank during the storm. In Fresh Creek, four small boats sank near the Andros Lighthouse, drowning more than 20 persons. Also, ten persons drowned in the area of the Southern Bight in Andros. Lord Baden-Powell arrived in the Bahamas at the Prince George Wharf in February 1930. On that occasion, Gordon O'Brien was presented with the Bronze Cross (the highest award for gallantry in Scouting) for his part in rescuing twelve women and children from a ship in distress during the hurricane of September 1929.[30]

Severe flooding on the grounds of the Montague Hotel after the Great Bahamas Hurricane of 1929 (Courtesy of the Charles Whelbell Collection-the Bahamas National Archives, Nassau, Bahamas).

Newspaper accounts gave evidence of the storm's impact on the city of Nassau. The Tribune of September 28, 1929, reported several deaths in Nassau, including Patrick Carr, May Thompson, Marsha Green, and Nathaniel Dean. In addition, many people were injured and about 30 were marooned on Athol Island, with one death reported there. There was a government quarantine station on Athol Island, where sick visitors were

---

[30]   *Monthly Weather Review-1929 (PDF)*. Retrieved 2012-11-09.

detained before being allowed entry into the city. Virulent diseases like Yellow Fever and Cholera could decimate the population in a short time, so the quarantine station was built to protect the public health. At the time, there were no antibiotics to treat these diseases. Penicillin was accidently discovered in 1928 but did not become widely available until 1948. Today we take these drugs for granted, but in 1929 there wasn't anywhere a person could go to get treatment for infectious diseases.

The Seventh Day Adventist Church on East Shirley Street showing the roof and building totally destroyed in the Great Bahamas Hurricane of 1929 (Courtesy of the Charles Whelbell Collection-the Bahamas National Archives, Nassau, Bahamas).

A 150 mph wind gusts was recorded near Key Largo, a barometric pressure reading of 989 mbar (29.21 inHg) was recorded in Key West, and a reading of 954 mbar (28.18 inHg) was recorded at Long Key. Damage in the Florida Keys was limited to swamped fishing boats and temporary loss in electricity and communications. The exact damage figures in the Florida Keys are unavailable.[31]

In Miami, a barometric pressure reading of 998 mbar (29.41 inHg) reading was recorded as the hurricane made landfall, and sustained wind speeds between 90 and 100 mph were recorded in Everglades City. The

---

[31] *Monthly Weather Review-1929* (PDF). Retrieved 2012-11-08.

hurricane spawned three tornadoes that touched down in Fort Lauderdale, Miami, and two other towns, with the Fort Lauderdale tornado being most the destructive. The tornado damaged a four story hotel, a railway office building and several cottages before dissipating 30 minutes after its formation. In southwestern Florida, there was damage to the orange and grapefruit crops. Three people were killed after ignoring warnings and trying to ride out the storm. Damage in the Florida Panhandle was moderate. The storm surge destroyed several wharves and damaged most of the oyster and fishing warehouses and canning plants. The storm surge also damaged part of the Gulf Coast Highway and left minimal damage to trees, homes and businesses. Throughout Florida, the hurricane caused 3 deaths and $676,000 in damage.

A weather station in Georgia reported a barometric pressure reading of 29.12 inches (994 mbar). However, there were few reports of damage and no reports of deaths when the extratropical remnants of the hurricane travelled up the East Coast of the United States. In Maine, heavy rains up to 2 inches (7 mm) flooded storm cellars and broke a prolonged dry spell in the state, though damage was minimal.[32]

After the storm, the Parliament passed a Special Act to render assistance to the storm-ravaged islands. The bill was called 'The Poor People's Housing Hurricane Act of 1929.' This bill was a stop-gap measure to meet some of the more urgent cases for hurricane relief. This special bill allowed the Government to lend the sum of £6,000 to tenants on a hire-purchase system. This also allowed the Government to purchase houses for as low as £40 per house to thousands of homeless families. This Hurricane Act provided at least 150 homes for many of the homeless persons. In addition to the Government action, the private sector stepped in to assist many others devastated by the storm. Various bodies, such as the Infant Welfare Association, the Royal Bank of Canada, the Bahamas Humane Society, the Wesleyan Methodist Society and the Daughters of the Empire all administered major organized relief efforts and provided much needed aid to the storm victims. This is in addition to one or two instances of help that had been generously extended from places outside of the Bahamas.

---

[32] *Monthly Weather Review-1929* (PDF). Retrieved 2012-11-08.

This storm was a 'turning point storm' in several ways. First, it changed the economy of the Bahamas. From the years 1926 to 1940, every year there were at least two storms to have a direct hit on the islands of the Bahamas (with the exception of 1930, which had none, and 1931, which only had one), and in 1933 there were 4 hurricanes and one tropical storm within that year to actually hit the Bahamas. This had a big impact on the economy of the Bahamas because the government of the day had to provide relief to the islands affected for this and other later storms at a considerable cost. A huge portion of the budget had to be allocated to the repair and rebuilding of homes, businesses, fishing and sponging boats. Infrastructures like roads, seawalls, docks and lightning systems in most cases had to be replaced or repaired, and in some cases they had to be totally upgraded at the same time. The Great Bahamas Hurricane of 1929 used up a significant portion of the Government's annual budget to assist in rebuilding efforts. In fact, at least 77% of the annual fiscal budget was used towards the rebuilding effort alone. To further escalate the economic problems of this storm, there was a significant drought in the Central and Southeast Bahamas at the time, hindering relying on these islands for any additional support or resources.

This hurricane forced the government of the Bahamas to examine the idea of having building codes with a view of strengthening homes and businesses to meet revised higher standards for hurricanes. There were new laws passed, and new building codes were enacted to ensure that buildings were built to much higher and rigorous standards to withstand hurricane force winds ranging from 75 to 185 mph. Some of these improvements and new requirements included mandatory use of hurricane straps or clips on all new roofs and mandatory use of tarpaper. In addition to that, vertical columns of steel reinforced concrete set at fixed intervals between blocks had to be in place for all new buildings. The footing of all new buildings had to be poured, and steel rods had to be embedded into the concrete beams. There were other additions, but these were some of the major changes made as a result of this hurricane. Better and more detailed evacuation plans were also further developed and enhanced because of the experience with this storm.

This hurricane also forced the government of the Bahamas to support and encourage agriculture and tourism as two basic industries of the

Bahamas, rather than simply relying on sponging as the major industry, which was more susceptible to future hurricanes. The government of the Bahamas had to provide a tremendous amount of relief aid to the affected islands. In addition, some additional aid was provided to the government by foreign governments such as England, Cuba, Jamaica, the United States and other unmentioned countries. The relief aid included cash donations, food items like sugar, flour, rice, and shortening and it also included building supplies like lumber, nails, and shingles. In addition, the government had to provide seeds to many of the farmers on the affected islands to replace the tremendous amount of crops damaged from this storm.

Many people who had experienced successive hurricanes here said that this one was the worst within their recollection, and although only a few persons actually went through the famous Great Bahamas Hurricane of 1866, it was becoming current gossip that it was the severest since that date. If the extent and nature of the damage are anything to go by, that opinion was probably correct, for the havoc that was brought about within those last few days was reckoned to exceed anything that had resulted from the recent storms.

CHAPTER EIGHT

The Great Bahamas Hurricane of 1929's Impact on the islands of the Bahamas.

Meteorological Track of the Great Bahamas Hurricane of 1929

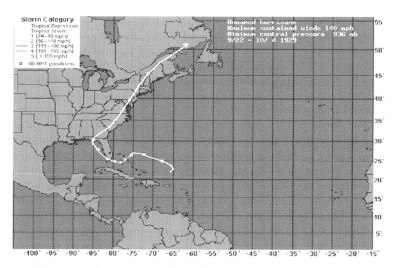

This map shows the track of the Great Bahamas Hurricane of 1929 (also called the Great Andros Island Hurricane) as it moved through the Bahamas (Information courtesy of Weather Underground).

DAMAGES

NASSAU

In the Bahamas, the hurricane destroyed the Ministry of Education mansion in Nassau, which was shortly rebuilt after the storm. Offshore, the wreckage of a steamship that sank during the storm was blown up because it was a hazard to shipping. In Florida, the damage from the hurricane knocked out rail service for a week. The United States Coast Guard provided mail service to Key West, an area hit hard by the hurricane. A special session was held by the House of Assembly from October 16-24, 1929, to assess damage and reconstruction needs. The members voted to support a measure authorizing expenditure to provide hurricane relief throughout the islands of the Bahamas. It was reported that in Nassau, 456 houses were destroyed and 640 were damaged, and this comprised about seventy-three percent of all homes and businesses. Certain sections of the hospital were so badly damaged that they had to be demolished and rebuilt. Long Wharf was totally destroyed. The roof of the police barracks was blown off, and large sections of the prison roof were blown away. For their own safety, 40 prisoners were released. The rebuilding of the prison was considered one of the most costly repairs. Potter's Cay was divided into two sections by the flood waters. There was a significant rise in food items and building supplies after the storm. After the hurricane, there was also a significant shortage of qualified carpenters throughout the island and as a result many of the qualified carpenters were charging exorbitant fees to get the work done. This forced the government to consider enacting a law to prevent this practice from happening in the future.

The eastern wing of Government House was unroofed on three sides and damaged to the extent that it was not fit for occupancy. His Excellency the Administrator and the Hon. Mrs. Dundas were in grave danger throughout the storm by pieces of falling roof, debris, crumbling ceiling and flying timber when whole sections of Government House blew in. Immediately after the storm, work began to restore Government House to its former glory.

Nine persons died in the capital of Nassau, and of the nine persons three died from drowning; the others died of various causes. Among the dead were Patrick Carr, age 34, an unidentified man buried by the Police, and another unidentified man drowned in the hurricane. Martha Green, age 45, Nathaniel Dean at Delaporte. Nathaniel Dean drowned near Laboushire while attempting to obtain food from the next village for the people of Gambier, who had ran out of supplies. Two additional unidentified bodies' locations unknown were taken to the hospital. An expedition was sent to Athol Island after the storm in the boat 'Caroline', headed by Dr. Cruickshank and Police Officer Lancaster. It was there that they found one death, 30 persons marooned and several persons injured. Constable Thompson's baby was killed and his wife's leg was broken while the family was fleeing from their home. Thompson had his wife on his arm and his baby on his back. The house fell at their heels; the baby was knocked from his back and crushed to death. Thompson took the limp body of his baby from under the debris and carried it away for a respectable burial.

In Nassau, there was chaos everywhere. Gardens, orchards and fields were devastated and to make matters worse, this was the fifth hurricane in the span of only three years to devastate the Bahamas. Few people throughout Andros and Nassau were unaffected. Crops everywhere were destroyed. Not a bird could be seen. Robert "Robbie" Burnside, who was in charge of the public gardens and the entire horticultural department of the Public Works department for years, was sent to Jamaica to obtain pairs of suitable wild birds to re-populate bird life in New Providence. Telephones were not operable, and telegraphs were also not able to be sent for quite a while after the storm. Also, the Board of Agriculture wrote to Jamaica and Trinidad, requesting a supply of an early maturing crop of vegetables commonly used in the Bahamas. This board also advised persons to plant the kind of vegetables they eat first before planting for the market. Many telephones were so bent, they had to be replaced, and major road repairs were required. Only a select few Out Island settlements had wireless stations, and overseas telephone calls were a long way off in the future. Various bodies, such as the Infant Welfare Association, the Bahamas Humane Society, the Wesleyan Methodist Missionary Society and the Daughters of the Empire all organized significant relief for the victims of the storm.

The east wall of Fort Montagu collapsed, and the canons tumbled down a considerable distance from where they were located. Western Esplanade was totally devastated after the storm as several large rock boulders and mounds of sand were washed onto the main thoroughfare. Many of the coastlines throughout the island of New Providence were completely altered, and many of the foreshores looked completely different than they did prior to the storm. In many cases, the road itself had been eaten into and torn up and debris large and small littered the highway. Everywhere along the route, battered and broken houses were to be seen on both sides of the road. On Village and Fox Hill Roads, there was a trail of devastation as all of the houses were destroyed. In some cases, there were still bits of furniture exposed among the debris. The telephones were also bent at right angles to the ground. Love and Charity Hall, one of the local meeting places, was reduced to rubbles. The Fox Hill fruit trees, which were both the pride and the main source of living of the neighbourhood, were blown down and the fruits destroyed. On Hog Island (now Paradise Island), the houses belonging to Mr. Philip Goster and Mr. Davis were swept away by the hurricane. The entire top of Mr. E.V. Solomon's house in East Bay Street was blown off. A stone house on East Street two or three hundred yards east of the Parade was completely collapsed with the exception of one room on the upper floor, which had no external wall to it.

Mr. Holmes' house on Bay Street was considerably damaged by water, and the kitchen was destroyed. The house of Ms. MacDonald, at the corner of East and Shirley Streets, lost part of its roof, including a dormer window that was blown right off. Mr. G.K.K. Brace's house, on the Montagu Foreshore, lost its front porch. The new warehouse that was being erected on Charlotte Street for Mr. Damianos had reached the 'skeleton' stage when the storm struck it, and it collapsed on its struts. Mrs. Twynam's home in East Shirley Street had its roof blown off and the walls badly damaged. Two other houses owned and rented by Mrs. Twynam on Mackey Street were unroofed, and in both cases the walls were badly damaged.

The sponge warehouse of Mr. G. Christolulacis on Bay Street was reported to be entirely demolished. A sponge warehouse on Heathfield Street belonging to Mr. Th. Tiliacos was so badly twisted that it had to be taken down and rebuilt. Several houses on Shirley Slope have been badly damaged, as have several of the garages there. Mr. Adams, who was in charge of the Industrial School, had his house damaged when a large tree fell on the roof. The tenants of Sturrup's cottage, near the Fort Montagu Hotel, found themselves surrounded by water and floating in their home during the storm; they eventually got into a boat and drifted into the house of Mr. Henderson Butler. The roof of 'The Hermitage' on the Coast Road several miles east of Nassau was reported to have been blown off. The residence of Mr. George Oliver on Montagu Foreshore roof was blown off. The Wesleyan Day School in Grant's Town was considerably damaged. A two-story building owned by Mr. William Dorsett from 'Over-The-Hill' was completely destroyed. Home Furniture store on Bay Street was badly damaged, and some of the furniture was destroyed; others had to be sold at a reduced price.

The roof of Ebenezer Chapel was blown off. The roof of Trinity Church also blew off. Several small boats were flung or floated on to East Bay Street. The roof of St. Ann's Church was blown off and the building completely destroyed. Two of the 'Jumper Churches' (Brother Enis and Brother Stanley's) in Grant's Town were demolished; two in the Freetown district were also leveled with the ground. The walls of Wesleyan meeting place were destroyed, and the building itself was leaning and the inside affected by flood waters. Salem Baptist Church on Parliament Street had its frontage badly torn and there was a gaping hole on top of the building. For a while after the storm, the services were conducted in the ruins of the church under a torn roof. The walls and the roof of Zion Baptist Church fell in, and the structure was more or less totally demolished. After the storm, the congregation of Zion Baptist Church on East and Shirley Street had to worship for months at Aurora Hall on Charlotte Street. A portion of the roof of St. Matthew's Church was blown off, the walls cracked, and the inside of the church was flooded in the storm. The roof was blown off St. Mary's Church in Virginia Street. The Seventh Day Adventists Church on East Shirley Street's roof and building were destroyed. About 300 people were sheltered in Our Lady's Chapel, the Roman Catholic Church in Grant's Town, throughout the storm, and many of them remained there for several weeks after the storm because their homes were destroyed in the storm. After the passage of the hurricane, the Sisters of Charity at St. Francis Xaviers Convent visited the poor districts and distributed food and clothing to the needy from their funds.

Long Wharf in ruins after the Great Bahamas Hurricane of 1929 (Courtesy of the Bahamas National Archives, Nassau, Bahamas).

The roof of the store of Messrs. H. and F. Pritchard on Bay Street was demolished. Mr. L.G. Dupuch's residence on Shirley Street sustained some damage; some of the frontal pillars were blown down and others twisted. Also, the house suffered some flood damage. Mrs. Augusta Neely's home on Dowdeswell Street was destroyed. The house of Mr. Cleveland H. Reeves, Secretary to the Board of Education, suffered considerable damage. The roof of the right wing was completely torn off, and the eastern side of the building was smashed in. Several windows were also broken and part of the house twisted. St. Hilda's School and the Western Police Station roofs were partly unroofed. The house of Mrs. Sarah Munnings on Dowdeswell Street lost its roof, and the kitchen and some other parts of the house were completely destroyed. The house of Mrs. Margaret Rogers on Dowdeswell Street lost part of its roof. The residence of Mr. Thomas S. Smith had its roof blown away. The store of Mr. Logan Dorsett in Deveaux Street was reported to be completely destroyed, along with part of the stock. A small quantity of liquor also went missing from the store. Mrs. Cedric Farrington's home on East Shirley Street was swept away. Mrs. Walter and her entire household had to move out of their house west of Nassau city during the storm. They had to move to Lucayan Baths, which Mrs. Walter so aptly named "The Ark" because of the significant amount of persons seeking refuge in her home during the storm. Schools that were scheduled to be re-opened in September, sadly, had to postpone the opening date to the much later date of October 7, 1929. This was because of the damages sustained to most of the school buildings. The remaining ones had to accommodate the homeless residents.

The pigsties and henhouses belonging to Mr. Pyfrom in West Street were destroyed. In several instances, people had to bore holes through the floors of their dwellings to drain the water out of the building. In some cases, it is said that the flood waters were as deep as 18 inches in the living rooms. In a bungalow near the Fort Montagu Hotel, the tenants had to take refuge through the manhole under the roof to escape the floodwaters on the ground floor. The office of the Munson Steamship Line on Bay Street lost its roof. On Dean's Lane, many houses were destroyed. Although the Leper Ward was practically reduced to ruins, the patients who were there were all safely cared for. The same applied to other portions of the hospital, including the lunatic asylum, which was also badly affected structurally. There was a great deal of homelessness in the 'Over-The-Hill' areas of Grant's Town and Bain Town. The hurricane made something in nature of a clean sweep, leaving total devastation and piled up debris in its wake. The same was reported in Fox Hill. It is worthy to note that the valuable library at Addington House was destroyed by the hurricane. The valuable picture of King Edward in the House of Assembly was damaged and had to be sent to England for restoration. In one insurance company alone, the insured losses were estimated at well over £100,000.

The House of Assembly report stated that 64 vessels were wrecked, including 10 motor boats, three pilot boats, three ocean-going vessels, nine sloops and other boats of various sorts. The Mailboat 'Princess Montagu' ran aground on Tony Rock and was badly damaged. The 'SS City of Nassau' replaced 'Princess Montagu' on its Miami-Nassau routine service. 'The Priscilla', which normally took the Abaco and Eleuthera mails, was dashed ashore and wrecked. The 'Ollie Forde', which normally looked after the Andros mail was totally destroyed, as was the schooner 'Magic', which had recently been doing the 'Ollie Forde's' work. These losses were significant because at the time the colony depended heavily on maritime commerce. Along the harbour-front, many boats lay on their sides, partially wrecked or just a mass of useless planks. A quite large motor boat buffeted by the winds and waves had crossed the Montagu foreshore and come to rest in the grounds of the almost completed Fort Montagu Beach Hotel.

On Thursday morning, when the water was 6 feet high on West Bay Street and mountainous boulders were rolling in over the bar, a young girl, Hattie Rolle, a native of Bimini and a passenger onboard the 'SS Priscilla', leaped overboard from this vessel into the high seas. While she swam onto the rocks, she held on for dear life. Behind Hattie came Leland Weech, who swam alongside her as they made their way to the shore. They swam to shore to summon assistance for their fellow passengers, who were in great peril. The police stationed at this point got busy, and a body of men led by Inspector Pembanton attempted time and time again to reach the SS Priscilla' in a small boat, but on each occasion the craft was overturned and hurled back on the land. Then young Gordon O'Brien, Bert North and Nigel Minnis volunteered to swim to the boat to get a life-line tied to the boat. At one moment, they were swallowed up in foam; at another, they were lost to view in the trough of the great waves that were rolling in from the bar; but on each occasion they reappeared on the crest of the wave. Eventually they reached their goal, and the most perilous part of the adventure was over. Connecting a life-line to the ship, they succeeded in pulling the open boat along this line, and in this way they landed everyone safely on shore. During this process, Hattie lost all of her money because it was tied around her neck; when she reached shore, it was gone.

There was flooding on the second floor of the Montagu Hotel, and it was reported that a piano floated out of the hotel onto the streets and that a boat was found inside the building. Nearby historic Fort Montagu was badly damaged when the walls were smashed in, and the cannons were moved quite a distance away. The roof of Mr. Bertram Johnson's house in Dowdswell Street was completely blown off. All of the chickens and poultry farms in Nassau were destroyed. Great damage was reported at the Bahamas General Hospital. Practically all the trees in vicinity of Fort Montagu and the hotel there have been blown away or stripped of their leaves and branches. The roof of Mrs. Evans' premises on West Street blew off and crashed into another nearby house. A house at the corner of Virginia and West Streets has been unroofed and reduced to wreckage.

Miss Moseley's house on East Street lost part of its roof, and the upper verandah has practically disappeared. After the hurricane, the government, with approval from the House of Assembly and Senate, built several houses throughout Nassau and Andros to replace the ones that were lost in the storm. Prices for the houses ranged from £40 to £60. They had to pay a down payment for the house, and the remainder had to be paid in monthly installments for a period of 4 years.

Practically the entire roof of Mr. Roland Cash's house on Union Street was destroyed. The cement shed that forms part of the Administration Building of the Water Supply Department, near the Colonial Hotel, has had its roof destroyed. The walls of the school at Fox Hill were badly cracked and the roof damaged. The Public School on Nassau Street was completely destroyed. The Eastern Central School sustained some broken windows and some flooding. The Manual Training Shop, which formed part of the Sandilands School at Fox Hill, was blown down. As a result of the hurricane, the Magistrate Court was closed for four days. Several persons were stranded on Hog Island during the storm, and some others took refuge in the Quarantine building on Athol Island. Mr. Asa Pritchard, M.H.A.'s, chicken farm was destroyed in the storm. He said that he was not disappointed because soon he would import 2,000 more chickens to replace those ones lost in the storm. A short time before the hurricane, he imported 800 one-day-old chicks from Detroit and raised 500 of them. The hurricane left him with only 90 of that total.

Significant and catastrophic damage was done to many of the Bahamian boats and schooners. Carl Brice's powerboat, *Matchbox*, secured for safety in the Fox Hill Creek, was found after the hurricane washed up a quarter mile away, on the high ridge near St Anne's Rectory, which was then east of the Hermitage. Spongers, fishermen, many men who made their living collecting and selling conch and sponges, lost their livelihoods, as well as their boats. The sponge fleet was decimated. Many men with their boats, which were anchored in Nassau Harbour, insisted on staying on board during the hurricane. Their boats were the only property they owned. Many had nothing else at all to call their own, so when the hurricane destroyed their boats, many were left with nothing but the clothes on their back. The angry wind and sea raced down the harbour and swept many boats over the bar, never to be seen again. Captain Fred Smith was hired by the Bahamas Government to inspect the sponging grounds in the Mud and to report these findings back to the Marine Products Board. Several of the hurricanes of the 1920s severely crippled the local boat-building industry at Abaco and Harbour Island, and it never really regained the momentum and status of the former days.

The Tribune was devastated by this storm. "This hurricane was not expected," reported The Tribune on September 28, 1929, on a tiny one-page sheet produced on a foot press after The Tribune building had been completely destroyed. "It is not the one from Puerto Rico," the report continued, "but believed to be of local origin and might have spent itself in the Bahamas. There are seven known deaths on this island, but Grant's Town is under water, and it is unknown if any are drowned over there." Then came the brave words of 30-year-old editor of The Tribune Etienne Dupuch: "The Tribune has been almost wiped off the map by this hurricane, but we are not discouraged, nor are we downhearted. We have our tools. We have our health and strength, and we still have faith and youth. That's plenty. If everyone who has suffered as badly as we, or even worse, will face the situation with a brave heart and determination to win through, the effect of this calamity may soon be entirely effaced. Today, we are printing a slip on a foot press; so as soon as we get electricity, we will return to normal size."

After this storm and the massive death toll incurred as a result, the British Government decided to put into law a Hurricane Warning Act to establish special hurricane signal flags that would be prominently displayed from the signal staffs on Forts Charlotte and Fincastle. Before this hurricane, signal flags were hoisted at the various forts but only randomly based on the location and strength of the hurricane. The new regulation required that signals be hoisted when the barometer fell below a certain point. In addition to this, it was required that there should be some means by which mariners should become acquainted with any information that was acquired by means of telegraph, so as to decrease the loss of life and property both at sea and on land. Because of this hurricane, all British Imperial Lighthouse Service light stations were issued a set of signal flags, which were kept ready once there was an approaching storm to warn incoming or outgoing ships and residents of the impending hurricane.

The official barometer reading at the Public Work building was 27.90 inches, and it occurred at 3am. The wind speed was estimated at 140 mph when the wind anemometer blew away.

Mayaguana

Andrew White, age 15 years, was taken with a bout of seizure while drawing water from a well in the settlement of Betsy Bay during the storm. He fell into the well and drowned. The body was not recovered until some hours later after the incident.

Cat Island

The storm was reported as not severe, and very light damage was reported. This island experienced gale force winds.

Ragged Island

From this island, it was reported that the public school house was blown down, but none of the private dwellings were seriously impacted.

Eleuthera

Some damage was reported, and North Eleuthera experienced wind speeds between 75 to 100 knots. At Harbour Island, a woman who died during the storm had to be wrapped and strapped to a board for burial because a coffin was not available at the time.

Abaco

There were 19 houses and 12 boats completely destroyed and many others badly damaged. Among the boats destroyed was the 'SS Domira.' It was reported that an American freighter that belonged to the Nelson Line of San Francisco, the 'Wisconsin Bridge', was lost off Abaco when sailing northeast of Hole-in-the Wall Light. This lighthouse was also damaged in this storm, and a boat was dispatched from Nassau with materials to repair it. The most serious damage was done to the massive glass plate in the lantern room. The crew of 34 took to the ship's lifeboats, and sadly they all drowned with one notable exception. The only member of the crew who was saved was the wireless operator who refused to leave the ship when others left because he said he thought it was too risky to battle the storm on the high seas with just a small lifeboat. The hurricane lasted for well over 36 hours, and the highest wind speeds were estimated to be between 75 to 100 mph.

Andros

Andros, which is the largest island in the Bahamas and just some 30 miles west of Nassau, was devastated in this storm. Some said that all 2,300 square miles were inundated with both salt and rain water from this storm. The Annual Report for the district of Andros for the 1929 fiscal year was submitted to the House of Assembly during a special session commencing on March 18, 1930, and ending July 7, 1930. In this report, it stated that the hurricane destroyed all of the crops and most of the fruit trees, livestock, and poultry. The sponge beds also suffered heavily, leaving people worse off than they had been in many years. Mr. Elgin Forsyth, the Commissioner for the entire island of Andros but stationed at Mangrove Cay, wrote a very detailed report on the impact of this storm on the island of Andros. His report stated that 16 sponging vessels and many unnumbered open boats ranching at Water Cay have all lost their sponges, and many of the boats were totally destroyed or badly damaged. The report stated that the storm had a disastrous impact on the sponging trade, as many of the sponge vessels were either destroyed or badly damaged in the storm. It also stated that 16 vessels and unnumbered open boats ranching at Water Cay lost all of their sponges when their boats were destroyed. The crew of Mr. P.C. Smith's schooner 'The Repeat' was lost with some of the crew perishing while they were trying to swim from one of the cays on the southern tip of Andros in the area of Grassy Creek back to the mainland. The great loss of the sponging vessels in this area had a tremendous impact on the entire Androsian population for many months after the storm.

The inside view of the rubble inside Trinity Church which stands on the corner of Frederick Street and Trinity Place after the Great Bahamas Hurricane of 1929 (Courtesy of the Charles Whelbell Collection-the Bahamas National Archives, Nassau, Bahamas).

In Stafford Creek, there were wreckages of many strange boats, including 'The Governor Shea' which floated ashore between Blanket Sound and Stafford Creek. The British ship 'SS Potomac' was wrecked off Andros, but fortunately all of her crew members were saved but the cargo lost. The 'SS Potomac', owned by the Anglo-American Oil Company, was en-route from Texas to London, transporting a cargo of oil. It ran ashore and split in two on a coral reef some three miles east-northeast of Mastic Point, Andros. Ten minutes after running ashore, her hull was split in two and her stern swung around in line with the bow. Realizing the danger of an explosion, the chief engineer returned to the engine room. At the risk of great personal danger to himself and the crew, he went in room and shut off the valves. The men in the stern of the ship by means of a rope swung themselves across the bow, which was in a less perilous position. The men remained on board until Sunday, when the sloop 'Memory' took ten of them off and brought them to the mainland. Another sloop came and got an additional fifteen more of the ship, but the captain remained with the ship. As pursuant to British laws, after the storm the Magistrate conducted an inquiry into the wreck of this British ship to find out if anyone was negligent or culpable.

In Blanket Sound, 13 houses were destroyed and others damaged. In Staniard Creek, 12 houses were completely destroyed, and every other house was badly damaged. The recently built bridge called the Staniard Creek Bridge, which was just recently built before the storm at a cost of about £400, was destroyed, and the Fisherman's Wharf was completely washed away. The storm surge from this hurricane was in the vicinity of 12 to 18 feet, and it swept across the entire western and southern coasts. In Love Hill and Small Hope, 5 houses were destroyed, while others were badly damaged, and all of the vessels there were damaged. In Calabash Bay, the teacher's residence, two society halls and 7 houses were flattened. The roof of the Roman Catholic Church blew off, and there were 22 coffins washed out of the graveyard. In Fresh Creek, 6 houses were completely flattened and at least 10 badly damaged. The seawall and the lighthouse were damaged. The poles of the wireless station blew down, and the building flooded to at least 4 feet deep. Cargill Creek had to be abandoned due to high water because only the hills were above water.

The lowest barometer reading was at Fresh Creek, with a reading of 28.70 inches on September 26th at 7am. Before it became dark, people were forced to leave their houses and find shelters with neighbours and churches. One of the hurricane shelters was the Wesleyan Mission House, where the Reverend Whitfield took care of the evacuated and distraught residents. During the storm, this building eventually became engulfed in water, so they had to seek refuge elsewhere in the school house and other private residences in the nearby vicinity. In Behring Point, there were twelve houses flattened and 15 people reported missing. In Mangrove Cay, many houses were reportedly destroyed, and the floodwaters were up to 20 feet deep; ten people drowned. In Mangrove Cay, several fishing sloops were totally destroyed, among them were 'Income,' 'Revive,' 'Trail,' 'Record,' 'Sasin,' and 'Glittering.' Two of the persons who drowned in one of these boats travelling from Nassau to North Andros were the husband and wife team of Mr. Charley and Mildred Woodside. Any boats that were left in the water were either damaged beyond repair or simply blown ashore several hundred feet from where they were anchored. Many of the sponging boats were blown into the Pine Barrens. Many of the pine trees were cut down and used as rollers to get the boats back out to the harbour. A lady was supposed to get married on the weekend of the storm in Mangrove Cay, and she and her bridal family were travelling by boat from Nassau en-route to Mangrove Cay to attend this wedding. A total of 18 persons drowned in this boat when it capsized during the storm.

In South Andros, in the settlement of Rolle Town, there were only 3 houses left standing and undamaged. During the storm, people had to escape to the hills for refuge from the floodwaters. In Black Point, 3 houses were left undamaged out of a total of 27 houses. All of the animals, livestock and nearby farms were destroyed. The Public Wharf at Deep Creek was washed away, and boats that were inland during the storm were simply washed out to sea. These boats held the communities together by providing a way of life for most of the men in the community. It also provided a means of employment for the local fishermen, so this storm, by destroying these boats, severely crippled this aspect of their lives for quite some time after the storm.

The Commissioner stationed at Mangrove Cay, Mr. Elgin.W.Forsyth, who was the Commissioner for the entire island of Andros, summed up the impact of this storm as such; "I regret exceedingly to report that on September 25th, 26th, and 27th, the most extreme destructive hurricane in the history of this district swept the Island. Its extreme duration and sustained violence is without precedent in my experience. The whole place appears as though burned with fire, and fields once full of promise are naked stripped of all vegetation. The situation is the most serious the island has ever had to face." After the storm, the Commissioner went around and gave the local residents corn and peas to replant in their farms. In addition, the government also sent assistance to the island in the form of labour, food, clothing and building supplies.

The schooner 'The Repeat' was lost, as the Commissioner's and House of Assembly Reports indicated, but not with all the crewmembers on board, as these reports suggested. A few of the crew members drowned, but the others survived by swimming back to the mainland of Andros. The schooner 'The Repeat' broke away from its mooring and drifted out to sea without any persons onboard with the exception of a stubborn dog named 'Busser', who refused to jump off the ship when he was instructed to do so by the crew members of 'The Repeat.' According to all the reports I have seen to this date, they all have all of the crew of 'The Repeat' being lost at sea. Fortunately, I was able to speak to two persons that were actually onboard the schooner during the storm, Mr. Illford Forbes and Mr. Daniel Rahming, both of whom lived in South Andros during the storm. Mr. Daniel Rahming and Mr. Illford Forbes have since passed away, but they both insisted that those reports were wrong because both of them were onboard the vessel 'The Repeat.'

Grand Bahama

No significant damage reported, but it experienced severe gale conditions.

CHAPTER NINE

How Bahamians Tracked and Monitored Hurricanes in the late 1800s and early 1900s.

Before the era of scientific understanding, religion and folklore played a critical role in perceptions of the day-to-day weather conditions and the seasons. A belief in the power of deities was commonplace, and observations formed the basis of many useful weather predictions. Today, meteorologists have an impressive array of technological devices and scientific techniques at their disposal in order to forecast or predict changing patterns of weather and climate. However, for thousands of years man has relied upon a combination of superstitions and observations to predict the weather. Over time, ideas that particular gods controlled various aspects of the weather were gradually complemented and superseded. They did this by looking at natural indicators such as wind speed and direction, cloud formations, the colour of the sky, certain optical effects and the behavior of plants and animals.

Weather folklore is indebted to oral traditions since most ancient peoples enjoyed minimal literacy. Predicting the weather accurately ensured their very survival. 'Old wives tales' and popular sayings underwent many changes as they were passed from one generation to the next, travelling widely and enjoying multiple distortions along the way. Many sayings simply relied on close observations of the skies and common sense. Clouds, for example, were called by various names depending on their changing appearance.

The ability to predict the weather was of great importance to many Bahamians, such as sailors, fishermen, farmers and others who lived of the land and the sea. Their very livelihoods, and even their lives, often depended upon weather conditions. Across the Bahamas, and particularly on the Family Islands, where conditions were most variable, almost every island developed its own weather lore. These weather lore often found expressions in many proverbs and sayings over the years. Some of these have no scientific groundings at all and rarely prove to be accurate. However, many of those relating to the short term, which was based on observations, still hold true to this day. Longer range forecasts, particularly those that are centered on particular days of the year and based on superstitious beliefs, also tend to be inaccurate. On the other hand, there are those that developed from long-term observations of seasonal weather patterns and other natural cycles, which continue to hold some truth.

Meteorology is a young science, and it is only in the last two centuries that we have learned how the sun's energy acts on the Earth's atmospheric envelope to produce the planet's diverse weather episodes and climatic zones; fortunately, we no longer believe, as primitive peoples did, that hurricanes, thunderstorms, rainbows and other atmospheric phenomena were omens sent by sky deities. We try to control the weather, to harness it extraordinary forces, yet we are still fascinated at nature's climatological handiwork. The tropics lie between the Tropic Of Cancer and the Tropic of Capricorn (latitude 23.5° north and south of the equator). It is only in this zone that the sun is directly overhead, which results in temperatures always being high. The seasons are marked only by changes in wind and rainfall, thus providing the perfect breeding grounds for hurricanes to form and survive.

Today, weather forecasting uses the application of science and technology to predict the state of the atmosphere for a future time and a given location. Hurricanes can be difficult to forecast. Nowadays, even with our advanced technology and satellites, forecasters have difficulty predicting the path of a storm. The responsibility of predicting these sometimes very erratic tracks falls on the shoulder of the National Hurricane Center (NHC) in Coral Gables, Florida (near Miami). The NHC forecasters have many tools at their disposal and receive data from many different sources, including, station data, satellite information, aircraft reconnaissance reports, ship reports, and radar, to name a few. One of the most useful tools forecasters have at their disposal is the use of 'super' computers. Several of these advanced computer programs have been created to simulate the atmospheric dynamics. The information that comes into the center is entered into these super computers, and an atmospheric model projection is produced. There are several computer models that are created. Some models are statistical, while others are dynamic. Statistical models use the climatological data of past hurricanes movements to predict the movement of the current storm. Dynamic models use equations to simulate atmospheric conditions at different levels to predict a storm's future movement.

In the past, human beings have attempted to forecast the weather informally for millennia, and formally since at least the nineteenth century. Weather forecasts are made by collecting quantitative data about the current state of the atmosphere and using scientific understanding of atmospheric process to project how the atmosphere will evolve. Our brief exploration into weather forecasting pretty much follows the techniques and methods developed by early weather wizards. From the earliest of times, hunters, farmers, warriors, shepherds, and sailors learned the importance of being able to tell what the weather might be up to next. Ancient civilizations appealed to the gods of the sky. The Egyptians looked to Ra, the sun god. The Greeks sought out the all-powerful Zeus. Then there was Thor, the god of thunder and lightning in ancient Nordic times. Between the 8th and 11th centuries, Norse, or Viking sailors from Scandinavia made a series of daring voyages of discovery, reaching as far as Greenland and North America. They attributed the storms they encountered on their journeys to Thor. They believed the thunder was the noise made by him as he raced through Middle Earth. Hurrikán was the Mayan god of hurricanes. Such societies, as the Aztecs used human sacrifice to satisfy the rain god Tlaloc who was thought to control the weather and hence hurricanes. Hurricanes were thought to be a sign of the gods' anger. Priests performed child sacrifices in attempt to appease them. Native American and Australian aborigines performed rain dances. Those who were able to predict the weather and seemed to influence its production were held in the highest esteem. After all, they appeared to be very well connected.

Even from biblical times, references to weather prediction are prevalent in both the Old and New Testaments. For the most part, they are instructive or cautionary rather than serving as mere descriptions.

The passages generally serve as reminders of God's power. One notable exception occurs in Matthew (KJV) 16:2-3, when Jesus instructs a group of fishermen: "When it is evening, you say, 'It will fair weather, for the sky is red.' And in the morning, 'It will be stormy, today, for the sky is red and threatening.'" More typical is the following verse from Psalm 107:25, 29: "For He commanded, and raised the stormy wind, which lifted up the waves thereof . . . He maketh the storm a calm, so that the waves thereof are still." Because the winds are invisible yet powerful, they make for a convenient expression of God's will on Earth: Exodus 10:12-13: ". . . And the Lord brought an east wind . . .(and) the east wind brought the locust." Exodus 14:21: "And the Lord caused the sea to go back by a strong east wind . . ." Genesis 8:1-2: ". . . And God made a wind to pass the Earth, and the waters assuaged . . . and the rain from the heaven was restrained." But the Lord's wrath can also express itself through the weather, and does so frequently: Psalm 78:47: "He destroyed . . . their sycamore trees with frost . . ." Psalm Psalm 18:12-14: "He shot out lightning, and discomfited them." 1 Kings 8:35-36 (2 Chronicles 6:26-27): "When heaven is shut up, and there is no rain, because they have sinned against thee; if they pray . . . and turn from their sin, when thou afflictest them: then hear thou . . . and give rain . . ." Psalm 78:47-48: "He destroyed their vines with hail . . . He gave up their cattle also to the hail . . ."

One of the earliest scientific approaches to weather prediction occurred around 300 B.C.E., documented in Aristotle's work, "Meteorologica." The ancient Greeks invented the term 'meteorology', which means the study of atmospheric disturbances or meteors. Aristotle tried to explain the weather through the interactions of Earth, fire, air, and water. His pupil Theophrastus really went to work and wrote the ultimate weather text 'The Book of Signs,' which contained a collection of weather lore and forecast signs. Amazingly, it served as the definitive weather book for 2,000 years. Theophrastus's weather lore included colours of the sky, rings and halos, and even sound. Hippocrates - also known as "the Father of Medicine" - was also very much involved with the weather. His work 'On Airs, Waters, and Places' became a medical classic, linking good health with favourable weather conditions. The opening of his work begins with the advice that those who wish to investigate medicine must first begin with an understanding of the seasons and weather. Weather forecasting advanced little from these ancient times to the Renaissance. Then beginning in the fifteenth century, Leonardo da Vinci designed an instrument for measuring humidity called a hygrometer. Later, Galileo Galilei invented the thermometer, and his student Evangelista Torricelli came up with the barometer for measuring air pressure. With these tools, people could monitor the atmosphere. Then Sir Isaac Newton derived the physics and mathematics that accurately described the atmosphere. Newton's work on motion remains 'The book of Signs' of modern meteorology. To this day, his principles form the foundation of all computer analyses and predictions.

Progress in understanding and predicting the weather is one of the great success stories of the Twentieth Century science. Advances in the basic understanding of weather dynamics and physics, the establishment of global observing system, and the advent of numerical weather prediction models have all put weather forecasting on a solid scientific foundation. The deployment of weather satellites and radar, together with emergency preparedness programs, have led to dramatic declines in deaths from severe weather phenomena, such as hurricanes and tornadoes. These days, an all-human endeavor based mainly upon changes in barometric pressure, current weather conditions, and sky conditions, forecast models is now used to determine future conditions. Nowadays, there are a variety of end users to weather forecasts. Weather warnings are important forecasts because they are used to protect life and property. Forecast based on temperature and precipitation is important to agriculture, and therefore to traders within the commodity markets. Temperature forecasts are used by utility companies to estimate demand over the upcoming days. On an everyday basis, people use weather forecasts to determine what to wear on a given day. Since outdoor activities are severely curtailed by heavy rain, strong winds and localized floods, forecasts can be used to plan activities around these events, as well as to plan ahead and survive them.

Today, hurricanes kill or injure people and destroy property and cause millions of dollars in damages. Preparations for hurricane landfalls also disrupt schedules and plans across much wider areas than those affected by high winds, storm surge or torrential rains. These preparations further impose substantial but poorly quantified economic costs. Contrary to initial expectations and popular belief, it is not the high winds but the moving water (the storm surge) that causes the most hurricane-related deaths. Historically, storm surge, where onshore hurricane winds push the sea or mound of water inland, has been the greatest cause of hurricane mortality. For example, The Great Bahamas Hurricane of 1866, The Great Nassau Hurricane of 1926, The Great Bahamas Hurricane of 1929, and the Great Bahamas Hurricane of 1932 killed hundreds of persons, and many were washed out to sea from their sea-side homes by the storm surge and wind driven flooding. At present, most of the hurricane-related deaths in the Bahamas have been caused simply by drowning in floods resulting from the torrential rainfall from the hurricane. Two recent examples of this are Matario Pintard, who died in the flood waters in Freeport, Grand Bahama, in Hurricane Wilma of 2005, and Kevin Milford, who died in Exuma in the flood waters from Hurricane Noel of 2007. However, this low death toll came about recently because of early evacuations and better and timelier hurricane forecast warnings for the impacted areas.

In the past, a forecast was considered successful if it specified the position and intensity of the hurricane for times ranging from 24 through 72 hours after the initial time. However, today the public at large has come to expect a great deal of specific details and pin-point accuracy from the local meteorologists, including spatial distribution of rainfall, winds, flooding and high seas, for times as long as 120 hours into the future. Meteorologists have over the recent years maintained reliable, homogenous statistics on forecast accuracy for more than half a century. These 'verification' statistics provide reliable metrics of meteorological performance over these years. In terms of results, late Twentieth Century forecasting methods prevents 90% of the hurricane related deaths that would occur with techniques used in the late 1800s and early 1900s, but it is difficult to demonstrate any effect on property damage. What was poorly known back then were the economic and human impacts of the response to impending hurricanes. Hurricane forecasting is a successful enterprise with demonstrably favorable benefit-to-cost returns. Compared with the early 1900s, today track forecasting accuracy is improving steadily, but intensity forecasting poses significant operational and technological challenges.

Since the turn of the century, hurricane-related deaths here in the Bahamas have dropped considerably, while property damage has increased in the extreme. The reason is obvious: hurricane forecasting has improved tremendously with time so that watches and warnings are getting to people with plenty of time to evacuate and prepare. We are getting out of harm's way when the hurricanes strike, but sadly, our property is getting ever closer to danger's edge. With the explosion of growth along our coastal regions, it is no wonder we have multi-million and billion dollar hurricanes.

We have seen the grief, hardship and devastation that recent hurricanes such as Irene, Sandy, Andrew, Wilma, Jeanne and Frances caused. Even though Grand Bahama and North Eleuthera were the focus of much attention in the wake of Andrew, Frances, Jeanne and Wilma, fortunately that has changed recently. There are other islands that are just as vulnerable to the effects of even minor hurricanes: Abaco, Long Island, Mayaguana, New Providence and many others in our chain of islands that now gather similar attention from the government and the private sector. Even our tourism industry is affected by these annual threats, and direct hit by a substantial hurricane in areas such as in Nassau or Grand Bahama would potentially harm our national economy and our number one industry of tourism in a significant way. Although the Bahamas has suffered from massive floods, lightning strikes, isolated tornado outbreaks, hurricanes pose a greater risk in any given year to our lives and our economy than all other natural disasters combined. Hurricanes have played a significant role in our nation's history, both in present day and during the colonial times, as this book will show. It's just a matter of time until the next 'big' one makes hurricane history.

Fortunately, man's prediction of the weather has come a long way in just the last century and a half. Today's meteorologists no longer look into a crystal balls or observe animals' and birds' behaviors to predict the onset of a hurricane; nowadays, he has far more sophisticated tools available to him, from satellite images to advanced Doppler radars. He can make fairly accurate predictions for the weather up to a week or more in advance. Yet, even with all of these early warnings, the coastal areas still sustains a lot of damage whenever a hurricane comes through because there is simply no time to fully prepare. A meteorologist can only make an educated guess, and even with this guess he can be wrong. At the moment, there are two ways that meteorologists predict hurricanes and they are: 1) seasonal probabilities; and 2) the track of a current hurricane. These two fields are very different in their methods and approaches.

A seasonal probability predicts the number of named storms and their breakdown by intensity (i.e. the number of hurricanes, tropical storms, intense hurricanes, etc.). They can also predict approximate wind speeds and intensity for these hurricanes. Named storms are typically predicted based on past occurrences and current measures of factors in the climate and in predicting them; they are only labeled as probabilities. On the other hand, once a hurricane has formed it can be tracked; and scientists can usually accurately predict its path for 3-5 days in advance. A hurricane's possible trajectory is usually represented as a cone, which shrinks over time as the error in the prediction decreases. To predict the path of these storms, meteorologists can use many different weather models in the North Atlantic. There have been great strides made in the science of forecasting hurricanes, but there is still a lot to do. One major problem is accuracy. The National Hurricane Center in Florida has been forecasting the paths of hurricanes since the early 1950's. They issue 120-hour, 96-hour, 72-hour, 48-hour, and 1-hour forecasts. The error decreases as the time before landfall decreases, and the error has also decreased over the years as models have become more accurate and advanced.

Today, the responsibility of forecasting the weather for the Bahamas rests on the shoulders of the Bahamas Department of Meteorology, based in Nassau, but that was not always the case. In 1935, the Bahamas Telecommunications Department, in conjunction with the United States Weather Bureau, organized a network of weather observing stations. The Bureau provided the instrumentation and forms to record the information, along with the necessary instructions and annual tours that were arranged to inspect and upkeep the instruments. The information was disseminated in accordance with international standards and practices. Aviation forecast began in 1943 during the Second World War, when the Royal Air Force established an Aviation Forecast Office at Oakes Field. At that time only a few Bahamian weather observers aided the Air Force, but the number increased in 1945 when the Aviation Forecast Office was transformed into a civilian Air Ministry Office.

Formation of the British Caribbean Meteorological Service in 1951 resulted in the transfer of the Bahamian weather observers from the Air Ministry. The comprehensive functions of the Service were: (a) collection and dissemination of meteorological information (b) provide services for aviation, the general public and research (c) provision of hurricane warnings, (d) provide advice to the government and its agencies for planning purposes, and (e) participation in the activities of the World Meteorological Organization (WMO) and the International Civil Aviation Organization (ICAO). Reconstitution of Caribbean Meteorological Service in 1962 prompted the Bahamas Government not to be associated with it anymore. In turn, the Bahamas Government established its own Meteorological Office as an autonomous section of the Department of Civil Aviation. This lasted from 1963 to 1972. The Bahamas Meteorological Service was created from 1963 to 1972. The Bahamas Meteorological Service was created as a separate Department of Government in 1973 while under the Ministry of Tourism. Since 1973, the Department of Meteorology has been under various Ministries but its mandate remained the same. The Department of Meteorology is committed to providing high quality meteorological and climatological information on a timely basis, to be used by special interests and the public at large for research, education and the protection of lives and property.

In 1929, many Bahamians depended heavily on weather lore and other natural signs to forecast the weather. Many of these weather traditions were simply passed down from generation to generation. The purposes of these weather lores were to instruct early farmers, sailors, fishermen, and others on how to predict the weather. Bahamians who made their living outdoors depended heavily on the weather, and that has always been the case during these times. Today, meteorologists make use of satellites, weather balloons, super computers, Doppler radars, and a complex communications network to produce reasonably accurate daily weather forecasts. However, in 1929 Bahamians had to rely on weather indicators to advise them on what kind of plans to make. Some of these indicators have a true correlation with factors that do affect the weather. Others have no relationship at all to the weather.

During the late 1800s up until the mid 1930s, there were several ways in which residents knew that a storm was approaching the Bahamas. Many of these methods were often weather folklores or simple deductions of the weather based on past experiences. Unfortunately, the warning system back then was not as effective or efficient as the warning system nowadays. Typically, coastal residents may have had less than a day or even hours to prepare or evacuate their homes from an approaching hurricane. For this reason, and because of more substandard housing, the damages sustained and the death toll back then were much higher than that of today.

Watching the sea rise or storm surge before the onset of the hurricane.

Before the onset of an approaching storm, the sea-level often rose to above normal positions. By watching this rise in the sea -level, the locals could tell whether there was an approaching storm. Today this rise in the sea -level just before the onset of the storm and during the storm is referred to as the storm surge. Just before the onset of an approaching hurricane, the seas would give these residents a small window of opportunity to prepare for a hurricane or to evacuate to a hurricane shelter.

Watching the clouds and other weather elements

The weather lore that follows has been derived from several sources, including older Bahamian fishermen and older persons within the Bahamian community. The sayings are very old and have been passed on from generation to generation. One of the first signs of an approaching hurricane is the clouds. These clouds often appeared in stages. First is the cirrus-form clouds, which is then changed to alto stratus or nimbostratus clouds, then to stratus-form clouds, and finally to cumulus and cumulonimbus clouds. These residents, especially on the Family Islands, might not have known the types of clouds or names of the clouds. They definitely knew the process by which these storm clouds appeared during a storm's arrival, and they used that as an indicator to prepare for an approaching storm. They also had the clouds in combination with the winds and the rainfall, which over time became stronger and heavier as the hurricane approached the islands.

According to other Bahamian fishermen, atmospheric pressure also helped them determine the weather. They said that knowing from which direction the wind was blowing helped them to locate where the highs and lows were relative to their position. For example, if they stood with their backs to the wind, a high pressure cell will probably be to their right. If their right was west, then they predicted fair or improving weather because weather systems usually move from west to east. Furthermore, the ways in which the wind direction changed also helped them to predict the weather. If the wind was out of the south, then it changes to the southwest, then west, then northwest, it is changing in a clockwise direction and they deduced that the wind was veering. If it changes in a clockwise direction, such as first blowing out of the west then southwest, then south, then southeast, the wind was said to be backing. Sometimes a backing wind is a sign of an approaching storm front, they speculated. The speed of the wind was also an indicator of the changing weather. A strong wind usually means a big differential in air pressure over a small space. This meant that a low pressure system was approaching, and it would in all likelihood be intense.

Many of the sayings of weather folklore made use of the correlation between these weather indicators and the effects they may have on observable phenomena. For example, as the humidity becomes higher, human hair becomes longer. It follows, then, that if your hair seems to curl up at the end and seems more unmanageable, it could be a sign of the rain. They also said another good sign of high humidity is salt. Salt tends to become sticky and clog the holes in the salt shaker if the humidity is high.

Placing signal flags in Nassau and on the Family Island lighthouses

All British Imperial Lighthouse Service light stations were issued a set of signal flags. These flags were kept ready once there was an approaching storm or hurricane to warn incoming or outgoing ships and residents of an approaching hurricane. For centuries before the invention of radio, sharing of information between ships from shore to shore and from sea to shore posed communications problems. The only way for mariners to pass a message from one ship to another or from ship to land was by visual signals. For many years preceding the invention of the telegraph (and during its invention), some type of semaphore signaling from high places, towers or forts was used to send messages between distant points. To this day, we still signal ships at sea with flags flown from shore-based towers and from other ships displaying storm warning flags.

On Hog Island (now called Paradise Island), there was a lighthouse located there and to the right of this lighthouse would be a flag and a flagpole displaying the Union Jack of Britain. If there was a known hurricane travelling near to or was scheduled to pass over the Bahamas, that flag would be removed and replaced with a specialty hurricane flag. This flag consisted of a red flag with a black square in the middle or a gale flag (two red triangle flags indicated gale warnings with winds from 34 to 47 knots) just before the onset of the hurricane or gale. The flag would be removed only after the hurricane or gale conditions had passed.

There were also hurricane flags placed on Forts Charlotte and Fincastle to warn residents of an impending storm. Similar events would also take place on Family Island Lighthouses if they had knowledge of an approaching hurricane. This signal flag also gave residents on Nassau and the Family Islands a small grace period to prepare for a storm. In this day and age of satellite communications and instant information, these flags are rarely used. Actually, there is a famous painting by the world famous artist Winslow Homer showing pastel coloured houses with the trees and hurricane signal flag and flagpole swaying in the winds near the light house on Paradise Island during a hurricane in 1899. This world famous water colour painting is now on display in the Metropolitan Museum of Art in New York.

The Parameter or Barometer shell

One of the ways local residents on some Family Islands tried to forecast the weather was by the use of a local shell called the 'Parameter' or 'Barometer Shell.' The shell got its name from the barometer instrument used for measuring atmospheric pressure. The content of the shell was allowed to dry out, and then the shell was painted in a blue dye called 'Iniqua Blue.' According to some local residents, they swore that this method of weather forecasting was indeed very accurate and quite reliable. The shell would be hanged up in most of the homes at the time, and if it was going to rain the shell turned speckled white. For heavy rain, the dots would turn significantly bigger and the colour of the blue ink would turn a deeper shade of blue. If the rain was light, the dots would become much smaller in size, and if it was calm or fair weather, the shell turned ashy white. As you can guess, this was an unreliable method to forecast the weather, as compared with the modern methods and instruments of today. Today, meteorologists still use an instrument called a barometer to measure air pressure.

Watching the birds and other animals

According to some residents, especially on the Family Islands, they would watch the birds, especially the sea birds making preparations for an approaching storm. They said that if there was a storm approaching the island, the sea birds would instinctively fly back in droves to the mainland from the various cays for shelter from the storm. Numerous Family Island residents said that these birds had a 'sixth sense' when it came to hurricane, because they would not return seaward until the hurricane had passed over that particular island. Others said that the caged and farm animals like the chickens, pigs and goats would start behaving differently just before the onset of a hurricane by trying to get out of their cages or simply making much louder noises than usual. This of course was a very unreliable method as compared to the methods of today and perhaps was one of the main reasons why the death toll was so high on many of the Family Islands.

Before giant waves slammed into the Bahamian coastline in the 1800s and 1900s, many Bahamian residents said that wild and domestic animals seemed to know what was about to happen and fled to higher ground for safety. According to several eyewitness accounts, they said that the following events happened just before the onset of a hurricane. First, wild and domestic animals such as hogs, chickens, goats, sheep and other animals screamed and ran to higher ground or away from the coastal areas. Second, dogs and cats would refuse to go outdoors or leave the yard. Egrets, wild pigeons, seagulls, frigate or hurricane birds, flamingos and other seabirds would abandon their low-lying breeding areas near or on the coast and would proceed to move to higher ground.

The belief that wild and domestic animals posses a sixth sense and that they knew in advance when a hurricane would strike has been around for centuries. Wildlife experts believe that animals' more acute hearing and other senses might enable them to hear or feel the Earth's pressure changes, tipping them off to an approaching hurricane long before humans realize what's going on. In most cases, after the passage of a hurricane over that particular island, many of these residents reported that relatively few animals had been reportedly found dead, reviving speculation that those animals can somehow sense an impending storm. On the beach, some Bahamians were washed away by the storm surge, but some of these residents reported seeing very few, if any animals washed ashore in the storm. In 1929, the Bahamian coast was home to a variety of animals, including crabs, iguanas, lizards, shore birds, seagulls, flamingos and other land animals. Quite a number of these residents reported that they did not see any animal carcasses, nor did they know of any, other than one or two fish caught up on the shore in the wake of the storm. Along the shore, many persons perished from the storm surge; however, many Family Islanders reported that the majority of the goats, sheep, cattle and dogs were found unharmed after the storm passage.

Flamingos, White Crown Pigeons and other birds that breed during the summer months on many of the Bahamian Islands, including, Andros, Abaco, Eleuthera, Inagua, and quite a few other islands as well, flew to higher and safer grounds ahead of time and away from the hurricane prone coastal areas. Many of these residents said that they, too, watched this movement and made preparations for the impending storm. South Andros native the late Mr. Daniel Rahming recalled watching the White Crown Pigeons and other seabirds frantically flying away just before the onset of the Great Bahamian Hurricanes of 1926 and 1929. Also, the late Mr. Illford Forbes, who lived on the coast in the settlement of High Rock, South Andros said his two dogs would not go for their daily walk before the hurricane in 1926 struck. "They are usually excited to go on this outing," he said, "But on this day of the hurricane, they refused to go for their walk and most probably saved my and their lives." Alan Rabinowitz, Director for science and exploration at the Bronx Zoo-based Wildlife Conservation Society in New York, says animals can sense impending danger by detecting subtle or abrupt shifts in the environment. "For example, earthquakes bring vibrational changes in the atmosphere," he said. "Some animals have acute senses of hearing, touch and smell that allow them to determine something in there." Did humans lose their sixth sense? At one time humans also had this sixth sense, Rabinowitz said, but they lost this ability when it was no longer needed or used.

Radio, Telegraph and Telephone

News about an impending storm was broadcast over the radio, but at this time radio was considered a luxury item out of the reach of the masses. The much needed radio service provided by ZNS never really began to operate as a broadcast medium until May 26, 1936. The telegraph was also another method of hurricane warning that came in handy for the Family Island residents. During the time of rapid change in the telegraph industry, the telephone was patented by Alexander Graham Bell in 1876. Although the telephone was originally expected to replace the telegraph completely, this turned out not to be the case: both industries thrived side by side for many decades.

On some of the major islands there was a local telegraph station, and this station provided a valuable link between the islands and New Providence, and indeed the rest of the world. The phone was also available but not to the masses, and at the time it was considered a luxury item that only the rich in the society could afford. Eventually, with ZNS coming on stream on May 26, 1936, it provided a valuable tool as a hurricane warning service. At the time, officials in the Bahamas Government were concerned that residents on the Family Islands were not getting timely weather reports and hurricane warnings. The end result of this was that many lives were lost in the process to these storms. Actually, one of ZNS Bahamas's first mandates was to provide a hurricane warning service to the major Family Islands around the Bahamas. As a result of this important mandate, many lives were saved.

Newspaper

Often news about an impending storm would be featured in the local newspapers of the Nassau Guardian, the Tribune and the Gazette. Many times, if some other island in the Caribbean experienced this storm and it was headed in the general direction of the Bahamas, it was given prominent front page coverage in these newspapers.

Barometer

The instrument used to measure atmospheric pressure is called a barometer. The change in the pressure and how fast it is changing are more indicative of the weather than the pressure itself. Pressure differences are caused by the uneven heating of the Earth's surface. Rapidly falling pressure or low pressure areas almost always means an approaching storm system. Rapidly rising pressure or high pressure areas almost always means clearing and cooler weather ahead. High pressure areas are produced by heavy, sinking air. They are characterized by pleasant weather and little or no precipitation. An area of high pressure is sometimes called a high pressure cell, or simply a 'high.' Low pressure cells are usually called 'lows.' As air rises, it cools, and cooler air can hold less moisture. So if the rising air reaches an altitude where it is too cool to hold the amount of moisture it had on the ground, that moisture condenses out as clouds and precipitation. Thus, low pressure areas produce cloudy and rainy weather.

The barometer in days gone by was the Bahamian residents' version of the radio and television of today. Many residential homes had as a staple in their homes a local barometer to warn them about impending hurricanes. However, these barometers gradually faded out of these homes once radios and televisions were introduced to the masses as a hurricane warning system. The majority of the fishing boats going out on sponging and fishing trips at sea often had a barometer on their boats, especially during the hurricane months of June through November, when the hurricanes were known to strike. Whenever there is a steep drop in atmospheric pressure, that would be the first sign of an approaching storm. They would immediately then make their way back to the mainland. Some of the fishermen would move their boats onto the land or into the mangrove swamps, where they would be protected from the storm.

The local Family Island Commissioner had a barometer stationed at his residence or in his office. If the barometer showed any indication that a storm was approaching that island by a steep drop in pressure, he would then go about informing the residents to start making the necessary preparations for the storm. In addition, those private residents who had a household barometer often took it upon themselves to warn other residents who didn't have a barometer of an approaching storm. That would mean battening down their houses and staying indoors or moving to the nearest hurricane shelter, which at the time was comprised mostly of churches and schools on the various islands.

Although Evangalista Torricelli, a student of Galileo, invented the mercury barometer in 1643, it was the discovery of the Aneroid Barometer in 1843 by Lucien Vidie that brought the barometer into common usage. This barometer was used in the Bahamas as early as 1854, but it came into widespread use during the late 1890s and early 1900s. Sponging was the number one industry in the Bahamas during this hurricane.

The following rules for the use of the barometer was explained by an unnamed observer, an inhabitant of Harbour Island:

1) *In the hurricane months, if the barometer falls with a N or NE wind, it should awake attention, and if it falls below 29.90 inches, it is almost certainly a gale approaching, even though it might be perhaps a 100 miles off.*

2) *During the approach, the barometer falls from noon until morning and then rises to noon again; every day falling lower than the previous day.*

3) *From sunrise to noon, any rise of less than 0.05 inches is unimportant, but the smallest fall during that period certainly indicates bad weather.*

4) *On the contrary, from noon to morning its fall is not conclusive of bad weather, but its rise certainly indicates improved weather.*

5) *Though the weather is ever so threatening at sunset, the rise of 0.05 inches or upward assures you that there will be no gale before morning.*

7) *Though the weather be ever so fair in the morning, the fall of 0.05 inches before noon, betokens a gale before night (provided it's already below 29.90 inches).*

A normal barometer reading in the Bahamas is 30.00 inches. An area of depression that is generally attended by winds varying from moderate to hurricane force causes a fall in the barometer at a rate varying with the rapidity of the approach of the storm. As the storm recedes and the depression fills the barometer and rises to normal, the distance away from the center can only be estimated.

Fall of Barometer per hour from:	Distance in Miles from the Storm Center:
0.02 to 0.06 ins.	250 to 150 miles.
0.06 to 0.08 ins.	150 to 100 miles.
0.08 to 0.12 ins.	100 to 80 miles.
0.12 to 0.15 ins.	80 to 50 miles.

The following may serve as a slight guide, but too much reliance should not be placed on it. In these latitudes storms travel at varying rates of progression, ranging from 5 to 20 miles per hour, generally decreasing as the storm track turns northward and recurves, increasing again as it reaches the North Atlantic. The storm area is usually small, the region of violent winds seldom extending more than 150 miles from the center. The barometer falls rapidly as one progresses from the circumference toward the center. There are two periods of high barometer readings each day, one occurring about 10am, the other at 10pm and two corresponding periods of low barometer reading at 4am and 4pm. [33]

These rules and guidelines were strictly adhered to by most of the residents and fishermen on the various Family Islands to give them some kind of indicator of an approaching weather system. These rules or laws governing the barometer usage remained in place until the 26th of May in 1936, when ZNS Radio Bahamas began broadcasting as a hurricane warning station.

---

[33]   Lawlor, J & A. Lawlor, (2008) *The Harbour Island Story*, Macmillan Publishers Ltd, Pg 206.

<u>Word of mouth</u>

This was a very effective form of a warning system for the residents on the various Family Islands. If there was a steep drop in pressure indicated on the barometer, an usual rise in the sea level, or if a resident read in the newspaper or by other means found out that there was a hurricane travelling, that person would take it upon himself to go around and warn residents that they needed to take the necessary precautions before the storm passed near to or over the island. This also meant that once the word was received in Nassau and on the Family Islands, this resident would proceed to warn other residents on the respective islands about an approaching storm.

CHAPTER TEN

Mr. Pierce.S. Rosenberg's Account of the Great Bahamas Hurricane of 1929

In August 25, 1970 Mr. Pierce S. Rosenberg, working at the United States AUTEC (Atlantic Undersea Test & Evaluation Center-US Navy) Base in North Andros, wrote a detailed report on the impact of the Great Bahamas Hurricane of 1929. It was such a compelling and detailed account of this storm that I decided to include it in this book. Below is his detailed report on this storm:

NATIONAL HURRICANE CENTER
P.O. BOX 8286
CORAL GABLES, FLORIDA 33124
25 August 1970

Mr. Pierce S. Rosenberg
RCA, AUTEC Environmental Science Section
<u>Through</u>
Captain W.P. Rochamel, Commanding Officer
Atlantic Underseas Test and Evaluation Center
3800 Southern Boulevard
West Palm Beach, FL 33406

Dear Mr. Rosenberg:

I have your report of the September 22-October 4, 1929, hurricane and have just gotten around to reading and checking all of the information and details which it contains.

We are in agreement that the official track as depicted by Technical Paper No. 55, Tropical Cyclones of North Atlantic Ocean is in error. The track will be corrected to show that from 27°N and 75°W, the hurricane moved southwestward through the Northeast Providence Channel, over Nassau (our lowest barometer reading at Nassau was 27.64 inches), thence over the center of Andros Island, thence to 24°N-80°W with no change thereafter.

We are indebted to you for your excellent report. Some data such as the high tide of 12 feet on Andros, the death toll of 25 plus on Andros and the 120 to 140 mph winds in Nassau, were not on our records at the National Hurricane Center.

We are taking action to correct the track and add this additional information to what we have on this important and great hurricane of 1929.

Sincerely,
R.H. Simpson
Director
c.c. A.L. Sugg
    L.G. Pardue
    RF
    F
    EDS

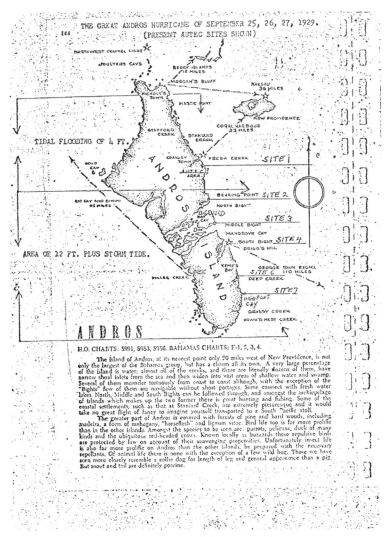

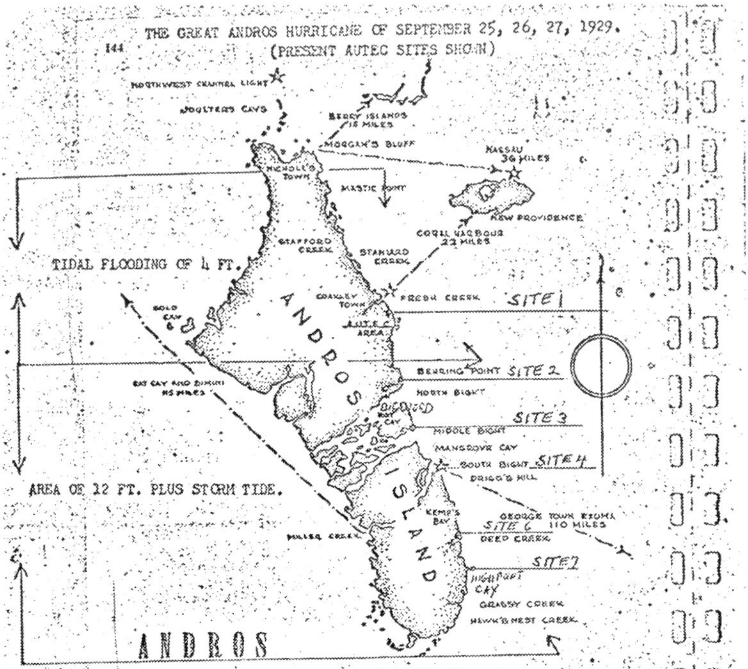
THE GREAT ANDROS HURRICANE OF SEPTEMBER 25, 26, 27, 1929.
144
(PRESENT AUTEC SITES SHOWN)
NORTHWEST CHANNEL LIGHT
JOULTERS CAYS
BERRY ISLANDS 15 MILES
MORGAN'S BLUFF
NASSAU 36 MILES
NICHOLL'S TOWN
MASTIC POINT
NEW PROVIDENCE
CORAL HARBOUR 23 MILES
STAFFORD CREEK
STANIARD CREEK
TIDAL FLOODING OF 4 FT.
COAKLEY TOWN
FRESH CREEK
SITE 1
ANDROS
AUTEC AREA
BEHRING POINT
SITE 2
NORTH BIGHT
SITE 3
MIDDLE BIGHT
MANGROVE CAY
SOUTH BIGHT
SITE 4
DRIGG'S HILL
AREA OF 12 FT. PLUS STORM TIDE.
KEMP'S BAY
GEORGE TOWN EXUMA 110 MILES
SITE 6
DEEP CREEK
ISLAND
SITE 7
HIGHPOINT CAY
GRASSY CREEK
HAWK'S NEST CREEK
ANDROS

H.O. CHARTS: 5991, 5953, 5958. BAHAMAS CHARTS: F-1, 2, 3, 4.

The Island of Andros, at its nearest point only 20 miles west of New Providence, is not only the largest of the Bahamas group, but has a charm all its own. A very large percentage of the island is water; almost all of the creeks, and there are literally dozens of them, have narrow shoal inlets from the sea and then widen into vast areas of shallow water and swamp. Several of them meander tortuously from coast to coast although, with the exception of the "Bights" few of them are navigable without short portages. Some connect with fresh water lakes. North, Middle and South Bights can be followed through, and amongst the archipelago of islands which makes up the two former there is great hunting and fishing. Some of the coastal settlements, such as that at Staniard Creek, are extremely picturesque and it would take no great flight of fancy to imagine yourself transported to a South Pacific atoll.

The greater part of Andros is covered with forests of pine and hard woods, including madeira, a form of mahogany, "horseflesh" and lignum vitae. Bird life too is far more prolific than in the other islands. Amongst the species to be seen are: parrots, pelicans, duck of many kinds and the ubiquitous red-headed crows. Known locally as buzzards these repulsive birds are protected by law on account of their scavenging propensities. Unfortunately insect life is also far more prolific on Andros than the other islands, be prepared with the necessary repellants. Of animal life there is none with the exception of a few wild hog. Those we have seen more closely resemble a collie dog for length of leg and general appearance than a pig. But snout and tail are definitely porcine.

A map showing the movement of the Great Bahamas Hurricane of 1929 as it moved over Nassau and Andros.

SYNOPSIS OF "THE GREAT ANDROS HURRICANE OF SEPTEMBER 25, 26, 27, 1929."

In the year of 1929, there were only 3 North Atlantic tropical storms recorded during the hurricane season. All reached hurricane force, and one of them, the second of the season, struck Andros Island dead center.

This storm was the most destructive of recent record (at least 100 years) for Andros. It completely devastated the island. There was a 12 ft. plus storm tide and terrific winds from Mangrove Cay south, lesser flooding north.

Hurricane winds and storm tides lasted nearly 48 hours as the storm slowed in forward speed from TOTO (Tongue Of The Ocean) to just west of Andros.

The area of hurricane force winds was about 50 miles in diameter during its passage southwestward down the Northeast Providence Channel and increased to about 100 miles in diameter as it remained nearly stationary over Andros.

It was first plotted as a tropical storm by the U.S. Weather Bureau on September 22, 1929, near Lat. 23.5°N, Long. 65.5°W. It moved west-northwest at 12-15 mph to Lat. 26.0°N Long. 70.0°W on September 23rd, where it reached hurricane intensity and continued at the same direction and speed on the 24th to Lat. 27.0°N Long. 74.0°W. Here, blocking action to the north caused it to change course and move southwest at a slower speed through the Northeast Providence Channel to New Providence Island. Its center passed over Nassau at 2030E on September 25th. The dead calm lasted two hours. The lowest barometer reading was 27.65 inches.

The center then moved over Andros on the 26th, just south of Fresh Creek, travelling at the rate of 2-3 mph, and this was the reason for the great havoc wrought.

By the morning of the 27th, it was about 60 miles west of the southern tip of Andros and then turned toward the Northwest with rapid acceleration, brushing the Florida Keys on September 28th. It passed inland near Apalachicola, Florida on the 30th, where it rapidly lost intensity.

It then changed direction toward the northeast, and as an extra-tropical storm moved rapidly northeastward through the Atlantic Coastal States and dissipated over Eastern Quebec Providence on October 4th.

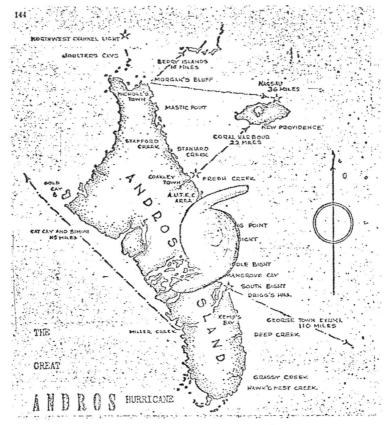

A map showing the movement of the Great Bahamas Hurricane of 1929 as it moved over Nassau and Andros.

FROM "THE NASSAU GUARDIAN", DATED SATURDAY, OCTOBER 12, 1929.

Data applies to the city of Nassau and New Providence Island.

First advisory from Washington, D.C., received Wednesday morning, September 25th.
"Disturbance apparently central about Latitude 26° north, Longitude 75° west or about 150 miles northeast of Nassau Disturbance moving 10mph."

Wind reached gale force by Wednesday noon and hurricane force by Wednesday evening.
Winds continued to increase to an estimated speed of 120-140 mph.
At 8:30pm, there was a dead calm that lasted 2 hours.
The lowest barometer readings ranged from 27.65 ins to 27.80 ins.

This was the first recorded hurricane to approach from the northeast.
Other devastating hurricanes occurred in 1866 and 1926.

FROM "THE NASSAU GUARDIAN" DATED SATURDAY, OCTOBER 12, 1929.

"The Commissioner at Mangrove Cay, Mr. E.W. Forsyth, writes":-

"I regret exceedingly to report that on September 25, 26, and 27, the most destructive hurricane in the history of this district swept the island. Its extreme duration and sustained violence was without precedent, in my experience. The whole place appears as though burned with fire, and fields once full of promise are naked and stripped of all vegetation. The situation is the most serious the island has ever had to face.

A tidal wave at least 12 feet high swept the whole west and south coast, driven by a terrific wind fully 20 miles inland. Little hope is felt for 8 persons missing and 15 also missing from Behring Point.

Fresh Creek felt the hurricane severely on the 25th to the 27th. The lowest barometer reading was 28.70 inches. Before dark, quite a number of people were obliged to leave their houses and take shelter with their neighbours. At midnight, the whole place was covered with water, the people crying to be saved. Seventy people took shelter in the Wesleyan Mission House, being fed and cared for by Rev. Whitfield and Captain Dingle, his guest. Every room in the house was covered by water, so as many as possible were removed to the school house. By noon, over 100 persons were in the school house. About 50 were collected in another house.

The following morning revealed scene of utter destruction:

- Staniard Creek was a waste and desolate; 12 houses destroyed and every other house badly damaged. Staniard Creek Bridge, which was just completed in May at a cost of over £400, was entirely gone and the wharf washed away.
- Blanket Sound: 13 houses down, all others damaged.
- Stafford Creek: wreckage of many strange boats, including 'Governor Shea,' floated ashore between Blanket Sound and Stafford Creek.
- Love Hill and Small Hope: 5 houses down, others badly damaged. All vessels damaged.

- Calabash Bay: teacher's residence, 2 society halls, and 7 houses flattened. Half of the roof of the Roman Catholic Church was blown off. 2 coffins washed out of the grave yard.
- Fresh Creek: 6 houses flattened, 10 very badly damaged, part of the Rectory blown down, window and door of the lighthouse blown away and lamp smashed. The roof of two cells of the Gaol were blown away. Commissioner's office damaged. Residency and out buildings damaged. Seawall damaged and poles of wireless station down, station out of commission.
- Behring Point: 12 houses down and the roads and streets in all settlements damaged. 15 people missing.
- Cargill Creek: abandoned due to high water. The street was just like a channel. No idea can be given of the height of the water flowed from the back of the settlement to the front, and just the hills are out.
- Black Point: 3 houses left standing out of 27 in total. Everything lost. Only 3 houses left in Rolle Town. The people left their houses for the hills to escape the flood. The public wharf at Deep Creek is gone. Boats were swept over the mainland into the ocean, and one was blown 18 miles away.

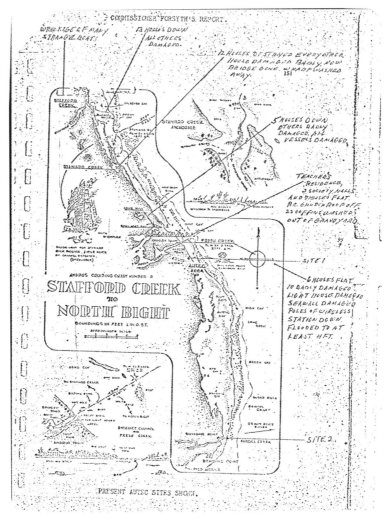

A map showing the damages sustained in Andros after the Great Bahamas Hurricane of 1929 as reported in Commissioner Elgin Forsyth's Report for the island of Andros.

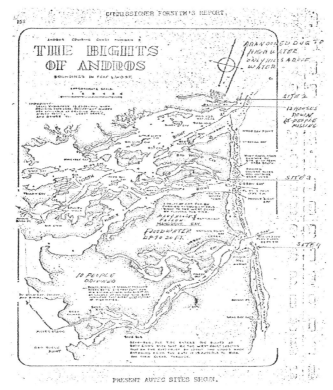

A map showing the damages sustained in the Bights of Andros after the Great Bahamas Hurricane of 1929 as reported in Commissioner Elgin Forsyth's Report for the island of Andros.

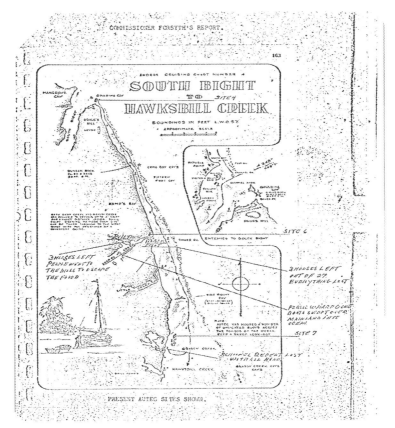

A map showing the damages sustained in the Southern Bight to Hawksbill Creek in Andros after the Great Bahamas Hurricane of 1929 as reported in Commissioner Elgin Forsyth's Report for the island of Andros.

FROM "THE NASSAU GUARDIAN", DATED SATURDAY, OCTOBER 19, 1929.

"THE HURRICNE AT ANDROS"

"I am trying to describe to you the recent hurricane that passed over this island. The hurricane started on Wednesday at 5am and did a lot of damage.

On Wednesday, the 25th, the Commissioner Mr. Forsyth sent down to let us know that the barometer was falling. We tried to secure our houses as best we could, and after doing so we waited to see what would happen.

Then about 10am, the wind shifted and the water started to come, it came until it was knee deep in our house before we decided to leave. Luckily we had a canoe, which was saved for a wise purpose, and we thought to get to the hills before worse came, fearing that the house might have been washed away and all would have perished, but thank God we did not. There are many fallen houses here and further south of Andros. One settlement in Deep Creek, Black Point, was swept away, leaving 3 houses standing.

During the storm, the Roman Catholic Church fell with over 100 people inside. All escaped any injuries except one man who could not get out in time. He was found later by the Catholic Priest buried under the ruins, but still alive.

The water rose to the hills and in some places was 20 feet deep. Mr. Moncur, the school teacher, was on the beach helping to secure boats, etc . . . and when he started for home, he had to swim to the hills.

Mr. P.Cavill was at Steamer Cay, and it seems that his boat scudded from the cay and he eventually came to the western part of Deep Creek in the Pine Yard. He was without food for 6 days. At last providence sent a crab to his rescue, which he caught and ate at once, not being able to even roast it. He told me that it was the sweetest thing he had ever tasted in his life.

Ten persons drowned in Southern Bight for their fields, and as far as we can judge they were drowned by the rush of water from the west side.

After the storm, the Commissioner went around to examine the damage and also to engage seed for planting. He was able to get about 6 bushels of Indian corn and bushels of peas from my mother to distribute to the people."

Lee Bowe
Mangrove Cay,
Andros
12th Oct. 1929.

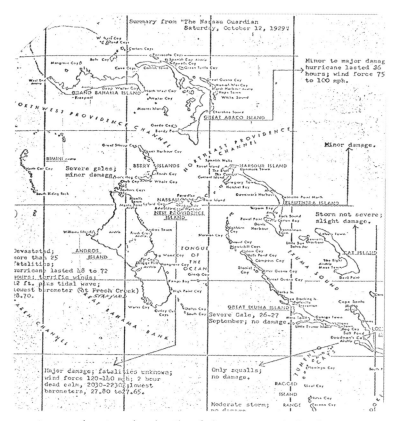

A map showing the details of the storm and the damages sustained in Nassau and Andros after the Great Bahamas Hurricane of 1929 as reported in Commissioner Elgin Forsyth's Report for the island of Andros and The Nassau Guardian.

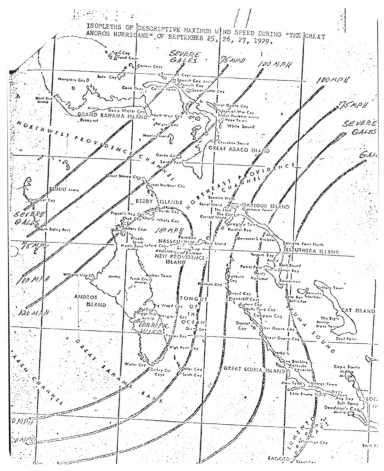

A map showing the sustained wind speeds throughout the
Bahamas during the Great Bahamas Hurricane of 1929.

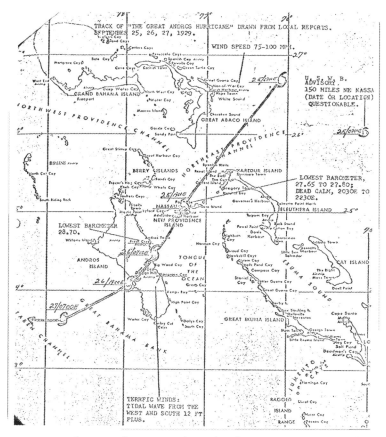

A map showing the meteorological information and track of
the Great Bahamas Hurricane of 1929 as it moved through
the Bahamas.

REFERENCES:

(1) The Nassau Guardian, Wednesday, October 9, 1929.
Commissioner Forsyth's report on the Andros Island disaster.

(2) The Nassau Guardian, Saturday, October 12, 1929.
   a. Commissioner Forsyth's complete report on the Andros Island disaster.
   b. Summary of damage to Nassau and New Providence Island.
   c. Summary of damage to the Northern and Central Bahama Islands.

(3) The Nassau Guardian, Saturday, October 19, 1929.
Description of disaster by Lee Bowe of Mangrove Cay, Andros Island.

(4) Record LN3698, "The Raunch Hands Pickin and Singing."
Calypso ballad, Run come see Jerusalem: Details the loss at sea of 3 boats, "The Ethel, Myrtle, and Pretoria with 33 souls aboard en-route from Nassau Harbour to Fresh Creek.

(5) U.S. Weather Bureau.
North Atlantic Tropical Storms originating in the period 1929.
Acknowledgements:
Bahamian workers at AUTEC, Site 1, who first told me about the storm.
Nassau Library.

CHAPTER ELEVEN

Personal Recollections of the Great Bahamas Hurricane of 1929

While researching this book, I spoke to a wide array of persons who had experienced this storm. What struck me and stays with me to this day is the way their body language immediately changed when I mentioned 'the Hurricane of 1929.' If they were smiling, for example, they suddenly became serious. It was clear that this hurricane had a very traumatic effect on their lives. As they recounted their experiences, some cried, others tried their best to hold back tears. After some 84 years, the vivid memory of this storm was still with them. And although most people I spoke to could recall other 'serious storms,' as they called them (for example, in October 1866, July and September 1926, August 1928 and several in the 1930s), very few could remember the exact dates, where they were and what they were doing when those storms hit. For example, the Nassau Hurricane of 1926 was just as powerful as the Great Bahamas Hurricane of 1929, and it affected more islands, but the 1929 storm was the most memorable and dangerous storm of the century.

I tried to get as many eyewitness accounts as possible from all strata of society in order to get a true picture of this terrible storm. That meant speaking to people in such diverse communities as Lyford Cay, Paradise Island, Bain Town, Mangrove Cay, South Andros, Yellow Elder, or the Eastern Road - wherever the research led me. It seemed that the storm had a more traumatic effect on the people living in Bain Town than those living on Paradise Island or the Eastern Road. Meeting those who had actually lived through the storm was the most enjoyable part of this project. But they were elderly and often sickly. I recall one individual suddenly falling asleep in the middle of a sentence and waking up about 10 minutes later to complete his story as if nothing had happened. I can also recall the eagerness in the faces of Daniel Rahming, Macushla Hazelwood, Dorothy Davis, and Illford Forbes, who obviously didn't have much longer to live but wanted to tell their story. I often had to do a lot of explaining to get people to talk, but once I mentioned the 1929 Hurricane it was generally smooth sailing after that. I recorded their recollections as they were told to me. Some accounts differ from others, but my job was simply to report what these eyewitnesses said and, when possible, to indicate the differences.

In 1929, sponging was the number one industry in the Bahamas, and most of the men I talked to were sponge fishermen at that time, while the women kept the house and farmed. In the early years of the last century, there was a huge worldwide demand for natural sea sponge, and the Bahamas was a major exporter. Greek traders set up a sponge exchange on Bay Street where the fishermen congregated. As a result, there are many Greek-Bahamian families here today. But the industry eventually succumbed to over-harvesting, disease and the introduction of synthetic sponges, although there are still small quantities of sponge being exported from areas like Mangrove Cay, Andros.

Another factor that made the Great Bahamas Hurricane of 1929 unique was its duration - it stayed over the Bahamas for three consecutive days with non-stop battering winds and rainfall. This had never happened before and has never happened since - including the devastating Hurricane Andrew in 1992. Typically, a hurricane makes landfall and the weather starts clearing about 12 hours later. That did not happen with the 1929 Hurricane, which explains why it had such a massive impact on people.

Message from the King of England George V

The following message from His Majesty the King was addressed to the Governor and the people of the Bahamas, which was received from the Secretary of State for the Colonies:

30th September, 1929.

> *His Majesty the King is deeply concerned at the news that the Colony has once more been ravaged by a hurricane. His Majesty anxiously awaits further tidings and desires, through you, to assure all sufferers of his personal sympathy.*

The Following reply was dispatched from Nassau to the Secretary of State for the Colonies:

> *On behalf of the Colony, I desire humbly to thank His Majesty for his gracious message of sympathy. Further reports confirm that New Providence and Andros have been the central points of devastation, but in both islands the casualties have been remarkably few. The main distress is occasioned by the destruction of the houses and the wreck of local craft. The public services are restored, and normal life is practically resumed. The population is facing disaster with fortitude and calm, and the situation is well in hand.*

The following remarks were made by Charles Dundas, Governor of the Bahamas, with regards to the hurricane.

> *I desire to express my deepest sympathy with all of those who have suffered in any way in this terrible disaster, more particularly with those who have suffered bodily injury and who count relatives among the victims of the storm. This disaster is extremely disappointing because up 'til now the prospects were singularly encouraging, and inevitably there will be a severe setback to the efforts of all those who have earnestly endeavored to promote the prosperity of the Colony. Nevertheless, it is vital that we should not be downhearted. The greater the calamity, the more need there is for courage and perseverance. I am speaking to a people injured to*

disasters and of a country in which there is manifestly no place for faint-hearted ones. I decline to despair despite the frustration of so much that we had hoped and striven for, and I sincerely believe that in this respect I shall have with me the stout hearts of the Bahamians. Going around the town on Friday, it was to me most heartening to witness much cheerful courage displayed in the midst of ruin and devastation. With staunchness and faith in ourselves, we shall set ourselves to repair the damage and prove to the world that Bahamians are undaunted.

Charles Dundas
Government House
September 28, 1929.

Special Session Of The House of Assembly-The Administrator's Charles Dundas Speech On The Great Bahamas Hurricane of 1929.

In accordance with his Proclamation calling the General Assembly together for a special session, His Excellency the Administrator, the Hon. Charles Dundas, O.B.E., met both Houses of the Legislature in the Council Chambers on Wednesday night and opened the session with a speech.

His Excellency, who was attended by his A.D.C., Captain Lancaster, M.C., was met at the entrance to the Council Chamber by His Honour the Acting Chief Justice, (Mr. G.H.F. Cannon) the Hon. Acting Colonial Secretary (Mr. C.P. Bethel, I.S.O., the Hon. Receiver General (Mr. N. Stafford Solomon), and the Hon. Acting Director of Medical Services (Dr. W.J. Woodman) and the Commandant of Police (Mr. C.J. Whelbell), who accompanied him to the Council Chamber. The members of the Legislature Council present were the Hon. W. Miller, I.S.O., the Hon. P. W. D. Armbrister, O.B.E. the Hon. Nigel B. Burnside, I.S.O.., the Hon. C.O. Anderson, and the Hon. Ronald Young.

The attendance of the Speaker and members of the House of Assembly, having been commanded by a message delivered by the A.D.C., the House, led by the Speaker preceded by the Sergeant-at-Arms bearing the Mace, arrived at the Bar of the Council Chamber, and His Excellency delivered the following speech:

Mr. President and Honourable Gentlemen of the Legislative Council.

Mr. Speaker and Gentlemen of the Honourable House of Assembly

> *I deeply deplore the catastrophe which has obligated me to summon you to a Special Session. That my first formal meeting with you should be occasioned by an emergency so distressing is a matter of sincere regret to me. Prior to the recent hurricane, I had reason to believe that if the Colony were spared from the adversity of the nature we have now sustained, her prospects were the brightest. It was also my earnest hope that the fourth century of the Bahamas as a British Colony would usher in an era of stable*

prosperity, that instead the anniversary for which preparation had been made with joy and pride should perforce be commemorated in the shadow of misfortune and privation is a circumstance that adds poignancy to our sorrow.

With havoc still painfully in evidence on all sides, one cannot be unmindful of the suffering and material loss caused to all sections of the community, and it is idle to gloss over the temporary check the Colony has sustained. But though I am keenly alive to these facts and in no way wish to minimize their consequences, and while it is due to you that I should make a full statement of the situation, I deprecate any inclination to harp on the disaster still less to magnify its discouraging aspects. It is rather my desire to divert attention from what has happened and give prominence to the constructive task now to be faced.

The praiseworthy spirit manifested by all sections of the community inspires me with confidence in the ability of the Colony to retrieve the situation, and if the work of reconstruction is undertaken with energy and with resolve to avert a far as possible the repetition of destruction on the same scale. I believe that the sore trial the Colony has experienced may be not devoid of its compensations. Every recurrence of hurricane devastation serves to demonstrate the need for sound construction, and that lesson be it said applies not only to works, but to the whole economic structure of the Colony. I am indeed tempted to say that given this teaching of nature is taken to heart and acted upon, God may yet come to evil.

The disaster has aroused widespread commiseration. His Majesty the King has with his wonted solicitude graciously expressed his anxiety and has commanded me to convey his sympathy to all those who have suffered. Numerous messages of condolence have reached me, notably from our sister Colonies of the western hemisphere. Offers of emergency aid came from the United States, and a generous donation from abroad enabled me to open a hurricane fund which will, I trust, afford relief to those most affected.

I am happy to say that on the majority of the Out Islands, the storm was either not felt at all or was so moderate as to cause no damage. In the case of a few islands, the effect was in fact beneficial in that the only result of the disturbance was much needed rainfall. The destructive range of the hurricane embraced the islands: Eleuthera, Harbour Island and Spanish Wells, Abaco and Andros, but serious damage is reported only in Andros, I have still no reliable data as to the loss of life and property on Andros, but I fear that it has been heavy and that the Sponging Industry must be severely affected by the destruction of boats and damage to the sponge bed. In a lesser degree, Abaco has suffered; twelve boats and nineteen houses are reported wrecked and damaged.

It is, however, probable that wherever the storm attained hurricane velocity, standing crops were entirely destroyed. It is not too late to repair this damage, the people have been encouraged to replant and have responded well, and steps have been taken to ensure an ample seed supply, some of which has already been issued. But it is to be feared that until fresh crops can be harvested, food shortage will prevail on some of the Out Islands, necessitating moderate rationing in return for labour.

It is an unfortunate coincidence that certain islands, as for instance Long Island and Long Cay, though not affected by the storm are suffering from food shortage due to prolonged drought. Now that rain has fallen, I hope that with the expenditure of monies already provided under the ordinary votes, distress in this area will be sufficiently alleviated.

I regard it as supreme importance that there should be no undue suspension of the progress made in respect to agricultural production. I am unable to subscribe to the view that the frequency of hurricanes rules out the possibility of prosperous peasant cultivation, rather does it seem to me that because of the greater hazards to other occupations arising from the same cause it is the more necessary to look to agriculture as a basic industry of the Colony. I have therefore endeavored to stimulate the cultivators to renewed effort, and their response to such encouragement is most gratifying.

I need not enter into deaths of the havoc caused in New Providence; suffice it to say that 456 houses were demolished and 640 damaged in varying degree. By singular good fortune, the loss of life and other casualties have been comparatively slight, the number of fatalities being seven, of which two were from drowning, while of serious injuries only twenty-two were reported.

The ultimate loss of shipping cannot be stated with accuracy since it remains to be seen how many of the sixty-four vessels of all types wrecked out of Nassau Harbour can be salvaged. Reports received immediately after the hurricane indicated the total loss of ten motor boats, three pilot boats, three ocean going motor vessels, nine sloops, and two lighters - twelve other motor vessels were doubtfully recoverable. The remainder, that is to say twenty-five craft of various sorts, were damaged and stranded. This is a heavy toll entailing substantial loss, not only to the owners, but to the Colony which so greatly depends on its marine transport facilities.

The lighting and telephone systems have been extensively damaged, and although everything has been done to repair the damage, there must be some lapse of time before these services can be completely restored. It is gratifying to note that the water supply has been barely interrupted and that the damage done to both the water and sewage works has been negligible, an indication, I presume, of sound construction. The fact that from the point of view of navigation the harbour has not been affected by the terrific seas that raged first from the one quarter and then from the other and that the wharf and shed have suffered only negligible injury prove that these works were capable of withstanding a maximum of strain. Most of the dilapidations of the shed roof were in evidence before the hurricane.

In other directions, however, the damage to public property has been most extensive. The arterial road of the island has been wholly or partly demolished over considerable stretches and has been seriously damaged in several sections.

This account was taken from the Monthly Weather Review of September 28, 1929, and it deals with the loss of life and property in Nassau:

The severest hurricane struck Nassau from the west at 1:30pm, Wednesday (September 25), followed by a 24-hour gale from the west in the early stages of the storm. The water rose very high, flooding roads and carrying away sea walls and houses. After seven hours, the winds blew from the west and southwest as the center passed over Nassau. The lull lasted for over four hours. It resumed at midnight, blowing harder than before from the southeast and east. Major damage occurred. It continued all Thursday (26th), and the barometer reading at the height of the storm was 27.64 inches, but the storm abated on Friday (27th). Still, the strong

*winds kept blowing. Damage to private property was enormous.
Few houses escaped, many unroofed, especially in the coloured
quarter. Stores, churches, and shipping were affected very severely.
The Mailboat 'Princess Montagu' was blown out of the harbour
and stranded on Tony Rock. The passengers and crew were safely
rescued of the boat. The mail vessel 'Ena K' was found safe in the
harbour. Many lives were lost and casualties numerous, however,
it is impossible to estimate yet. No news from the Out Islands, but
it is feared that they suffered severely.*

This Account of the Great Bahamas Hurricane of 1929's impact on the
city of Nassau was reported by the editor of The Tribune on Wednesday,
October 2, 1929:

*At 10am on Tuesday last, Washington reported that a tropical
disturbance was apparently central about latitude 26 degrees north,
longitude 75 degrees west (approximately 100 miles northeast of
Governor's Harbour) moving west or west northwest, and that it
was quite likely that the disturbance was increasing in intensity.
Reports from the Out Islands in the vicinity of the disturbance
were far from alarming.*

*No one dared to believe that the storm would touch this
island, and if it did, it was thought to be only a minor disturbance.
A few people took the precaution to batten up their homes and
business places and to secure their boats. So little thought was given
to the storm, however, that even the Imperial Lighthouse Tender
'Firebird' remained at the dock and did not attempt to go to her
hurricane moorings in the harbour.*

*On Wednesday morning, the storm warning from Washington
indicated that the disturbance of hurricane force was expected
to reach the Florida coast between Palm Beach and Daytona,
Florida, sometime that afternoon. Messages were broadcast over
the radio from Miami up to the afternoon on Wednesday, and
it led everyone here to believe that the hurricane had passed over
this island and was well on its way to Miami. Even at that point,
they did not believe the hurricane was a dangerous one, as one
broadcaster stated that it was quite safe for the children in Miami
to go to school that day and that the Red Cross was standing by
only in case they were needed.*

By 1:30pm on Wednesday, the wind had raised sufficiently to cause the more cautious to secure their property. Rain was then falling in torrents, and there was even a rumble of thunder and an occasional flash of lightning (it is commonly believed that this is a sign that the storm is broken). The siren gave out a long, loud scream, as if in alarm, but it was only that two wires had crossed somewhere. The siren on the S.S. Princess Montagu also summoned assistance just about this time as she started to drag away from the wharf. She was secured again but eventually dragged away and finished the storm on Tony Rock. It was at 1:30pm that we saw the latest advisories on the storm (received about 1 pm) to the effect that "a tropical storm is centered this morning at the southern end of Great Abaco and apparently moving slowly westward, gradually increasing in intensity. The wind is apparently of hurricane force close to the storm centre. If the course does not change, it will reach the Florida coast between Jupiter and Miami late tonight." Armed with this cable, we traced the course of the hurricane on a chart, along with an authority on hurricanes, and it was clearly evident from this cable that the storm was at Abaco and that it would follow the course of the 1915 hurricane. At 1:10pm, the barometer in the Public Works Department registered 29.38ins, a drop of 6 ½ tenths from the previous day.

The wireless, electric light and telephone services were still functioning, and we returned to our office and made an effort to finish the printing of the paper for that day. It was about 2:30pm before we began to realize that the situation appeared more serious than was generally believed, and by then the Telegraph Department had received information that the storm was coming direct for Nassau, and radio broadcasters in Miami were fairly screaming the information through the transmitter. By then everyone was bestirring themselves. The wind gradually increased, the rain fell in long, slashing sweeps, the tide rose higher and higher until the water was several feet deep on Bay Street. All this time, the barometer dropped at a startling pace.

At about 9pm, there was a sudden - almost a dead- calm. A few stars straggled out, and an electric storm developed soon after. Sometimes almost bright, sometimes overcast and threatening, with an occasional roll of thunder and flash of lightning, the weather was far from settled, but people came out in the streets, and after looking around at the comparatively small amount of damage that had been done, returned to their homes and beds, feeling thankful that it wasn't such a bad show after all. They felt doubly reassured because it is commonly believed that lightning was a sure sign that everything was over. But the barometer kept falling.

It was soon after midnight when the wind started to rise from the southeast, the opposite direction to that from which it had blown all day, and people with any knowledge of the laws of hurricanes realized immediately that the centre of the hurricane had passed over the island (the centre of a hurricane is calm, and when the second half of the storm begins it comes from the opposite direction to that in which it originated) and that the worst was yet to come. The wind puffed and 'blowed' and screamed and howled until it is estimated that it reached a velocity of 140 miles an hour. There is no accurate estimate of the wind force, however, as the anemometer was blown clear away. The needle on our barometer dropped until it could drop no lower, and we shook it to see whether it was a 'dead' thing. But no, it was still very much 'alive' and functioning. The instrument in the meteorological department recorded until there was no more room for it on the chart, and then it ran off the reel; but the barometer in the Telegraph Department registered 27.65ins between 10pm and 11pm Wednesday, and the barometer in the Public Works Department registered 27.90ins at 3 am on Thursday.

Thursday morning 'dawned' dark. The wind had not abated, and rain was still pouring down with a cruel, cutting force. All day Thursday, the wind was high and rain fell. By Thursday night the barometer had slowly climbed back to a reassuring point, but when in the afternoon the wind had started to rise again, it was reported that another hurricane was coming. The wind remained high all night Thursday until late Friday morning, when it slowly died out, but the rain continued to fall heavily until early Saturday morning.

Saturday morning was dark, but after a brave effort the sun peeped out. The work of destruction was over, and the task of reconstruction began.

Every square inch of Nassau might have provided material for a column of newspaper description, for this hurricane had stolen on us 'like a thief in the night', stayed longer, blew harder, and worked more havoc than any hurricane on record. Ships were thrown bodily into the interior of the island; government buildings and property were torn and battered; private buildings were destroyed or damaged; and even the churches were not overlooked by this angel of destruction. Anyone who saw Nassau on Saturday morning would not have recognized it. It looked like a city in France during the World War, after a long siege had been lifted. Nor would anyone who saw Nassau on Saturday morning and then looked at it again today recognize the place, so rapidly has the work of reconstruction progressed.

Led by His Excellency, the Hon. Charles Dundas, O.B.E., everyone has set to work with grim courage and determination to efface in a miraculously short time all effects of this calamity.

The roof of Trinity Methodist Church destroyed during the Great Bahamas Hurricane of 1929 as it moved through the Bahamas (Courtesy of the Charles Whelbell Collection-Bahamas National Archives, Nassau, Bahamas).

This account was taken from the Nassau Guardian of September 28, 1929:

The storm which began to be felt on Thursday and reached gale intensity during the daytime on Wednesday resolved itself definitely into a hurricane before Thursday morning, and sweeping through Nassau it has left a trail of destruction and devastation in its wake. We have not got meteorological particulars, but it is evident that an exceedingly high velocity must have been reached.

Guesswork puts the figure at 150 miles an hour, but this may not be accurate. Many people who have experienced successive hurricanes here say that this one is the worst within their recollection, and although few persons now here actually went through the famous 1866 storm, it is becoming current gossip that this is the severest since that date.

If the extent and nature of the damage are anything to go by, this opinion is probably correct, for the havoc which has been brought about within the last few days is reckoned to exceed anything which resulted from the recent storms. Complete particulars of all the damage are not at hand, but generally speaking it is common to find damaged shops and premises in every direction, and the outlying villages from Nassau are said to have suffered very badly and in some cases to have been practically wiped out. Within Nassau itself, many houses have been severely handled by the hurricane, and in certain cases are actually razed to the ground. Many of the churches and chapels also have fared rather badly.

Zion Baptist Church on East and Shirley Streets totally destroyed in the Great Bahamas Hurricane of 1929(Courtesy of the Bahamas National Archives, Nassau, Bahamas).

H.E. Sir Orville Turnquest

The former Governor General of the Bahamas, Sir Orville Turnquest, said, "We here in Nassau have really been lucky in the sense that we didn't have any major hurricanes since the Hurricanes of 1929 and 1926 to affect the entire Bahamas. I think this is because of our geographical location within the Bahamas. Nassau seems to be sheltered from these dangerous storms. In the late 1930's and 1940's, I recalled that Bahamians were more radio prone. At this time, I was a young boy of 8 to 10 years old growing up, and I recalled that residents would gather at public points to listen to the radio (for news of impending storms and more) and one of those gathering places was at the British Legion Headquarters just below the hill on Blue Hill Road near the Government Clinic. There was a radio receiver in the building, and crowds would gather there to listen to the radio. People on the Family Islands were even more radio savvy because the radio was one of the few things that kept the islands linked with the capital of Nassau, so they really relied greatly on the radio for communications. I can recall minor storms over the years (I was only a few months old when the Hurricane of 1929 struck the Bahamas and was too young to remember this storm). However, my most memorable hurricane was that of Hurricane Andrew in 1992."

H.E. Arthur D. Hanna

The former Governor General and Deputy Prime Minister of the Bahamas said that the 1929 Hurricane was a very powerful storm and that many persons died in this storm. I experienced several storms while growing up as a boy in The Bight on the island of Acklins. Among them was a powerful hurricane in 1936, where I actually saw the water going out of the harbour, leaving all the boats stranded and sitting on the sand. By midday a few hours later, the water came rushing back onto the land. Growing up on Acklins, we were not as fortunate as the people of today to get advanced storm warnings, with all of the sophisticated weather equipments that the meteorologists have nowadays. To make matters worse, no one on Acklins had a radio to give them any kind of advanced warnings. During my childhood years, we had three ways in which to determine when a hurricane was travelling or approaching Acklins. The first was the use of a barometer, and all seamen had a trusty barometer on their ships, and they would never leave the shore without it. They would watch the barometer at sea, and if there was a steep drop in pressure, the seamen would immediately make their way back to shore and make preparations for a hurricane. Secondly, they knew a storm was approaching Acklins was by watching the movement and types of clouds ahead of the hurricane. Most residents didn't know the names of the clouds, but they certainly knew the types of clouds associated with a hurricane. Lastly, they knew a storm was approaching Acklins was by watching the behavior of seagulls. Just before the onset of a hurricane, the seagulls always flew in from out at sea in large flocks and made their way onto the mainland in search of a safe resting area. Armed with this information, we would start the process of battening down our houses. Strangely enough, after the storm the birds would make their way back out to sea, unharmed.

Part of the roof of Salem Baptist Church during the Great Bahamas Hurricane of 1929 (Courtesy of the Bahamas National Archives, Nassau, Bahamas).

Hilbert Pinder

I was about 7 years old at the time when the Great Bahamas Hurricane of 1929 hit the Bahamas. The storm started at midday and came out of the northeast and blew consistently for 3 days. At the time, I lived with my father on Yamacraw Hill Road, and I can distinctly recall the water from the storm was over six feet deep and that it stretched from the eastern shores of New Providence, near present day Port New Providence, all the way to South Beach, and it was all salt water. The water was so deep that my father was growing watermelons and cantaloupes and they floated onto the streets from the farm and he had to go and collect them. We lived in Camperdown Heights, but this hurricane destroyed our home there, so we moved into a house on Yamacraw Road. My father had just recently built this new home, and sadly the hurricane came along and destroyed it.

My father used the building materials from the destroyed house in Camperdown to build the new one in Yamacraw. The winds were so strong in this storm that it split the house in two, and one half was deposited over 150 feet away from its original location. All of my father's sheep and goats were killed in this storm. The only thing that was untouched was my father's car, which was in the garage; however, the garage roof was also blown off. There was so much water on the streets after the storm that my father could not drive his car for quite a while. The main reason my father's house was destroyed was because it blew hurricane force winds consistently for three days. My family knew the storm was coming because my father heard it on his radio from a Florida radio station. In fact, he was one of the first persons to own a radio in the Bahamas. It was a bulky Kent Radio; however, there were not much radio stations to listen to, with the rare exception of one or two stations located in Florida. There were no meteorological offices nor any radio stations located in the Bahamas at the time to warn us of any impending storms. When we found out a storm was travelling, we quickly battened up the house the best we could, but that didn't do us any good because the hurricane still destroyed it.

Sponging was the number one industry in the Bahamas at the time, and there were many sponging schooners which were blown in from out at sea into the pine barrens of Andros miles away. To get them out, they had to cut down pine trees to make way for the boats and use some pine trees as rollers to roll the boats out to the water front, which was a very difficult task in itself. After the storm, it took six to nine months for our family to return to some degree of normalcy. The only thing we had left to eat after the storm were sweet potatoes, yellow corn grits and pigeon peas. We lived of pigeon peas soup for months after the storm. Things were so bad that my dad went to the Red Cross, which was giving out free food and blankets. When he got there and asked for some blankets for his family, the clerk told him to leave because those blankets were for people who could not work to support themselves. This storm was so destructive for us that I can recall this storm more vividly that I can remember the more recent Hurricane Floyd in 1999 or Hurricane Andrew in 1992.

Jackson Burnside

I first learned about this storm by listening to older persons in the community talking about this giant of a storm. I also learned about this storm by reading a book called *Their Eyes Were Watching God,* by well noted American author Zora Neale Hurston. This book was made into a movie starring Halle Berry, who starred as the main character Janie. It was a made- for- TV movie which aired for the first time on March 6, 2005, and was produced and developed by Quincy Jones and Oprah Winfrey. The TV movie was watched by an estimated 24.6 million viewers, further entrenching the novel in the public consciousness and in the American literary canon. Zora Neale Hurston encountered this hurricane in the Bahamas while she did research for this book. From New Orleans, she travelled to South Florida and on to the Bahamas. Her stay here in the Bahamas was devoted mostly to the collection of native songs and learning about the Jumping Dance. During her stay in the Bahamas in 1929, she experienced this powerful three-day hurricane, which resulted in the deaths of many persons and animals and the washing away of hundreds of homes. Hurston called on the memory a few years later to develop and duplicate the terror in her Everglades hurricane in *Their Eyes Were Watching God,* which is actually based on the Great Lake Okeechobee Hurricane, which struck Florida in 1928 and caused severe flooding. She repeated her trips to the Bahamas during the latter part of the 1920s and early 1930s. Today, *Their Eyes Were Watching God* is widely regarded as a literary masterpiece.

Vera Bethell

The two most dangerous storms to affect this country were the Hurricanes of 1926 and 1929. In the 1929 storm, seven people died from the settlement of the Bluff and two from the settlement of Smith's Hill. This storm lasted for three days and three nights, and I can distinctly recall the small lull lasting only 15 to 20 minutes when the eye passed over Andros. During this lull, we all assumed that the hurricane was over. The others and I went to pick up coconuts on the beach that had fallen during the storm. However, my father realized that the storm was not over and came and brought us back in the house. Shortly thereafter, the winds and rain from the hurricane came roaring back with even greater ferocity than before. Had it not been for my father's quick thinking we would have all surely been caught in the midst of the deadly storm. During this three-day storm, we moved from house to house as the hurricane continued to blow the roofs off the houses, until we finally settled in my grandmother's house (along with two other families). Her house was much more secure than ours was, so we stayed there until the storm was over. After the storm, I cried because of the great devastation everywhere on the island; most of the houses suffered major damages from this storm. Fortunately, most of the roofs of the houses in my settlement were made of straw, so they were easily replaced with new straw. This storm will always be memorable for me because of the extent of the damage it caused to the island of Andros.

The Munson Steamship Line building totally destroyed in Downtown Nassau next to the Royal Bank of Canada (Courtesy of the Bahamas National Archives, Nassau, Bahamas).

Cleo Deveaux Dean

Mrs. Dean, who now lives in the settlement of Kemp's Bay, South Andros, said that she was a child at the time the Hurricane of 1929 occurred and she recalls many details about this storm. This storm was so dangerous because it lasted for three days and three nights. This country had never had experienced a storm like that before, and has never had a storm of this magnitude since. For that reprieve, I thank God because this country couldn't take another storm of this magnitude. The communities of South Andros and Mangrove Cay had quite a number of boats destroyed in this storm. One of the boats that went down was called 'The Electric'; it went down near Cay Lobos and was never heard from again. My cousin and several other crewmembers went down with the boat in the storm. Of the crewmembers, I can recall George Johnson and a man by the name of Alfred but the others I can't remember. The Lighthouse Keepers on Cay Lobos reported that they saw when the storm carried the boat out to sea in the east, but they were helpless to rescue it.

My father had a dinghy boat, 'The AC,' named after my youngest sister. After the hurricane left Andros, water was everywhere (up to 20 feet in some instances), and my dad used the boat to rescue people from their homes and take them to dry land. The Catholic Church came to Andros in the late 1920s, and at the time, they held church services in the home of a man by the name of John Rolle in Kemp's Bay. Unfortunately, the hurricane destroyed his house and they had to move into Mrs. Ellen Forbes' home to have church services for several months after the storm.

Initially, the storm started to blow really hard, I heard a loud noise which sounded like a train and I began shouting repeatedly, "Lord I am in your care!" The water came and flooded the entire community, and my father's house was completely flooded up to its roof. After this storm, the western and eastern shores of Andros were joined together because of the vast amount of water on the land. The winds were so strong that a large grape tree fell between our house and the well. The settlement, had only one road, which was called the Bay Road. After the storm, the elders in the settlement had to find another route to our homes because the hurricane had eroded and washed away the original road. The Commissioner for the island of Andros, Mr. Elgin Forsyth, was stationed in Mangrove Cay. After the storm, he came over to South Andros and provided many of the residents, with food, clothing and seeds to replant on their farms. After the storm, many of the residents in South Andros were near starvation because the storm had destroyed everything they had, including their farms and livestock, which they greatly depended upon for survival.

Most residents had to start life all over again because nothing was left after the storm. I can distinctly recall that during the lull of the storm, me and many of the neighborhood children and I became curious about the storm and ventured outside to look at the storm damage. One of the things we saw after the storm was a coconut tree that had fallen on top of a man's house by the name of Mr. Thomas, destroying it. Also, another coconut tree fell on the neighbour's John Forbes' house. The vessel 'The Pretoria' went down in this storm, and most of the persons on board drowned, with the exception of the captain and two crew members. They survived by clinging onto a pig, which was being taken to Andros by the captain to start a pig farm. In addition to the three vessels Blind Blake sang about in his popular tune 'Run Come See Jerusalem', there were two other vessels which went down in this storm, and they were 'The Bright Eyes' and 'The Andros.'

A badly damaged sponging schooner in Nassau Harbour during the Great Bahamas Hurricane of 1929 (Courtesy of the Bahamas National Archives, Nassau, Bahamas).

Francita Rolle

I can recall living in the settlement of The Bluff, South Andros, during the 1929 Hurricane. During the hurricane, I stayed with my family in a cave called 'Lumbo Hole.' We stayed in this sheltered cave for 3 to 4 days with about 100 other persons. This group comprised mostly of women and children because most of the men were out at sea on a sponging trip in the area of the Mud and the southern tip of South Andros. In this cave along with me were my mother Sarah Rolle, my sister Elizabeth Rolle, Token Lewis, Verna Stubbs, Dick Solomon, Simeon Davis, Florence Rolle and her Family, Kita Johnson and many more persons. Simeon Davis, who was the pastor of Friendship Native Baptist Church in the Bluff, held church services in the cave for the three to four days we stayed in this cave. Throughout the storm, we sang spiritual hymns, prayed and asked God for His divine protection. We cooked in this cave and were able to grind corn and eat corn grits. When we got out of the cave, we were surprised to find out that most of the houses in the settlement were destroyed and there was floodwater everywhere. There was so much water on the land that the two seas of the western and eastern shores of Andros were joined together. After the storm, Commissioner Elgin Forsyth came and gave many of the residents food, clothing and seeds to replant their farms because all of their crops were destroyed by the hurricane.

My father, Prince 'Papa-Warthy' Rolle, told me how he was able to survive in this storm by clinging onto a dog by the name of '*Speak Your Mind.*' The storm blew the schooner '*The Repeat*' out to sea, and my father along with others were forced to swim back to the mainland. He said initially the dog kept swimming around him while they were swimming into the land. He became very tired, and he then grabbed the dog by its tail. He held onto the dog's back and held onto that dog for his dear life because he realized that if he ever let that dog go, he would surely drown. The dog swam him into the shore. When he got to the shore, the dog caught a crab, and he ate the body of the crab and gave the back of the crab to the dog, and that was how they were able to survive. My uncle Lewis drowned trying to swim to the shore. Furthermore, a man by the name of Simeon Davis, who had a son named Josh Davis, who also drowned in this storm. Two other men named James Smith and Sam Black also drowned trying to swim from one cay to the next during this storm. There were also 2 men from the settlement of Smith's Hill who drowned in this storm, and if my memory serves me correct, a lady named Missy also died in the storm.

Before the storm, my father and other crew members were onboard the schooner '*The Repeat*', playing checkers, cooking, eating dumpling soup and pancakes. However, unknown to them the barometer indicator got stuck while they were in the vicinity of Grassy Creek in South Andros. Unfortunately, they were unable to get a precise or accurate reading after this occurred, and so they had to try and get back to the mainland when they realized a storm was travelling. It was doing this time that some of the men drowned when they tried to swim from Beach Cay to the Andros mainland. Fortunately, the surviving crew members were able to survive when they swam back to the shore. They came ashore at a lady name Arfee's, who lived in the settlement of Hawk's Nest. She cooked a hot meal for them and gave them some clothing to wear because they were starving and naked. Their clothing went out to sea on '*The Repeat*' during the storm. In fact, Arfee gave my dad a dress to wear because that was all she had, and he gladly took the dress and was happy to put it on because he had nothing to wear.

A badly damaged Princess Montagu Mailboat was blown out of the harbour and stranded on Tony Rock during the Great Bahamas Hurricane of 1929 (Courtesy of the Bahamas National Archives, Nassau, Bahamas).

Ruben Green

In 1929, most people in Andros simply referred to this deadly storm as the '*1929 Gale*.' I was 11 years old at the time when this storm hit Andros. I recalled a boat by the name of the '*The Repeat*', which went down in this storm. This boat was owned by Hardy McKinney, and they were on a sponging trip in the area of the southern tip of Andros. The storm caught them by surprise on this sponging trip because their barometer, which they had on their boat, somehow was broken so it was not able to provide the crew with an accurate reading. Because the storm caught them by surprise, they were forced to swim from Beach Cay back to the Andros mainland. While they were swimming back to the land, a number of the men drowned. After the weather subsided, a search team was organized and went back up to the Grassy Creek and Beach Cay areas to look for the dead bodies. They found their bodies scattered several hundred feet inland at Grassy Creek. They brought the bodies back to the Andros mainland and put them all in a large dinghy boat and buried them in a mass grave in St Andrew's Cemetery. What was usual about this incident I recalled was that after the hurricane, the top mass of '*The Repeat*' drifted all the way down to the settlement of McKinney Hill, directly in the front of the boat's Captain Hardy McKinney's house. After the storm, there was devastation everywhere, and most of the roofs of the houses were blown off. Most of the roofs were made of straw, so they simply had to go out and gather new straw and replaced the old ones with the new ones. This hurricane destroyed most of the farms, so to survive everyone had to go out and pick up coconuts that the hurricane had blown off the trees. One thing that I will always remember was the fact that all of the trees were wiped out. All of the leaves were blown off the remaining trees, and the entire settlement looked as if it had been burned by fire. In fact, during the storm I saw the top of a coconut tree flying through the air like a bird.

There were several ways that residents of Andros knew a hurricane was travelling. The first was by the Family Island Commissioner and the police who went about informing residents that a storm was approaching the island and that they should make preparations for a storm. Another way was by watching the rising sea-level; most persons could look at this rising sea level before the storm and saw that a storm was travelling. Another way they could tell a storm was approaching was by watching the clouds and their movements. Finally, most experienced navigators could look at the sea bottom and tell if there was a storm travelling. Once we realized that a hurricane was approaching the Andros mainland, we would go out and immediately tie the house down with a strong rope and batten down the house.

I can recall that in the Settlement of Red Bays, North Andros, several persons died in the storm when they were washed away from their homes and boats, never to be seen again. As a memorial to the ones who had died in this storm, they erected three large crosses at the entrance of the settlement. This was the worst storm to ever hit this country, and I hope that there will never be another storm like this one ever again.

Dorothy Davis

I can recall at the time of the storm, I lived in Nassau. I lived with my family in a wooden house just off Bain Town. I can still remember the vivid details of this storm as if it was an event that took place just last year. My father was a finish carpenter, and after the storm left Nassau his services were in such great demand by the local residents. A lot of repair work had to be done to their individual homes, businesses and fishing schooners. As we were staying in our house that night, the roof of the house blew off and we all had to run out of the house into the strong winds and heavy rainfall to our neighbour's Mr. Thompson's house. Soon after arriving, the hurricane blew his roof off, and we were once again forced to leave his house and run to another neighbour's house, where we rode out the rest of the storm. What was significant about this storm was the fact that the storm took forever to pass over the island of Nassau. It remained nearly stationary over Nassau for over three days. After this storm, movement around Nassau was severely restricted because the streets were flooded. My father had to use a dinghy boat to navigate the streets of Nassau, as they were severely flooded. The streets were so flooded that the people who had houses left had to remain in them for several days after the hurricane.

Sir Durwood Knowles

I was twelve years old at the time of this storm and can distinctly remember finding out about this storm by looking at the household barometer falling rapidly. This was a clear indication that a storm was approaching the city of Nassau. My family went about quickly to make preparations for this approaching storm. This meant we had to move the harbour pilots' boats to safe moorings at Fox Hill Creek. After the storm, the floodwaters were about six feet deep, but it drained away very quickly. Our home was located on the waterfront, but fortunately it sustained little damage. One of the pilot boats was found on Paradise Island, some considerable distance from where it had been anchored.

Glica Christofillis

I recalled the event of this storm as a very frightening experience. I was living on Paradise Island at the time of the storm. I lived with my father, who was the foreman at Symonette's Shipyard. I remember hearing about the approaching storm on our radio from a radio station located in Florida. It was then that we made all of the necessary preparations for the storm, including, battening down our doors and windows of the home. Fortunately, Paradise Island was not heavily flooded like Nassau, and the standing water drained away quickly. Paradise Island was not really built up as it is today and only two families lived there. Our family home weathered the storm well, but I recalled that Nassau was totally flooded and the landscape of the harbour significantly changed, which led to the reclaiming of some coastal areas. In fact, Bay Street as we know it today was reclaimed land as a result of this storm.

June Maura

Mrs. Maura is active in the Bahamas Historical Society. I can recall the tales my grandfather told me about the 1929 Hurricane. My grandparents lived in a wooden house on Mackey Street, opposite the Salvation Army. This building provided shelter to a dozen or more neighbors who were forced from their homes during the storm. This points to one of the main reasons why this storm was so memorable. So many people had to flee their homes and move from house to house in search of safety - a terrifying experience. Everyone was similarly affected, no matter where they lived.

Jerry Gibson

(Mr. Gibson is my grandfather, and I can vividly recall growing up in South Andros how he and my grandmother, the late Joanna Gibson, frequently talked about this storm and its significant impact on the island of Andros). At the time of this storm, I was living in the Bluff, South Andros. During the storm, God kept us safe in the midst of a tremendous disaster. This was a very powerful storm. It was a rare storm and was one of the only times I could recall where the two seas on the western and eastern shores of Andros met because of massive amounts of water that the hurricane dumped over Andros. This storm lasted for three long, grueling days. Many areas were flooded with some four feet of water for several days after the storm. Our family home was blown down, and we were forced to seek shelter in a neighbour's house to weather the remainder of the storm. When the eye passed over South Andros, the men went into the farms to salvage as many crops as they could. I can remember my father returning in waist-high water with cassava, corn and sweet potatoes in his bag. But others were caught in the storm and drowned before they could get back to the safety of their homes. The family's hogs and dogs were kept in the house with us during the storm, and afterwards my father wouldn't let anyone go out because the water was everywhere. Somehow, curiosity got the better part of us because we sneaked out to look at the damage, which was shocking. My grandfather was the first person to tell me the story about the courageous act of the dog 'Speak Your Mind,' which we will hear about later.

Florence Stubbs-Rolle

Mrs. Rolle still lives in the Bluff, South Andros. This was a powerful and massive storm, and I can recall this storm as if it was yesterday. When my family and others heard that this storm was approaching Andros, we went and hid in a cave at the back of our yard called Lumbo Hole. There were more than 30 people with us in the cave, and we brought all of our belongings in the cave with us out of the fear that they would be destroyed in the hurricane. I recalled securing the family's corn mill in the cave. Most of the men from the settlement were not present, as they were busy on a sponging trip to an area called Bulla Hill, at the extreme southern end of the island. This storm was so large that it made that the two seas on the western and eastern shores of Andros meet inland, and many persons drowned as a result. Among the names I remembered were Bulla Lewis and Sam Black. When my family and other persons came out of Lumbo Hole after three days, there were flood-waters everywhere. All of the cassava and potatoes were destroyed. We made molasses syrup from the destroyed sugar cane and used it to sweeten tea and bread. Despite the difficulties, I consider this time of my life as the 'good ole days.'

Daniel Rahming Sr.

I can distinctly remember the Great Hurricane of 1929, because of the significant impact it had on my life while on a sponging trip. During the storm, I along with other spongers went up to Grassy Creek on the southern tip of South Andros on a sponging trip. The sponging trip started while we were sailing on the schooner 'The Repeat', which was captained by Mr. Hardy McKinney from the settlement of The Bluff, South Andros. I could tell that a hurricane was approaching by the use of the ship's barometer when the pressure started rapidly falling and the hand indicator was pointing to a hurricane on the dial. We also sensed that a storm was approaching because the seas were beginning to get very rough. It was at this time that the captain told us that it was time to head back to the shore.

We went into Grassy Creek and anchored the schooner 'The Repeat' in the harbour at Grassy Creek. We then took the sponges off the schooner and the dinghy boats and put them in the kraals. While we were at Grassy Creek, the schooner 'The Repeat' drifted out of the harbour, breaking away from the anchor holding her and going out to sea with the dinghy boats in tow. So, after this unfortunate turn of events we decided to swim to the nearest cay called Beach Cay to get back to the mainland. Several of the men drowned in this attempt to get back home, including a man named James Smith. I only survived because I was with a strong swimmer named Ditmus Dames, who the locals affectionately referred to as 'Ba-Did.' After the storm, vessels that were not damaged were able to rescue us from Beach Cay. When we got to our settlement of the Bluff, we were surprised to find out that many of the houses were destroyed and the entire settlement was flooded. To make matters worse, the two seas on the western and eastern sides of the island had joined together during the storm.

Melsheva Ferguson

This great storm affected everyone in South Andros, blowing down all of the trees and houses and severely flooding the area for many days. During the time of the storm, I was a little girl living in my parent's home in the Bluff. This storm in some way or the other affected everyone living in the settlement of the Bluff and the entire community of South Andros. This storm helped me meet and marry my late husband Isaac Ferguson, who was forced to move to the Bluff with his family. During the storm, he lived in an exposed settlement at the extreme southern tip of South Andros, but his entire family was forced to move further north because this storm devastated this exposed settlement, and everyone in this settlement was forced to leave abruptly and move further north. To this day, most of the houses that were abandoned or destroyed because of this hurricane can still be seen just to the extreme south of the settlement of Mars Bay in South Andros.

Nimi Nottage

I experienced this storm while living in a wooden house on Peter Street, here in Nassau. I can recall the heavy rainfall and strong winds, which toppled a big almond tree onto the front porch and destroyed it. My family decided to stay in the severely damaged house and ride out the storm, which for me was the most terrifying and longest three nights of my life and one that I would not want to repeat. What I can most clearly remember about this storm was the damage it did and the length of time it lingered over the islands. When all was said and done, all of the trees and buildings were blown down on Peter Street.

Macushla Hazelwood

I remember living in the area of Sans Souci in Nassau with my father, the late Sir Asa H. Pritchard, when we experienced this memorable hurricane. At the time, we didn't have any radios or televisions to warn us about an approaching storm, but we relied on a man by the name of Mr. Carl Brice to give us ample warnings. He simply had a knack for predicting an approaching storm. I recalled him informing Dad about this storm and telling him to get ready, and he immediately came home and began preparing for this storm by battening down the house. Our family lived on a hilltop, and eventually the strong winds became so great that Dad took me and my eight- year- old brother Emmett to the nearby home of Mr. Darling Bethel, which was more protected from the wind. It was a terrifying time, and I remembered my dad moving so fast that our little feet hardly touched the ground. The house next door was completely flooded, and the hurricane had blown the family car to the bottom of the hill.

Many persons were taken by surprise after the passage of the eye because the structure of a hurricane was poorly understood, and by that I mean many persons never knew that when the eye passed, many never knew that the strong winds would come again with even greater fury, but from the opposite direction. Our house suffered considerable damage: - the roof was twisted so badly that all the corners had been forced open. One partition was leaning against the grand piano, and dirt and debris were scattered everywhere. I can recall my dad starting a chicken and egg farm just before the hurricane with about 1000 chickens, but the hurricane destroyed most of them, and there were dead chickens and feathers scattered everywhere after this hurricane. Of the 1000 chickens my father raised, only about 90 of them survived the storm. This destruction did not deter my father; in fact, after the storm my father imported an additional 2,000 chickens. My father had a store on Bay Street in the Beaumont House, and the roof of the shop was blown off and a huge shipment of rice was destroyed by the rain and flood waters. This storm eventually evolved into John Bull and Asa H. Pritchard, two of the largest merchant stores in the Bahamas today.

Emmett Pritchard

I can recall that most of the stores on Bay Street were either destroyed of flooded with water, like City Pharmacy and Black's Candy Kitchen. I can distinctly remember that the water came in waves, and not many people knew what to expect when a hurricane passed because they were caught by surprise on the outside when the eye passed over the island. What stayed with me was the way the hurricane destroyed my father's chicken farm. After the storm destroyed the building on the farm, I saw many of my father's chickens walking around with absolutely no feathers on their body because the strong winds literally blew the feathers off their skin.

Illford Forbes

I lived in the settlement of High Rock, South Andros, and was a sponge fisherman on the schooner *'The Repeat.'* I can recall trying to take shelter from the approaching storm at Grassy Creek, on the southern tip of South Andros. However, we couldn't get the vessel as far into the creek as we would have liked, so we put five anchors down on the sea bottom to hold her steady. We left the vessel empty except for a dog by the name of Busser. Unfortunately, the vessel broke away from its mooring and drifted out to sea. At this point, I called for Busser to jump off the boat, but the dog refused and was lost with the vessel. I can also recall a dog named

Speak Your Mind, who was on the vessel (this dog was a true hero, but his exploits would have gone unreported had I not decided to write this book). *Speak Your Mind* belonged to a man named Berse, who perished in the storm.

At Grassy Creek, a man named Prince Rolle (the locals called him Warthy or Papa Warthy) suggested that we swim to Beach Cay, which was closer to the mainland. At the time, *Speak Your Mind* was with me, Elon, Jim, Dan and Travis Taylor. Not all of us made it to Beach Cay, including a man named Josh Smith, who became exhausted while swimming and drowned right in front of us. Warthy then yelled out, "Oh my God, he drown now!" At this point, I was swimming with Herman Rolle, Preston Smith, and Jim Smith. Jim told the group he couldn't make it any further either, and he also drowned in the front of us. I can further recall his last words were, "For God so loved the world that He gave His only begotten Son, that whosoever believeth in Him shall not perish but have everlasting life!" This scripture was taken from John 3:16, and then he sank and drowned. Nick Rolle also gave up and drowned, along with two other men named Lewis and Phillips. Also swimming were Falcom and Urm Taylor, and Urm swam with his clothes on top of his head. Although some men were swimming together, no-one was strong enough to rescue anyone else in the heavy seas. Rip -currents were also very strong.

Warthy was able to hang onto *Speak Your Mind*, who swam with him on his back to shore. When Warthy and *Speak Your Mind* got to the shore, the dog once again came to his rescue by going into the bushes and catching a land crab, which they both ate raw. Warthy said it was the best tasting crab he had ever ate, and had it not been for *Speak Your Mind* he would have surely died. I can further recall that either the stern or bow of the schooner somehow found its way all the way back to the Bluff, at McKinney Hill to be exact (where it was built). The top mast of the schooner turned up at Long Road, in High Rock, and the hull was found on Bel-Tongue Bank. *The Catherine*, another vessel lost in the storm, was found at Money Rock, in The Bluff. Both vessels were lost at Grassy Creek, some 30 miles away from where they were later found.

Edward Bain

I was seven years old at the time and living in the settlement of Victoria Point, Mangrove Cay, Andros, with my father Herbert Bain. This storm was a very powerful and destructive storm and lasted for three days and three nights with terrible winds and heavy rainfall. I can recall the neighbours running into our house wrapped in blankets, and before the storm was over at least three families took refuge in our home during the storm. Our house was spared because my father, a carpenter by trade, built his newly built house very sturdy to withstand hurricane force winds. I remember my father killing the family goats just before the hurricane because he feared they would not survive the storm. My grandfather's schooner, 'The Cherry Vine', was lost in the storm on its way to The Bight and was found several years later miles away. The three crewmen, including my uncle Uskine, were never found. After the storm, the government distributed food, seeds and lumber to the people of Mangrove Cay because this community was totally devastated by this storm. A lady was supposed to get married on the weekend after the storm in Mangrove Cay, and she and her bridal family were travelling from Nassau to Mangrove Cay to attend this wedding. A total of 18 persons went down in this boat, and they all drowned in the storm.

Bastian Miller

Mrs. Miller who was also from Victoria Point, Mangrove Cay, recalls the locals singing a song about this storm. "In 1929 as the sun crossed the line, it was a great storm and the storm refused to cease, he wounded some, he took some away and leave some still to pray!" This song was called 'The 1929 Storm Song' and became the most popular song for years after the storm. This storm took a lot of lives in Mangrove Cay, and many persons lost their homes in this storm and had to start from scratch with the rebuilding of their homes with a little effort from the government of the day. I recalled my father, Mr. Bartholomew Bastian, had the only barometer in the settlement, which everyone relied on for weather forecasts in the days before transistor radios and meteorological offices. A total of 18 persons died in a boat travelling from Nassau to Mangrove Cay.

Fernley Palmer

My parents often spoke to me as a child about how destructive the Great Hurricane of 1929 was to the Bahamas. My parents were members of Zion Baptist Church, and unfortunately the hurricane destroyed the roof of Zion Baptist Church. The church had to take up a special collection and held several fund-raising exercises to collect money to replace the roof.

CONCLUSION

Every year from June to November, Bahamians listen intently to news reports about approaching hurricanes and tropical storms. The history of every civilization includes stories about disasters caused by weather. The strong winds, high seas and torrential rainfall of hurricanes have always fascinated us here in the Bahamas and across the region. They are what make them so dangerous and deadly. Today, meteorologists understand hurricanes in depth. We know that they are part of a massive worldwide heat engine at work. The boiler house is in the equatorial regions, and the cooling system is at the poles. Excess heat from the sun is transported away from the tropics by fast- moving air and slower ocean currents.

Interest in the weather is near universal, and perhaps a primitive feature in the make-up of mankind that reflects the intimate relationship of all living things within our natural environment. Weather patterns occurring in any one country are connected to systems occurring elsewhere around the planet. Nowhere is the concept of 'One Earth' better demonstrated than in the behavior of our atmosphere and the resulting patterns of climate. Science has provided us with the capability to monitor the varying behavior of the atmosphere to our advantage. It enables us to be forewarned about impending dangers that can threaten our lives and livelihoods.

The Great Bahamas Hurricane of 1929 will not be the last to cause such massive devastation and havoc. A storm of similar strength could appear this year, next year, or 10 years from now, but there is no way to know when. The bitter lessons learned from this storm have provided us with more than enough experience to survive the next big one. Meteorologists know that science will never provide a full solution to the problems of hurricane safety because the rapid development of coastal regions has placed hundreds of thousands of people with little or no hurricane experience directly in the path of these lethal storms.

Hurricanes impact people's lives every day in different ways. From this hurricane to Hurricanes Andrew or Floyd and others that hit various islands in the Bahamas, all brought with them significant damage to the islands in their direct path. When this Great Hurricane of 1929 reached land, it uprooted massive trees, flooded the land with over 18 feet of floodwaters, and basically destroyed any and everything in its path, including many of the residential homes and businesses along the coasts of New Providence, Abaco and Andros. To make matters worse, it even killed over 134 persons. In order to have the formation of a hurricane, first there must be moisture, heat and pressure. Usually, hurricanes are formed over large bodies of water, like the Atlantic Ocean for us here in the North Atlantic. One hurricane that affected many lives is the Great Bahamas Hurricane of 1929. This massive hurricane of Category 4 strength hit New Providence and Andros in September of 1929 at peak intensity, creating much terror and misery in its path.

The positive aspects of hurricanes in the natural environment are that these storms help to circulate the air and redistribute heat from the equator to the poles. In actual fact, there are really not a whole lot of great things that can come out of a hurricane. Negative aspects of having a hurricane hit land are that it can certainly destroy anything in its path and destroy lives as well. Hurricanes do indeed change lives and destroy the environment as well. The only way to prevent further damage is to prepare ahead of time and educate ourselves about the safety and the precautions that go into play when properly preparing for a hurricane. Potentially catastrophic hurricanes require the government to act quickly to implement disaster recovery plans and improvise creative solutions to address unforeseen difficulties. Not every eventuality can be anticipated or prevented, but preparation and practice can help lower the odds of being taken by surprise.

Having spent the last 10 years travelling throughout the Bahamas, interviewing hundreds of persons affected by hurricanes, I have come to the disturbing conclusion that this country is far more vulnerable to hurricane damage today than it was in 1929. The main, but not only, reason is complacency. Hurricane survivors tell me over and over again that they didn't prepare because they thought a storm of that magnitude would never hit them. When it did, they had to rely on others, especially the government, to bring their lives back to some degree of normalcy.

This is a dangerous situation if, as some meteorologists predict, we are entering an ominous period of increased hurricane activity, similar to the decades of the 1920s and '30s. This could see the Bahamas frequently suffering devastating damage in the coming years unless - we as individuals, corporations, non-government organizations and the government-take action. My main goal as a meteorologist and author is to help make the science of hurricanes more useful and relevant to people, especially by helping them understand the risks and how to prepare for them. As well, I want to support and promote policies and programmes that could help reduce our vulnerability to hurricanes and lessen the costs associated with cleaning up after they have passed. I have come to the disturbing conclusion that the Bahamas is more vulnerable today than ever before because too many people choose to live in hurricane-prone coastal areas without considering the magnitude of the risks they are taking. As a result, public education and community preparedness must be the key to saving lives and lessening the effects of hurricanes on our society.

REFERENCES

❖ *"HURRICANE!" A Familiarization Booklet by NOAA, April, 1993.*

❖ Chris Landsea, et al. (2003). *"Documentation of Atlantic Tropical Cyclones Changes in HURDAT: 1900-1930"*. NHC-Hurricane Research Division. http://www.aoml.noaa.gov/hrd/hurdat/metadata_1929-30.htm#1929_3.

❖ Chris Landsea, et al. (2003). *"Raw Observations for Hurricane #2, 1929"* (XLS). Hurricane Research Division. http://www.aoml.noaa.gov/hrd/hurdat/excelfiles_centerfix/1929/1929_3.XLS. E.B. Garriott (September 1929). *"Monthly Weather Review"* (PDF). U.S. Weather Bureau. http://www.aoml.noaa.gov/hrd/hurdat/mwr_pdf/1929.pdf.

❖ Chris Landsea, et al. (2011). *"Raw Observations for Hurricane #2, 1929"* (XLS). Hurricane Research Division.

❖ Chris Landsea, et al. (2011). *"Documentation of Atlantic Tropical Cyclones Changes in HURDAT: 1929 Hurricane Season"*. NHC-Hurricane Research Division.

❖ *The Governor's Dispatches-CO-23 January-December, 1929,*

❖ *Votes of the House of Assembly-1929 & 1930-Bahamas Department of Archives.*

❖ *The Bahamas Journal of Science Vol. 6 No.1 Historic Weather at Nassau-*Ronald V. Shaklee, Media Publishing Ltd.

❖ *The Bahamas Journal of Science Vol. 5 No.1 Historical Hurricane Impacts on The Bahamas, Part I: 1500-1749* Ronald V. Shaklee, Media Publishing Ltd.

❖ *The Bahamas Journal of Science Vol. 5 No.2 Historical Hurricane Impacts on The Bahamas, Part II: 1750-1799* Ronald V. Shaklee, Media Publishing Ltd.

❖ *The Bahamas Journal of Science Vol. 8 No.1 Historical Hurricane Impacts on The Bahamas: Floyd on San Salvador & Early Nineteenth Century Hurricanes 1800-1850* Ronald V. Shaklee, Media Publishing Ltd.

❖ *The Sponging Industry Booklet-Department of Archives Exhibition 18-22 February, 1974. Pgs 1-31.*

❖ *A Columbus Casebook-A Supplement to "Where Columbus Found the New World"* National Geographic Magazine, November 1986.

❖ *The Nassau Guardian, Saturday, September 28, 1929 pg 1-'The Hurricane,' 'Hurricane Briefs' & 'Message from the Administrator.'*

❖ *The Nassau Guardian, Wednesday, October 2, 1929 pgs 1,2&3-'The Hurricane,' 'Message from the King,' & 'Hurricane Briefs.'*

❖ *The Nassau Guardian, Saturday, October 5, 1929 pg 1-'Hurricane Relief,' 'Trail of the Storm' & 'Hurricane Briefs.'*

❖ *The Nassau Guardian, Saturday, October 19, 1929 pg 1-'Special Session-The Administrator's Speech.'*

❖ *The Nassau Daily Tribune, Saturday, September 28, 1929 pgs 1&2-'Courage.'*

❖ *The Nassau Daily Tribune, Saturday, October 5, 1929 pg1&2-'Government making estimates of hurricane damage to lay before Legislature', 'The Bahamas Hurricane Relief Fund 1929' & 'Here and There.'*

❖ *The Nassau Daily Tribune, Wednesday, October 9, 1929 pg 1-'Here and There,' & 'Captain and crew saved from Storm-Driven "Wisconsin Bridge."'*

❖ *The Nassau Daily Tribune, Saturday, October 1, 1929 pg 1-'Here and There,' & 'Hurricane Reconstruction.'*

❖ *The Nassau Daily Tribune, Wednesday, October 2, 1929 pg 1-'All traces of hurricane damage are being quickly effaced by cheerful workers.'*

❖ *The Nassau Daily Tribune, Saturday, October 19, 1929 pg 1-'Here and There,' & 'It can be done is the verdict of Asa Pritchard, M.H.A.'*

❖ *The Nassau Daily Tribune, Saturday, October 26, 1929 pg 1-'Here and There,' & 'Hurricane Relief.'*

❖ Ahrens, D. (2000) *Meteorology Today, An Introduction to Weather, Climate, and The Environment*, USA, Brooks/Cole Publishing.

❖ Albury, P. (1975) *The Story of The Bahamas*, London, Macmillan Education Ltd. Pgs. 163-169.

❖ Barnes, J. (2007) *Florida's Hurricane History*, Chapel Hill, The University of North Carolina Press.

❖ Barratt, P. (2003) *Bahama Saga-The Epic Story of the Bahama Islands*, Indiana, Authorhouse Publishers.

❖ Burroughs, Crowder, Robertson, et al. (1996) *The Nature Company Guides to Weather*, Singapore, Time-Life Publishing Inc.

❖ Butler, K. *The History of Bahamian Boat Builders from 1800-2000*, Unpublished.

❖ Butler, E. (1980) *Natural Disasters*, Australia, Heinemann Educational Books Ltd.

❖ Challoner, J. (2000) *Hurricane and Tornado*, Great Britain, Dorling Kindersley.

❖ Clarke, P., Smith, A. (2001) *Usborne Spotter's Guide To Weather*, England, Usborne Publishing Ltd.

❖ Craton, M. (1986) *A History of The Bahamas*, Canada, San Salvador Press. Pgs 236-238, 250-254.

❖ Davis, K. (2005) *Don't Know Much About World Myths*, HarperCollins Publishers.

❖ Domenici, D. (2008) *The Aztecs-History and Treasures of an Ancient Civilization*, White Star Publishing.

❖ Douglas.S.M. (1958) *Hurricane,* USA, Rinehart and Company Inc.

❖ Duedall, I., Williams, J. (2002) *Florida Hurricanes and Tropical Storms 1871-2001,* USA, University Press Of Florida.

❖ Durschmied, E. (2001) *The Weather Factor-How Nature has changed History*, New York, Arcade Publishing, Inc.

❖ Emanuel, K. (2005) *Divine Wind-The History and Science of Hurricanes,* New York, Oxford University Press.

❖ Fitzpatrick, J.P. (1999) *Natural Disasters-Hurricanes,* USA, ABC-CLIO, Inc.

❖ Green, J., MacDonald, F., Steele, P. & Stotter, M. (2001) *The Encyclopedia of the Americas*, London, South Water Publishing.

❖ Hairr, J. (2008) *The Great Hurricanes of North Carolina*, United Kingdom, The History Press. Pgs 81–104.

❖ Horvitz, A.L. (2007) *The Essential Book of Weather Lore*, New York, The Reader's Digest Association, Inc.

❖ J.D. Jarrell, Max Mayfield, Edward Rappaport, & Chris Landsea *NOAA Technical Memorandum NWS TPC-1 The Deadliest, Costliest, and Most Intense United States Hurricanes from 1900 to 2000(And Other Frequently Requested Hurricane Facts).*

❖ Jones W. (2005) *Hurricane-A Force of Nature*, Bahamas, Jones Communications Intl Ltd. Publication.

❖ Kahl, J. (1998) *National Audubon Society First Field Guide To Weather,* Hong Kong, Scholastic Inc.

❖ Keegan, W., (1992) *The People Who Discovered Columbus-The Prehistory of the Bahamas*, Tallahassee, University Press of Florida.

❖ Kindersley, D., (2002) *Eyewitness Weather*, London, Dorling Kindersley Ltd.

❖ Lauber, P. (1996) *Hurricanes: Earth's Mightiest Storms*, Singapore, Scholastic Press.

❖ Lawlor, J & A., (2008) *The Harbour Island Story,* Oxford, Macmillan Caribbean Publishers Ltd, pgs 154-177, 203-226.

❖ Lightbourn, G. R. (2005) *Reminiscing I & II-Photographs of Old Nassau*, Nassau, Ronald Lightbourn Publisher.

❖ Lloyd, J. (2007) *Weather-The Forces of Nature that Shape Our World.* United Kingdom, Parragon Publishing.

❖ Ludlum, D. M., (1989) *Early American Hurricanes 1492-1870*. Boston, MA: American Meteorological Society.

❖ Lyons, A.W. (1997) *The Handy Science Weather Answer Book,* Detroit, Visible Ink Press.

❖ MacPherson, J. (1967) *Caribbean Lands-A Geography Of The West Indies,* 2nd Edition, London, Longmans, Green and Co Ltd.

❖ Malone, S. and Roberts, R. *Nostalgic Nassau-Picture Postcards-1900-1940.*

❖ Millas C.J. (1968) *Hurricanes of The Caribbean and Adjacent Regions 1492-1800*, Edward Brothers Inc/ Academy of the Arts and Sciences of the Americas Miami, Florida.

❖ Pearce, A.E., Smith G.C. (1998) *The Hutchinson World Weather Guide,* Great Britain, Helicon Publishing Ltd.

- Phillips, C. (2007) *The illustrated Encyclopedia of the Aztec & Maya,* London, Lorenz Books.
- Redfield; W.C., 1846, *On Three Several Hurricanes of the Atlantic and their relations to the Northers of Mexico and Central America*, New Haven.
- Reynolds, R., (2000) *Philip's Guide To Weather*, London, Octopus Publishing Group Ltd.
- Rouse, I., (1992) *The Tainos-The rise and decline of the people who greeted Columbus*, New Haven, Yale University Press.
- Saunders, A. (2006) *History of Bimini Volume 2*, Bahamas, New World Press.
- Saunders, G. (1983) *Bahamian Loyalists and Their Slaves*, London, MacMillan Education Ltd, pg 2.
- Saunders, G. (2010) *Historic Bahamas*, Bahamas, D. Gail Saunders. Pgs 85-87.
- Saunders, G, and Craton, M. (1998*) Islanders in the Stream: A History of the Bahamian People Volume 2*, USA, University of Georgia Press. Pgs 43-44, 79 & 237.
- Triana, P.(1987) San Salvador-The Forgotten Island, Spain, Ediciones Beramar.
- Williams, P.,(1999) *Chronological Highlights in the History of the Bahamas 600 to 1900*, Nassau, Bahamas Historical Society. Pgs 1, 54.
- www.noaa.gov
- www.nasa.gov
- www.weather.unisys.com
- www.wunderground.com
- www.wikipedia.org
- www.hurricanecity.com
- www.nationalgeographic.com
- www.weathersavvy.com
- http://agora.ex.nii.ac.jp/digital-typhoon/help/world.html.en

The writing of this book has been a highly satisfying project, made so not only by the subject itself but also by the people who have helped and assisted me in some way or the other, so here are the persons I wish to thank: -

My Father and Mother Lofton and Francita Neely
My Aunt and Uncle Coleman and Diana Andrews and family
The late Mrs. Joanna Gibson
Ms. Deatrice Adderley
Mr. Christopher Landsea
Ms. Stephanie Hanna
Mr. Ray Duncombe
Mr. Ethric Bowe
Mr. Rupert Roberts
Mr. Peter Graham
Mr. Leroy Lowe
The late Mr. William Holowesko
The Hon. Glenys Hanna-Martin
Mr. Murrio Ducille
Mr. Charles and Eddie Carter
Dr. Gail Saunders
Mr. Joshua Taylor and family
Mrs. Patrice Wells
Mrs. Jan Roberts
Ms. Jeffarah Gibson
Mrs. Shavaughn Moss
Ms. Kristina McNeil
The late Mrs. Macushla Hazelwood
Mrs. Suzette Moss-Hall
Mr. Rodger Demeritte
Mr. Michael and Phillip Stubbs
Mr. Orson Nixon
Mr. Neil Sealey
Dr. Myles Munroe
Dr. Timothy Barrett
Rev. Theo and Blooming Neely and family

Staff and Management of The Nassau Guardian Newspaper
Staff and Management of Media Enterprises
Staff and Management of The Tribune Newspaper
Staff of IslandFM Radio Station
Staff of the Broadcasting Corporation of the Bahamas (ZNS)
Staff of the Cable12 News
Staff of the Department of Archives
Staff of the Department of Meteorology
Staff of NOAA and National Hurricane Center in Miami
Mr. Phil Klotzbach
Mr. Bryan Norcross
Dr. Steve Lyons
Mr. Jack and Karen Andrews
Mrs. Margaret Jeffers

The good people of the Bahamas who opened their doors, hearts and minds to assist me with this project and provided me with overwhelming research materials, and many others too numerous to mention who gave me their take on this devastating hurricane.

Contact Information:

Mr. Wayne Neely
P.O. Box EE-16637
Nassau, Bahamas
E-Mail:
wayneneely@hotmail.com
wayneneely@yahoo.com

I would like to sincerely thank each one of these sponsors, both individual and corporate who assisted me financially and in other ways in making this book project a reality. Without them this book would have not been possible, so from the bottom of my heart I thank each and every one of you:

34 Collins Ave.
P.O. Box N-8337
Nassau, Bahamas
Tel: 242-322-2341
E-Mail: info@jsjohnson.com
www.jsjohnson.com

Crawford St. Oakes Field
P.O. Box N-8170
Nassau, Bahamas
Tel: 242-323-5171
E-Mail: rduncombe@cavalierbahamas.com
www.bobcatbahamas.com

SUPER VALUE FOOD STORES LTD.

P.O. Box N-3039
Nassau, Bahamas
Phone: 242-361-5220-4
Fax: 242-361-5583
E-Mail: svfsltd@batelnet.bs

#432 East Bay Street
P.O. Box CR-54288 | Nassau, N.P. Bahamas
Tel: 242-322-6735 | 242-322-6736 | Fax: 242-322-6793
Email: admin@afsbahamas.com| Facebook: AFSBahamas |
Twitter@AFSBahamas